FIESTA TIME IN LATIN AMERICA

FIESTA TIME. IN
LATIN AMERICA

BY JEAN MILNE

THE WARD RITCHIE PRESS • LOS ANGELES

Copyright © 1965 by Jean Milne
Library of Congress Catalog Card Number 65-24170
Designed by Ward Ritchie
Illustrated by Mario Casetta

Lithographed in the United States of America
by Anderson, Ritchie and Simon

TABLE OF CONTENTS

v

FIESTA TIME IN LATIN AMERICA

THE EARLY MORNING stillness of the sleepy little Latin American town is suddenly shattered by the ringing of church bells. They clang wildly with a din like that of the beating of dishpans on New Year's Eve. Bursts of gunfire follow, each one louder than the one before. It must be a revolution! A quick glance reveals, however, not soldiers with rifles to their shoulders but a group of men in front of the church lighting firecrackers and homemade rockets. Of course! Today is the day of the town's patron saint. There will be a fiesta, so why not get started early?

The preceding scene could be taking place almost any day and almost any place, because it's always fiesta time somewhere in Latin America. Every day is a saint's day, and each town has its special patron who must be honored annually. In addition, each locality celebrates several other holy days, and sometimes there are civic celebrations as well. In some countries hardly a week passes when a villager cannot attend one fiesta or more either in his own town or in a neighboring one.

Some North Americans tend to think of a fiesta as a carefree or perhaps even giddy social affair at which there is loud music, gay dancing, and laughter of happy people. For the most part, however, a fiesta is not just a wild spree. Church bells may raise a great clamor and fireworks fill the air with their explosions, but the general tone of the affair is surprisingly serious. In fact, some of the Indian fiestas are even sad. What, then, is a fiesta? As used in this book, the term means merely an annual community celebration of some very special event.

Fiestas, *festas* (Brazil), or *fêtes* (Haiti) are given for just about every reason that one might think of and may be roughly divided into three groups: religious, civic, and tribal. Patriotic celebrations on national holidays, which are characterized mainly by speeches, athletic contests, and parades of school children, labor unions, women's organizations, soldiers, or police, are not discussed in the present work unless they include something out of the ordinary. Tribal celebrations, which may have as their excuse such things as a harvest, the bringing of rain, the roofing of a house, or a child's first haircut, have likewise been omitted unless they occur annually at more or less the same time of the year. It is the religious fiesta with which this book is most concerned.

All religious fiestas have a dual purpose—devotion and diversion. Generally, the more remote the village the more emphasis there is on the former, and the more urban the fiesta the more emphasis on the latter. Every fiesta includes special masses and at least one procession in which the holy image or images are carried through the town with great ceremony. Usually there is a market, because out-of-towners must combine business with pleasure, and there is no better time to display their local produce and handmade articles. Fireworks too are a necessity and may range from simple firecrackers to elaborate set pieces known as *castillos* (castles). Communities that can afford to bring in a few bulls love to stage a *corrida de toros*. These local affairs bear little resemblance to the artistic performances of Mexico City or Lima, however, and the bulls are seldom killed. These are usually free-for-alls in which all males who wish to prove their valor jump into the ring and bait the bulls.

A fiesta which lasts for a week or more, and especially one associated with a religious pilgrimage, is often called a *feria*. At fairs the market is much larger than usual, and in the open space around the church are food stalls, gambling concessions, and perhaps a Ferris wheel or merry-go-round. In very small towns the latter are often primitive affairs, made with benches instead of horses and propelled by the feet of many small boys.

In some countries (notably Mexico, Guatemala, El Salvador, and the Andean countries of South America) dancing is an integral part of the religious fiesta. Travelers are often treated to the sight of huge feather headdresses swaying to the primitive strains of flute and drum, flashing swords in mock combat, or grotesque masks bobbing around to an endlessly repeated rhythm. Nearly two hundred different dances have been recorded in the Andean countries alone, and there are at least that many in Mexico and Central America. Some are modified primitive rituals that were offered to pagan gods before the Conquest; others are definitely of European origin.

Spanish priests, though horrified at the symbolism of the fertility dances, realized the importance of this medium for their own proselyting. Some of the dances were immediately suppressed, but others were adapted for use in the church festivals. Many new dances were added at this time. Thus we find, even today, Indians all over Mexico and Central America regularly performing the Dance of the Moors and Christians, though they haven't the slightest idea who the Moors were.

At present-day fiestas, ritual dances are often performed in the atrium of the church or within the church itself. They may begin at three o'clock in the morning and continue until sundown or even go on for several consecutive days and nights. Dancers appear tireless and usually quite unaffected by the large quantities of alcohol that are consumed during each brief rest. The participants are generally important men of the community, chosen as an honor or permitted to take part to fulfill a sacred vow. They must have great physical endurance in order to undergo long months of preparation as well as the grueling performance itself. They must also be men of some means or they could not devote long hours daily to rehearsals. Women do not take part in ritual dances; feminine parts, if any, are danced by men. The ritual dance is a serious affair involving dramatization and often dialogue and presented for some special purpose such as to honor a saint or to bring rain or good crops. The folk dance, on the other hand, is a social affair with no other purpose than to bring pleasure to the participants, and it is usually performed by couples or by a group of women.

Fiestas differ greatly in different countries and in different parts of the same country. In general, the best place to see a festival is in the interior where customs change slowly and where local celebrations have not yet been commercialized. Indian communities can almost always be counted on for colorful festivities, as can those sections in which there is a large concentration of Negroes; for instance, along the shores of the Caribbean and in the northeastern part of Brazil.

Although both Indians and Negroes have accepted Catholicism, they have never given up completely their old beliefs; their religion today shows the blending of Christian ritual and faith with the ancient pagan ones. What they have accepted is not so much the Christian faith as we understand it but the glittering rituals of its church. The Indians love the holy images, pray to them, believe in their miracles, and make them gifts; few, however, have any idea of their divine representation. After praying to the Christian God and saints, they repair to hilltop altars to pay their respects to their pagan gods.

In the Andean countries Christian saints and pagan gods have become inextricably entangled. The Indian sees little if any difference between the Virgin and Pacha-Mama (Mother Earth). St. James, who was made patron saint of lightning, has become quite indistinguishable from Apu Allu, the lightning god of the Incas.

In Haiti, the Black Republic, most of the population are professed Catholics, yet many of those attending early mass in the churches have come there directly from all-night voodoo ceremonies. The voodoo rites themselves show the influence of Catholicism. Many of the popular saints are identified with the *loa* (African deities) and their pictures appear on voodoo altars. It is not unusual to find the entire assembly at a voodoo service chanting the Pater Noster, the Credo, and the Confiteor. The Cross of Christ doubles for the symbol of the treacherous crossroads, guarded over by the African Legba. This same infusion of Christianity in the ancient African religion is found in the *candomblé* and *macumba* of Brazil and in the *santería* of Cuba.

Whether the fiesta-makers are one hundred per cent Christian or not, they are always the humble folk, and a fiesta is the one dash of color in their otherwise drab lives. In contrast to our way of life where time is linear and each moment points to some new experience or goal, the humble peasant's or Indian's life is an endless circle. The boredom of everyday labor leads into the magic experience of religious ritual only to have the ritual dissolve again into the everyday labor that began the cycle. Inhabitants of small villages practice the strictest economy all year in order to finance a magnificent celebration on the day of their patron saint. The fiesta is more than a show of devotion; it is a work of art to which everyone contributes the best he is able to create whether it be decoration, food, dances, music, drama, costumes, or fireworks.

The actual burden of the fiesta rests on one certain group or individual. In Guatemala and El Salvador there are permanent organizations called *cofradías*, each one in charge of a certain saint. They spend the whole year preparing for that saint's fiesta, and besides contributing financially themselves they solicit from others in the neighborhood. In Mexico and many other countries, special fiesta committees called *mayordomías* are formed. In some places one man is specially selected to take charge. In order to put on a really splashy celebration he will sell animals, tools, or other possessions, even though it may mean his financial ruin. He will have his reward as he walks at the head of the procession or occupies his special place of honor, knowing that everyone is admiring and envying him, secretly hoping that it will be said that his fiesta was the most successful yet. Fiestas often act as the balance wheel of communal economics; they take from those who have in order to make all men have-nots. By leveling the surpluses of wealth, they also inhibit the growth of class distinctions.

Fiestas have undergone many changes during the last fifty years. They have felt the effect of such competing amusements as movies, radio, and now television. Automobiles with their blaring loudspeakers have added a jarring note to the celebrations. Time itself has taken away or modified some of their original character. Costumes especially have been simplified or corrupted; modern steps have been injected into some of the old dances. Whole fiestas have disappeared because the government decided they were not good publicity for the country; because it was thought unsafe to let people congregate during political crises; or, because too many people were killed in the exuberance of the festivities. Several years ago the government of Mexico, in an attempt to break the hold of the Catholic Church, prohibited all outdoor religious ceremonies. It was very difficult to enforce the regulation, however, because religion is so much a part of the life of the common person that it cannot be taken away without depriving him of life itself.

For every fiesta that has been lost a new one has appeared. In recent years vintage festivals and others related to important crops have been springing up all over South America. Religious fiestas too are still being born. A few years ago some boys in Amatitlán, Guatemala, accidentally broke a large branch off a mango tree. In the cut thus revealed was a Virgin, clearly outlined in the natural formation of the tree. The tree soon became a shrine, and the anniversary of its discovery is celebrated each year by a fiesta.

Fiesta-hunting in Latin America can be a very rewarding experience but a very frustrating one too. Though clearly marked on the calendar of saints' days or on the festival list supplied by the local tourist office, some fiestas just do not materialize. The saint's day may fall on a weekday and the men are too busy to celebrate until the following Sunday, or it may coincide with a fiesta in a neighboring town that they all wish to attend. Sometimes the saints will still be marching strong several days after a celebration was supposed to have ended.

In general, most of the fiestas listed in the appendix of this book will occur regularly on the date indicated. Since it is impossible to do justice to them all, a few have been selected for each month and will be described in the following chapters.

FIESTA TIME IN LATIN AMERICA

JANUARY

PILGRIMAGE TO CHALMA

THE FIRST FIVE DAYS of January are exciting ones in Chalma, Mexico, a tiny town located in a deep canyon between breathtaking cliffs and a turbulent river. Roads leading in this direction are packed with a moving tide of humanity—some squeezed into lurching trucks or busses, some riding horses or sad-eyed burros, others plodding along on foot. At night the nearby forest trails, packed hard by the feet of countless pilgrims, are ablaze with hundreds of moving torchlights. Everyone is anxious to get to the shrine of the Señor de Chalma to ask his blessing for the coming year or to express gratitude for favors received during the past one. Whole villages often come in a group. Those who have recently begun the journey are gay, sometimes performing dances along the way. The weary, who may have been walking for nearly a week, keep pushing ahead, stopping only long enough to cut a piece of sugar cane with which to quench their thirst.

The last part of the journey must be made on foot on trails which lead through lush, tropical vegetation. Except for modern-day dress, the scene must be very much like that which took place some five hundred years ago when the Aztecs made pilgrimages to this place. To a cave not far from the present shrine, offerings of flowers, incense, and at times still warm human hearts were brought to a stone idol called Otzocteotl, God of the Caves.

As the story goes, not long after the Conquest of Mexico two Augustinian missionaries, who had tried in vain to get the people to give up their pagan god, arrived with a huge wooden cross with which they hoped to replace the idol. On entering the cave they found the image broken to bits and in its place a life-sized figure of the crucified Christ. News of the miracle spread, and the natives agreed to accept the new faith. As time went on, the cave could no longer accommodate the increasing number of pilgrims. In 1683, against the wishes of many pious Catholics, the Señor de Chalma (as this image is now called) was moved to the recently completed church and placed on the altar where it now stands.

As they walk along the trail, the pilgrims are mindful of the belief that he who is not truly repentant of his sins will be turned into a stone and remain that way until the feet of the faithful have kicked him all the way to the sanctuary. At last the church comes into sight, its white towers and dome dwarfed by the towering rocks all around it. The hard dirt changes to cobblestone as the pilgrims enter the tiny town of Chalma. The new arrivals push their way through the crowds surrounding the booths where vendors are exhibiting pictures of the miraculous image, candles, and tiny silver objects made to represent every part of the human body. The latter are offered as testimonials for cures received, and parts of the shrine are covered with thousands of these figures.

The town seems ready to burst, yet this is one of the smaller fiestas. Pilgrimages also take place in February,

August, September, and usually during Holy Week and Christmas. At the most popular ones as many as thirty thousand people gather here. The convent with its cloisters and cells for pilgrims soon fills to the bursting point, and families overflow into the atrium of the church. Every bit of available space around the town and hillsides is utilized. Here they cook, eat, and sleep in the open.

When the pilgrims arrive at the church, many of them crawling painfully on their knees, they leave their offerings of flowers or other things as close as possible to the image, pray for His mercy and a remedy for their ills. Many remain kneeling for hours with rapt expression and unseeing eyes. Even the poorest has a candle to offer, and after some fiestas enough wax has been collected to fill a room. There are many services, each one singularly lovely with the fine singing of the student priests, the flickering lights of the candles, and the sensuous odor of incense.

Outside the church, dancers and musicians compete with the skyrockets, which continue to explode all day and a part of the night. Various groups of brilliantly costumed Indians hop backward and forward for hours, completely unaware of the performance of the others, interested only in paying homage to the Señor de Chalma. At some fiestas as many as thirty or forty different dances may be seen.

On the last day, the priests are busier than ever blessing little images, medals, or pictures that will be taken home and cherished or given to someone less fortunate who had not been able to make the journey. The dancers put aside their elaborate suits and headdresses, and the pilgrims pack up their few belongings. Everyone begins the homeward journey assured that the Señor will be looking after him in the months to come.

Día de Negritos

In Popayán, Colombia, the Mardi Gras-like festivities of January 5 and 6 mark the end of the Christmas season. Although in honor of the Three Kings or Wise Men, who presumably reached their destination on the sixth day of the month, January 5 is generally called the Día de Negritos (Day of the Black Ones) and January 6 the Fiesta de los Blanquitos (Festival of the White Ones). The tourist in Popayán soon learns, however, that the names of these fiestas refer not to the color of the original Eastern dignitaries but to that of the unsuspecting visitor who carelessly ventures forth on one of these two days.

In the morning of the fifth, little boys armed with black shoe polish chase the squealing girls and decorate them with their grimy hands; in the afternoon and evening, the bigger boys chase the bigger girls and anyone else who happens to be around. No one is safe no matter how old or how important.

In olden times this was done with much more finesse. Gentlemen paraded beneath the balconies of the fair señoritas tossing serpentine at them, and they were rewarded when the young ladies came to the door and allowed a beauty spot to be painted on their cheek or forehead. This custom gradually degenerated, and the spirit of rowdyism that prevails today keeps a good part of the population behind tightly-closed doors. Nevertheless, there continue to be parades of cars in the afternoon, groups of people in masquerade costumes, and the music of *chirimías* (ambulating groups who play the latest Colombian *bambucos* and *pasillos*) on primitive instruments. Usually at least one member of each *chirimía* dresses as a devil and runs through the crowd flourishing a spike or horsewhip. The poor jam the main square where the *tasajo* takes place. This is the distribution of beef and other foodstuffs donated by the rich hacendados. When night comes, the gay masqueraders get together in different homes or at one of the social clubs to dance and continue the merrymaking until dawn.

Fiesta de los Blanquitos

The next day everything in Popayán changes from black to white. Boys now chase the girls with white powder and wheat flour. Many young people get together and ride through the streets in trucks or other vehicles pelting everyone in sight with the stuff. People on balconies collaborate by throwing great quantities of water on the helpless victims, and soon everyone is streaked with the gooey mixture. There is much drinking and loud music, and the resulting bacchanalia is most distasteful to the many Colombians who remember the beauty of the religious festivities with which this day used to be celebrated.

Día de los Reyes

In most Latin American countries the sixth of January is called simply Día de los Reyes, or Day of the Kings. Known as either Epiphany or Twelfth Day, this festival has been celebrated for centuries in the English-speaking world, changing from one of great solemnity during the Middle Ages to boisterous and lawless revels during the reign of Queen Elizabeth I and then gradually losing its importance after that.

In most parts of Latin America, this is primarily a children's holiday. For weeks ahead they write letters to the Three Kings as our own children write to Santa Claus, and on the eve of the sixth they place their shoes on the balcony or in front of the door. The more thoughtful also leave a little hay and water for the Wise Men's camels. The next morning, of course, the children find their shoes filled with toys or good things to eat.

In Mexico there are many children's parties with the traditional *piñata*, a clay jar filled with goodies and decorated with crepe paper to represent some animal, person, or object. One by one the children, blindfolded, swing at it with a stick until it is finally broken and they all scramble for their reward. Sometimes a special crown-shaped pastry is served, and inside it is baked a doll representing the baby Jesus. Each child hopes that his piece will be the lucky one.

In many places, the ceremonies are more elaborate and the adults take part too. In the Dominican Republic, where

7

festivals are fewer and less spontaneous than in most Latin American countries, the eve of Epiphany is an exciting time. The sound of firecrackers, whistles, and horns fills the air, and sparklers glow on all sides. A parade of Oriental splendor passes slowly through the capital. Leading it are men carrying blazing torches. A platoon of incense-bearing Egyptians is followed by colorfully costumed dark-skinned swordbearers. Finally come the Three Kings, luxuriously clad and bearing gifts for the Holy Child.

This pageant is also a familiar sight throughout Venezuela where the Kings, on horseback, are accompanied by the music of guitar, drum, and maracas. As they ride majestically through the streets throwing toys and candies, singing men, women, and children attach themselves to the court. The procession ends at the church, where all attend mass. This festival reaches its height in the city of Independencia (Táchira State) where the play goes on all day and consists not only of the arrival of the Wise Men but also of such episodes as the Beheading of the Innocents and the Death of King Herod.

A similar religious play has been seen in Cuzco, Peru. To give a new twist to an old story, there is one Ethiopian King, one Inca, and one Spaniard. Various scenes depict events in the early life of Christ. When Herod orders all newborn male infants killed, horsemen rush through the crowd and snatch from the women spectators babies made of paper which they dramatically behead. This drama is barely finished when a second pageant begins, and the spectator finds himself in the midst of the ancient and glorious Inca empire. Fantastically bedecked Indians re-enact the important events in Inca history, sing the songs of their ancestors, and perform the age-old Inca dances.

In too many places the feast of the Three Kings has lost its original religious significance. In Sicuani, Peru, the three Indians masked and costumed to represent the white, black, and Indian king run a race on spirited horses. If the white one wins there will be bad crops and hunger; if the black one comes in first there will be epidemics. When the Indian king wins there is great rejoicing, for it is a sign of good crops and prosperity.

In the small towns of Paraguay the day begins with a mass and a procession during which the images that were left in the church overnight are carried back to the homes of their owners. Following this are horse races and games on horseback, bow-and-arrow shooting contests, and such competitive sports as climbing a greased pole. Prizes of either food or money are awarded to the winners. In Tobatí, the religious procession is accompanied by a small band of drums, flutes, and cymbals and by masked clowns called *negritos* or *cambá ra'angá*. Their masks are fantastic representations of animals, humans, or a mixture of both, some merely comical and others unbelievably ugly. They are never used more than once unless in another place, because the identity of the clowns must remain a secret. Their heads are completely covered, and even gloves are worn to prevent any possibility of recognition. Though the representations may be female, only men take part. They talk, sing, dance, and tell obscene jokes in falsetto voices. Because of their profanity they must always remain outside when the procession enters the church.

In the northeast of Brazil there is a pageant associated with the sixth of January called *Bumba meu boi*. Its theme appears to be a mixture of African symbolism, the Christian ceremony of communion, and the Indian sacrificial feast in which each member of the victorious tribe ate a portion of a captive in order to partake of the strength of the defeated tribe. Originally the cast included only the Apostle Matthew, the *boi* (ox), and such local personages as a *vaqueiro* (cowboy), *padre* (priest), and doctor. Today, however, after generations of Indian and Negro embellishments, one can see almost everything from sorcerers to snakes. Though the initial incidents vary and have more or less to do with the theme, Matthew eventually kills the ox (a wooden framework adorned with horns and covered with some brightly colored material and propelled by a man underneath). One of the cast, usually the *vaqueiro*, sings an endless ballad lamenting the death of his ox and bequeaths to the rest of the cast, as a sort of last will and testament, some part of the body of the ox. After the symbolic communion, the ox comes to life and the performance ends with joyous dancing and singing. This same play also takes place on St. John's Day and occasionally during Carnival, at Christmas, or on St. Peter's Day.

The republic of Haiti celebrates not so much the day itself as the eve of the sixth of January, and the festivities take the form of indoor parties with the traditional "Twelfth Cake." A bean is put into the cake prior to baking, and the person who discovers it in his piece becomes the king or queen of the evening. He chooses a partner from among his court, and during his reign everyone must obey him. It is the duty of the king to make the party as gay as possible.

El Cristo de Esquipulas

Where Guatemala, El Salvador, and Honduras meet there is a place called Esquipulas. Long before the Conquest, Indians used to gather at this spot to trade and to perform their pagan religious ceremonies. Unlike so many others, Chief Esquipulas, the ruler of the tribes in this region, realized the futility of resisting the invading Spaniards and thereby avoided the slaughter of his people. To reward him for his cooperation, the Spaniards established a village on this spot and gave his name to it. A church was erected, and the priests commissioned the famous colonial sculptor, Quirio Cataño, to make a figure of the Saviour. Because the Indians believed that all white men were evil, the priests asked that the image be made of balsam wood, whose color closely resembles the complexion of the Indians. Since that time nearly 400 years ago, the continuous smoke from candles and burning incense has turned the wood quite black.

Long before the fifteenth of January, which is the day of the Christ of Esquipulas, people set out from all over Central

10

America and even Mexico and South America, for this is one of the most important pilgrimages of our neighbors to the south. Here, as at other shrines, many of the Indians have made the entire journey on foot and look with scorn upon those who come on horseback or by car. The Esquipulas pilgrims are easily recognized along the roads by their wide straw hats decorated with gray Spanish moss and yellow gourd-like fruit called *chiches* (breasts) because of their shape and texture. Pilgrims from Quezaltenango stain their hands black with a certain kind of fruit juice in the belief that it helps the Black Christ bear his burden of suffering.

Near the village of Esquipulas are two boulders, one on top of the other, called "The Rock of the Compadres." *Compadres* is the word used to designate a godparent and parent of the same child, and *compadres* have always been forbidden to have more than a spiritual relationship with one another. It is believed that the boulders were at one time real life *compadres* who, having sinned, were turned to stone. Every good pilgrim comes well supplied with small rocks which he throws at them in passing. If he does not show his disapproval in this way, his prayers to the Black Christ will not be answered.

Another of the many legends that have grown up around the Black Christ concerns a rich merchant of Antigua who became incurably blind. As a last resort he made the pilgrimage to Esquipulas and laid a heavy gold chain at the feet of the Christ. Immediately his sight was restored.

"What a joke on the doctors who said that nothing could cure me," he told his friends later.

"You are cured, thanks to our Saviour," they reminded him.

"Thanks to our Saviour? You mean, thanks to the gold chain!" And with those words the merchant once more became blind, and in his hand appeared the chain.

Throughout the hills surrounding the valley in which Esquipulas is located are numerous altar-like structures built of stones brought by the pilgrims. Here the Indians pray on their arrival, and here again they make their last prayer before departing for home. It has often been rumored that the church itself was built over a well-hidden idol and that this is the reason for the Indians' fervent belief in the sanctity of the place. It is certainly significant that many of the sacred rites, such as dressing the image for the annual ceremonies, are performed only by Quiché Indians from Chichicastenango and Nahualá in the highlands of western Guatemala. These are said to be the only Indians in the country whose blood is untainted by mixture with whites, and in their own villages no one, not even the priest, is allowed to interfere with their pagan ceremonies. One can't help wondering whether these Indians would travel clear across Guatemala to take part in a purely Christian ceremony. White men as well as Indians come to the shrine, however, and every social and economic level is well represented. The lowly peon, the Indian in his gaudy dress, the middle-class *ladino*, the wealthy landowner—all kneel together inside the impressive and beautifully decorated church with enough combined faith to move mountains.

On the opposite side of the country of El Salvador, the town of San Vicente also holds elaborate festivities in honor of the Christ of Esquipulas. A day or two before the fifteenth, a group of Indians from Apastepeque arrives with great pomp and clamor. Following those playing the fife and drum are the five men who will take part in the performance called *La Partesana*. The first two carry long wooden poles with sharp metal tips called *picas*. Following them comes an Indian with a shorter pole, about seven feet long, which ends in a metal cross and lance; this is the *partesana*. One of the remaining men carries an *arquito*, or small bow, trimmed with ribbons and the other a red *banderilla*, or dart such as those used in bullfights. A curious crowd follows them to the church where they begin their strange performance.

The first two men toss their *picas* in such a way that they come back to earth point first. Catching them skillfully, they toss them again several times. The men then lay their *picas* on the ground, take off their hats and kneel opposite the large door of the church before returning to their places. The one with the *partesana* comes forward next and gives an even more dextrous demonstration of lance-tossing. He makes the same genuflections as the others, and the man with the *arquito* takes his place. Placing one end of the bow on the ground, he gives it several half turns, first to the left and then to the right. The man with the *banderilla* is content to describe figure 8's with it in the air. All the preceding is done to the accompaniment of fife and drum. Also coming from the town of Apastepeque are two young men carrying a small tree trunk whose branches are laden with bright colored flowers and fruits for the Señor de Esquipulas.

At midday on the fourteenth of January, the group from Apastepeque goes up to Calvario to met a similar group coming from San Pedro. When they join, they all dance together before going to the sanctuary. Dancing and general celebrating continue through January 15.

El Cristo de Esquipulas de Antón

Also on January 15, the picturesque town of Antón in Panama is the scene of a pilgrimage to the Christ of Esquipulas. In spite of the name, however, there seems to be no relation between this image and the one farther north. Some say that the image was found in the water along the coast of Antón shortly after the wreck of a ship bound for Esquipulas in Quatemala. The most popular story of its origin, however, is the following.

During the colonial era when Antón was nothing more than a few scattered cottages, a mysterious stranger appeared one day and offered to carve a sacred image of Christ for the people living there. The only condition was that he was to be left completely alone with his work. The people gladly consented and did nothing more than hand him food every day through a tiny window in his improvised workshop. One day the stranger did not open his window to receive the food. Fearing that some harm had befallen him, the inhabitants of Antón broke open the door. There before their eyes stood a beautiful image of Christ on the Cross. There was no trace of the mysterious stranger, and all the food he had been given was found untouched. The residents of Antón feel sure that he was a Divine Being sent especially to carve this image which has been worshipped there ever since.

San Antonio Abad

Anyone wandering around rural Mexico on the seventeenth of January might suddenly come upon a pair of burros with bright red stripes, a polka dot cow, or chickens bobbing along in starched pinafores and poke bonnets. Groups of children walk along the dusty roads carrying a variety of pets in their arms: a hoopskirted rabbit, a tiny dog in velvet breeches, baby chicks dyed like Easter eggs, a blue and white striped kitten, a parrot with an enormous bow tie. It's the Day of St. Anthony, and they are taking their pets to the church to be blessed.

The open space in front of the church is bedlam as moos, brays, quacks, honks, meows, barks, and chirps meld in one gigantic potpourri of noise. From a safe place atop the churchyard wall the priest holds his vessel of holy water and generously sprinkles the animals and humans that pass beneath. The water is soon exhausted, and an altar boy brings a fresh vessel. Before long the priest is also exhausted, and a new one is sent into the ring. Though this ceremony is especially colorful at such places as Oaxaca, Taxco, and Ajijic, it can also be seen close to Mexico City at Tlalpam and at the church of San Bernardino in Xochimilco.

In El Salvador, the little town of San Antonio Abad celebrates the day of its saint in quite a different manner. The religious procession in which the image is carried through town is preceded by small girls in blue dresses with silver ribbons and flowers. They carry long reeds and cry copiously each time the procession pauses along the route. This is done as part of a vow that their mothers have made to God so that He will shower blessings on them during the coming year. During the day masked Indian dances are also performed.

San Sebastián

The day of St. Sebastian, January 20, is celebrated in many parts of Latin America, but one of the most unusual fiestas is that which takes place in Tenosique, Mexico. It features the rarely seen *El Pocho*, a dance-drama in which everyone eventually takes part. The dancers (from fifteen to sixty or more) are divided into three groups: *pochoveras*, *cojoes*, and *tigres*. The *pochoveras* are women, generally of advanced age, who wear blouses with embroidered borders, colorful, long, full skirts, red capes, and wide-brimmed palm hats adorned with fresh tulips and tropical flowers. The *cojoes* are men with silly hats perched atop crude wooden masks that have either regular or grotesque features and exaggerated eyebrows, mustaches, and beards of pig bristles. These men are the center of the whole fiesta, for in addition to their part in the dance, they must keep things lively by constantly making witty remarks and ridiculing present-day affairs. The *tigres* are also men and wear only a loin cloth. Their bodies have been covered with a layer of yellow clay which quickly hardens, and black spots painted over that—spots, not stripes, because the American tiger is really a jaguar. Some men have a puma skin on their back, complete with head, tail, and claws while others have a tiger's head over their own. There is always one *tigresa* among them, and she jealously guards her *tigrito*.

The fiesta takes place at some house in town chosen several days ahead of time in the following way. At nine o'clock the leader of the *pocho*, who was elected the year before, presents himself with his beribboned staff of authority and announces that this particular house has been chosen for the event. Permission is never denied, although it carries with it the obligation of furnishing refreshments for the whole crowd.

On the evening of the twentieth, the sound of fife and drum in the main square calls the people together. They quickly go to the scheduled place, and the ceremony begins. The first act is a mazurka-like dance by the *pochoveras* who enter carrying the banner of the *pocho*, a red flag adorned with tulips. The music changes, and for the next fifteen minutes, the *cojoes* take over with great noise and ridiculous remarks, always in time with the music.

All at once the fife announces the approach of the tigers. The *cojoes* in great panic run to get ropes which they stretch across the doorways. With great agility the tigers leap over these and enter to perform their dance which is done in bent-over position. Soon the tigers are dancing inside a circle of *cojoes* with the *pochoveras* forming an exterior ring. Suddenly the *cojoes* flee, trying to hide among the spectators, but the tigers find them and bring them back to the center of the room. After alternately dancing and throwing themselves on their captives, the tigers climb to the rafters of the house. When the *cojoes* regain consciousness, they hunt the tigers with old shotguns, bringing the bodies down on stout ropes that have been tossed over the rafters and laying them face down on the ground. Then the *cojoes* fan them back to life again with their hats. In the end, the *cojoes* and the *tigres* unite in pairs to pursue the spectators. Thus everyone gets into the final act. When someone is caught, he is dragged to the nearest *cantina* to buy a drink for his captors. Usually some enthusiastic spectators manage to abduct the *tigrito*, and when they are caught, they must reward the tigress with whatever she wishes.

In another town of Mexico, Chiapa de Corzo, the day of San Sebastian is given over to a group known as *Parachicos* (literally, "for children"). This group of masked men on horseback has the sole purpose of frightening or trying to frighten the children of the place.

In El Salvador, the town of Villa Delgado celebrates the

day with the lively *Torito Pinto* dance, a bullfight farce which is found in nearly all the Latin American countries. One of the five men taking part wears a framework representing the body of a bull, with a tail at one end and a wooden head or skull at the other. One of the men tries to lasso the bull while the others wave bullfighter capes at him and flee from his vigorous attacks. Everything is acted out to the accompaniment of fife and drum and the laughter of the spectators.

Santa Inés

The Mayas of Yucatán, who are noted for their striking features and beautiful costumes, have some of the most interesting and least touristed fiestas in all Mexico. The little town of Dzitas, not far from the famous ruins of Chichen Itzá, has a week-long celebration in January honoring Santa Inés, of which the most important day is the Sunday nearest January 21.

On the Wednesday just preceding the fiesta, the preparation of the festal foods is begun by the wives of the *cargadores*, or men previously chosen to take charge of the fiesta. Most important of all is the grinding of the maize for the cakes called *arepas* which are baked the next day. Some are eaten immediately by the *cargadores* and their helpers, and some are offered to people who drop by during these first few days. These people in turn are expected to contribute something to the cost of the fiesta.

The main attraction of the Dzitas fiesta, as of all those that are purely Mayan, is an organized dance known as a *jarana*. The number of these depends upon the size and wealth of the community, and in Dzitas there are usually at least two —one held on Saturday night and the other on Sunday.

Soon after nightfall, people begin to congregate at a thatched enclosure erected especially for the *jarana*. The Maya girls with their high cheekbones, narrow forehead, and almond-shaped eyes are ravishing in white, square-necked huipils embroidered with a cross-stitched fret or profusion of tropical flowers and ending in a wide lace ruffle just above the ankle. A few older couples are present, but the young people are in the majority, for this is their big opportunity to make acquaintances of the opposite sex.

Before long the music starts and couples eagerly dance to the gay *sones* played by brasses, drums, and a ukulele-like instrument. The couples dance opposite one another, the man with his hands behind his back and the girl raising her skirts slightly. From time to time they pass each other with arms curved upward, snapping their fingers as in the Spanish jota. Two hundred or more couples may dance at a time, and it seems to be a kind of marathon. Couples drop out one by one, and the winners are acclaimed with loud cheers.

The first *jarana* reaches a climax with the ritualistic turkey dance performed by about fifteen men wearing turkey-feather headdresses and each carrying a live turkey under his arm. As they dance they wring the turkeys' necks, and it is said that if one of the turkeys is found alive after the dance it is beaten to death against the head of the negligent dancer.

On Sunday a second ritual, known as the pig's head dance, usually takes place. Odd-numbered dancers carry roasted pigs' heads adorned with colored paper flags; even-numbered ones bear wooden frames called *ramilletes* decorated with strips of colored paper and the little cakes called *arepas*. The dance ends with the transference of authority to those who will prepare the following year's fiesta. Each new *cargador* receives from his predecessor one of the pigs' heads, a *ramillete*, a certain number of *arepas*, and vessels of turkey broth from the birds sacrificed the night before.

Many times a bullfight also takes place in connection with this fiesta, and in that case the dance is called a *vaquería* instead of a *jarana*. The boys, who go out to get the bulls and later fight them, are called *vaqueros*; the girls are known as *vaqueras* since they wear the boys' hats during the dance. Each *vaquería* ends with the *Torito*, a dance in which the girl simulates the bull and her partner the bullfighter.

At the end of the evening, the shaman-priest or *h-men* makes ritual offerings of corn gruel to the Yuntzilob (supernatural beings that guard the village) and to X-Juan-Thul, who is supposed to protect the bullfighters. Formerly the *vaqueras* were brought to the *h-men* to be cleansed of the evil winds to which dancing and close association with men had exposed them. Oldtimers still remember seeing the girls being beaten on the back with twisted handkerchiefs, but this custom no longer exists in Dzitas.

Alacitas Fair

For hundreds of years before the arrival of the Spanish conquerors, the Aymará Indians of Bolivia held an annual fair in honor of their god of prosperity, Ekeko. The plump, smiling god was a favorite of everyone, and no Indian home was without his image. When the conquerors won their great victory at La Paz in 1781, the governor attributed it to the intervention of the Virgin of La Paz and instituted a festival in her honor. To assure good attendance at this festival, he placed it on the same day as Ekeko's Fair. Though the church considers January 24 the day of the Virgin of La Paz, the Indians have always remained faithful to Ekeko and it is generally considered his day.

Several days before January 24, the beautiful main square of La Paz breaks out in a patchwork of booths filled with all sorts of fascinating Indian crafts. Most engaging of all are the figures of the god himself, a potbellied little man with open mouth and extended arms. On his head is a multicolored knitted cap with earflaps, and over that a felt hat with a bird's wing on it. The pack on his back is filled to overflowing with tiny sacks of sugar, coffee, and other foodstuffs, bits of clothing, cigarettes, matches, kettles, dishes, and many other objects which the needy Aymará family might find useful. According to very old tradition, Ekeko has the power to bring to every house into which he is brought an abundance of everything with which he is laden.

Many people also carry small images of him in their pockets or on their watch chains to bring them luck.

The religious part of this fiesta has almost been forgotten, though several indigenous dances are still performed in which fruits, pottery, and various other items are offered to Ekeko. The chief importance of the fiesta now lies in its commercial aspects, and the name has recently been changed to Alacitas, an Indian term meaning "come and buy."

There is hardly anything one can think of that is not represented here in miniature. At one booth a farmer may buy sheep, horses, cows, and even a haughty llama or two. Nearby a carpenter or a shoemaker can find dainty little tools like those used in his trade. Housewives pore over the latest designs in dishes, silverware, and cooking utensils. There are tiny crispy-looking loaves of bread, tempting cheeses, and other foods; diminutive articles of clothing, cigarettes, and even newspapers carefully printed and completely readable. At times the latter contain inflammatory editorials gravely offered to Ekeko in hope that he will do something about the political situation.

Although, like most fiestas, the Alacitas Fair is primarily for adults, the expectant look on the faces of the children in the crowd clearly suggests that not all of the miniatures are bought to hang on some already over-burdened Ekeko. Surely many of the beautifully furnished doll houses, complete with gardens and fountains, and the exquisitely dressed dolls were meant for little girls, not gods.

FEBRUARY

CANDELARIA

FEBRUARY 2, known in English-speaking countries as either Candlemas or the Feast of the Purification of the Blessed Virgin, has been celebrated all over the world for over a thousand years. From early Christian times all the candles and tapers to be used in the church during the year were consecrated on this day, and lighted candles were carried in solemn procession. Known in Spanish-speaking countries as Candelaria, the day is celebrated most enthusiastically by those countries with a large Indian population.

In Bolivia the Virgen de Candelaria is the patroness of the whole country, and people flock to her shrine at Copacabana. The August fiestas, also in honor of this virgin, are perhaps better attended because people are free for the Independence holidays, but the February festivities are by no means lacking in local color.

A fiesta in the Andean countries is among the most spontaneous, exuberant, and confusing to be found anywhere—a sort of ten-ring circus. Anyone having visited the sleepy little town of Copacabana under normal circumstances would find it difficult to recognize during the first week of February.

As in all Indian celebrations, there is no definite beginning or ending of activities. From the arrival of the first out-of-towner nearly a week ahead of time, there is one continuous pageant of color and sound. Probably the first to arrive are groups of Aymará Indians—the broad-faced men in ponchos and pointed woolen caps staring solemnly ahead, the full-skirted women spinning yarn from great bags of wool tucked under their arms. Many Quechuas, recognizable by their finer features and more cheerful manner, also stream in from all directions. A group of Chiriwanos from the forest regions arrives playing strange long-tubed, double-rowed panpipes and enormous drums. Wearing long black wigs and bands across their foreheads, they begin a strange dance, bending forward and then suddenly straightening up, looking for all the world like Hollywood Comanches circling a covered wagon train. Before long there is a steady stream of Indians arriving, many of whom begin to dance almost immediately and seem not to stop, except for a drink, until the fiesta is ended.

Women on ladders busily decorate the arches at the entrance to the church; hawkers set up their wares in the main square just opposite. Many of the newcomers stroll around looking at the various things offered for sale: handmade blankets, woolen caps, pottery, little hands carved out of bone or stone and guaranteed to bring good luck to their owners, bracelets of dried meat to free children of worms, fetuses of pigs or llamas to place in the foundation of a new house for protection. Before they have time to make even one purchase, they are distracted by the sound of drums and pipes coming their way. Musicians in plumed hats and spangled coats cut like bullfighters' jackets are followed by couples moving slowly around the square with courtly steps. At intervals they join hands and make a figure-eight turn.

The women in their derby hats, shawls, and layers of brightly colored skirts seem hypnotized by the rhythm of their own movements.

As time goes on, it becomes more and more difficult to push through the milling crowd in the square. In one particularly noisy section a bullfighting game is taking place. Masked men in the familiar wooden contraption with horns are being taunted by "toreros" armed with whips and wooden swords. But this is not the harmless play usually seen in such performances. The toreros are knocked down and viciously jabbed, and from time to time the bulls charge blindly through the crowd attacking anyone who happens to be in the way. Everyone is by now so gloriously drunk that no one seems to mind the rough play.

A steady stream of people flows up the steep hill to the Calvary where many deposit small stones at the foot of the first cross. Professional prayer chanters are busy blessing the people in various Indian tongues. If someone wishes to get married, special "notaries" will perform the ceremony with a proxy and give him a certificate guaranteed to make the real marriage come true within a year. If it's a house or farm he wishes, a "deed" will be made out as soon as the proper amount of Bolivianos is paid.

The inside of the church is even more crowded than the square. The Virgin, a large Indian-looking figure made of maguey, wood, and plaster, looks down at the multitude from her lofty perch above the main altar. Though Indian garments are painted on the Virgin, both she and the Infant have been dressed for the occasion in costly robes and precious jewels. The image stands on a revolving platform so that it can be turned to face either the church or the chapel behind the altar. In the chapel, which is reached by a flight of stairs, she is closer to the people and they can watch her face, which changes under various lighting effects from an expression of happiness to tears. In a small passageway just off the nave, hundreds of candles burn brightly; crouching sorcerers watch their light in order to foretell the future of the donors. A group of dancers in silk tunics and plumed headdresses nearly three feet high comes into the church, kneels to pray, and leaves again dancing.

Outside they continue their marathon, and those who swayed drunkenly on walking into the church are now performing their parts without missing a single step. In the center of one group of spectators is one of the most elaborate dances seen yet—that of the Incas of Oruro. All the characters of the discovery and conquest of Peru are present: Pizarro, Almagro, the priest Valverde, Atahualpa, Huáscar, Virgins of the Sun, Chasquis or royal messengers, Inca fortunetellers, and many others. The Incas, speaking in Quechua, are magnificent in black velvet robes with silver trimmings; the Spaniards, who answer in Spanish, are very simply attired. At the end of a long discussion Atahualpa is sentenced to death, and to the beat of drums he obligingly steps forward and drops dead on a cloth spread on the ground to protect his costume. There is a long, sad part during which the Indians weep over their dead ruler, but the drama ends happily when Atahualpa is miraculously brought back to life.

On the day of the fiesta the long-awaited procession begins to materialize. The military band which will lead it assembles on the church steps. There is a stir by the main door as the big statue appears and bows its way under the arch. The Virgin, who is greeted by joyous shouts from the crowd, is not the one on the altar but a duplicate decked out in the same manner. It was noticed long ago that the real Virgin does not wish to leave the church, for every time she was moved there were great storms and calamities of one kind or another. The pedestal on which the image is borne is surrounded by a group of priests dressed in silver and gold. Firecrackers pop on all sides and a rain of confetti flutters down on the bearers and their precious cargo. The crowd opens up just enough to let the procession pass and then closes again while dancers and others try to follow the image along its entire route.

After the procession, things return to their former frenzied pitch and reach a climax in the evening with a display of fireworks that goes on for hours. Indians stand motionless, watching with a sort of haggard ecstasy the thrilling exhibition. Dancers still pass back and forth between the square and the church, but the music has died down. Indian women crouch in corners sobbing disconsolately over their last empty bottle, and it is easy to see that the fiesta is just about over.

In Puno, Peru, there is another Virgen de la Candelaria who is feted in much the same manner. The day before the second of February is usually a big market day. Derby-hatted and brilliantly-skirted women squat in two rows facing each other with their merchandise between them. Working in pairs they place their potatoes, corn, or other products side by side. If both parties are satisfied, the exchange takes place without a word and usually some little gift is added in appreciation. This silent barter is typical of Andean markets and so different from that of Mexican markets where vendors talk and laugh as they haggle over prices.

All day long dancers roam the streets, stopping to perform at the door of the church of San Juan where the Virgin is housed. In the afternoon, Aymarás from the community of Ichu swarm in by the hundreds. The village dignitaries lead the way, carrying large silver-encrusted canes and doing elbow swings with one another. Following them, the rest of the mob enters dancing and yelling like demons.

On the morning of the second, the various groups continue to dance at the door of the church. Young boys and girls in vivid costumes perform the dance of the *Llameros*, making graceful figures with their shepherds' slings. Sicuri dancers in bullfighter suits and feathered headdresses circle a drum with small, trotting steps. There are dancers wearing animal skins and masks and others in elegant Spanish colonial costumes. Through it all runs the haunting sound of the panpipes and the beating of drums. In the *Choquela* dance from Ichu, women carry tall poles with feathers on top joined by colored strands of wool. The dance is supposed to represent a hunt for an escaped vicuña, and the poles carried by the women represent the traps.

Early in the afternoon the Virgin, much tinier than her Bolivian counterpart, is carried in a colorful procession. Visiting first the altars at the four corners of the Plaza de Armas, the procession continues through the streets where Indian women strew the path with petals of yellow wild flowers. People also throw flowers from windows and balconies along the route. After the procession, dancers resume their performance in the plazas and adjoining streets, and many groups continue for a whole week.

Eight days after the first procession a similar one takes place, and then begin the elaborate *despedidas*, or leavetakings. Each day the group whose turn it is to leave has a special mass followed by a banquet. At the Independence Arch on the hill, the leader of the group delivers a farewell address and the men now begin to dance with their female companions—through the streets, around the two plazas, and on to their homes.

The popular Virgin of Candelaria is also the patron saint of Cartagena, Colombia, and as expected, her day is an occasion for general merriment as well as religious observances. For nine days before the second, thousands of people carrying lighted candles swarm up La Popa, a hill about 500 feet in height and the highest point in the city. On top is a small restored church that is part of an old Spanish convent dating from colonial times. It is said that the nuns, on seeing a pirate fleet enter the harbor, often plunged to death over the cliffs to avoid falling into the hands of the marauders.

At night public dances and other festivities take place at the foot of the hill. Most popular of all is the *cumbia*, whose maddening rhythm goes on for hours. The musicians, most of them playing wind instruments, sit in the open while couples dance around them in a circle. Each woman holds at shoulder height a bundle of three or four lighted candles, and her partner dances around her. The dance goes on without any pause. When one couple gives out, another immediately takes its place, and musicians are replaced in the same way.

In Mexico most localities have some sort of celebration on February 2, but there are three that are of particular interest. In Tlacotalpan, in the state of Veracruz, the fiesta begins near the end of January and lasts for a whole week. Charros from nearby towns participate in a grand rodeo, and on February 1 there is an interesting parade of grotesque figures. On the following day there are religious ceremonies in honor of Nuestra Señora de la Candelaria, who happens to be the patron saint of this town also.

Among the interesting features of this week-long fiesta are the *huapangos*. Like the *jarana* of Yucatan, the *huapango* is both an organized social dance and the dance step typical of the region. The *huapango* takes place on a wooden platform raised off the ground or laid over hollow earthen jars for greater resonance. When the music begins, the young men step in front of the girls with whom they wish to dance, raise their hats in silence, and the girls follow them onto the floor. The dancers, who are usually in two lines facing each other, keep their bodies rigid and show no signs of coquetry as they pass to exchange places. The steps are rhythmic and simple—usually one stamp with the heel and two with the toe—and the musicians accent the rhythm by striking the strings of their instruments with an open hand on the last beat of the measure.

Often the men sing improvised verses to the music, and two men who are interested in the same girl may have an elaborate and amusing vocal duel. Different songs are played for different purposes. During *"El Caimán"* or *"La Bamba,"* dancers show off their skill by balancing a glass of water or bottle of liquor on their head, or by tying a knot in a sash with their feet as they dance. *"El Torito"* is the signal for the men to produce huge handkerchiefs and play at bullfighting with their partners. When the musicians want to rest, they play *"Los Panaderos"* as a hint to the men to invite the girls for refreshments. Some *huapangos* last for days and, as at the *jaranas*, many young people find their future mates.

At San Juan de los Lagos, Mexico, the fair honoring the Virgin of Candlemas lasts for two whole weeks. This tiny, vegetable paste figure is greatly loved, and at least a half-million pilgrims come to pay homage to her. One of the interesting tales about her is that she often sneaks out to the hills to play marbles which she makes herself. The place where she gets the mud for them is called El Pocito de la Virgen (Little Well of the Virgin), and the sick and injured rub the mud from it on the aching parts of their bodies.

Among the several native dances to be seen during the two weeks is the popular *Moros y Cristianos*. Sometimes on horseback and sometimes on foot, the dance-drama begins with long speaking passages and eventually leads up to a heated battle between the two forces. The Moors, of course, are always defeated. Wooden machetes are used in place of steel weapons in case the performers let their enthusiasm run away with them.

Tzintzuntzan, whose musical name means "Place of the Hummingbird," is another Mexican town that devotes at least a week to honoring the Virgin of Candlemas. Canoes from the different villages along the shores of Lake Pátzcuaro are decorated with flowers and candles and participate in a colorful regatta. At the church, seeds as well as candles are blessed and the agricultural dance of *Las Sembradoras* (The Sowers) is usually performed. It is a dance of thanksgiving for the harvest just completed and of hope for the new crop about to go in. The men carry hoes, shovels, or other farming implements, while the women hold baskets of corn, wheat, and other products which they throw to the spectators from time to time. The costumes are striking. The men wear clean white shirt and pants, sometimes elaborately embroidered, and hang a black and white fringed serape over their left shoulder. The women use an embroidered blouse and a voluminous skirt pulled straight in front and gathered into as many small box pleats as possible in back. The skirt is held in place by a wide, colored sash, and a blue and white striped rebozo is draped over the shoulders. Colored ribbons in the women's long braids accentuate the black of the hair. The couples dance side by side around a yoke of oxen decorated with ears of corn, flowers, and ribbons, and the women scatter flower petals over the ground with the movements used in sowing the fields. Finally the animals are led away, and the dance ends with a gay *jarabe*.

The Tzintzuntzan fair is also a good place to witness the comical *Viejitos* dance familiar throughout Michoacán. The *Viejitos* (little old men) are really youths who do their best to look decrepit. Wearing white suits with embroidered cuffs, flat wide-brimmed hats decorated with ribbons, heavy serapes, silk kerchiefs, and wooden masks with fibre hair, each dancer carries a strong staff and tries to outdo the others in intricate steps and clowning.

In Central America the most important celebration on February 2 is the pilgrimage to Chiantla in Guatemala. Many years ago a Spaniard named Almengor presented to the church in this village a figure of the Virgin of Candelaria made from the silver of his mines. Before long he became so fabulously rich that he decided to return to Spain. During a last visit to his mine, a Negro slave suddenly shouted to him to come out. He had barely come out of the entrance when the whole mine caved in. This was adjudged an act of the Virgin, who wished not only to save the life of her benefactor but to make it impossible for anyone else to profit from the silver in that mine. Since then the Virgin's fame has spread, and the pilgrimage to her shrine is now one of the three largest in the country.

Nombre de Jesús

The little town of San Pedro Nonualco in El Salvador celebrates the first fifteen days of February with a fair called

Nombre de Jesús. The patrons of the fiesta are two images of the Christ Child which are brought with great ceremony from the nearby town of Cojutepeque. One image has black hair and black eyes and the other blond hair and blue eyes. The fair-haired child seems to be the favorite, and money and gifts are showered upon it as it passes. It is a great privilege to house this image, and the major-domo of the fiesta is usually the lucky host. Various native dances are performed, some of them in a circle around the veiled figure of the blond infant. Catholic priests have tried to suppress this performance and place the images in the church, but their efforts have constantly been thwarted. Typical of this fiesta is a dove-shaped candy called *chancaca*, made of ground corn and sugar, which every young man is supposed to present to his sweetheart.

San Blas

On February 3, the country of Paraguay honors its patron saint, San Blas. Asunción and some of the larger towns have only religious processions, but in small villages far from the capital the center of attraction is a "bullfight" in the main square. The bull is decorated with flowers and colored streamers and has several paper *guaranís* (the national currency) tied to his tail. There is no attempt to kill the bull. The whole thing is a burlesque of bullfighting techniques, and the aim of the bullfighter is to get hold of the bull and remove the money without being wounded.

Balserías

On or about February 12 the Guaymí tribes of Chiriquí Province in Panama meet at various places to hold fiestas and transact tribal business. The most important business of all is that of choosing mates and is accomplished by means of grueling contests known as *balserías*. Men of two different tribes, their bodies and faces painted, line up facing each other. Each man holds a log of balsa wood and, to the excited rhythm of the accompanying music, hurls it at the ankles of the man opposite him in an effort to eliminate him from the contest. The blow may not be diverted by hands or arms but must be avoided by leaps and skillful footwork requiring unusual agility. Those who emerge from the fray without broken bones or other injuries are given their choice of the most desirable maidens.

San Isidro

The tiny country of Costa Rica is famous for its painted oxcarts, and one of the best times to see them is on February 15 in the village of San Isidro de Coronado. Each part of the country has its favorite design and color, but in general the vivid shades of red, orange, yellow, and blue predominate. Each ox-cart is not only a work of art but is carefully constructed so that it will "sing" or rattle in a certain way as it rolls. Country people claim that they can tell who is approaching at night by the sound of his cart. For the fiesta in San Isidro, the oxen as well as the carts are decorated with flowers and ribbons and are blessed by the priest in a solemn ceremony. There are music and dancing in the market place, and often many colorful costumes are seen.

Pisa

In the southern coastal region of Peru, the gayest fiestas are those in connection with the pruning of the grape vines in July (*poda*) and the pressing of the grapes (*pisa*) at the end of February. At both times the workers organize themselves in military fashion with a captain in charge and a sergeant assisting him. Besides the common soldiers there is a mulatto to run errands and an executioner to punish those whose work is not acceptable. The owner of the vineyard is called the general and his wife the generala.

Early the first morning there is a simple service in which the helpers ask for the Lord's blessing followed by a recitation of verses asking for a drink to mitigate the cold morning air. The grapes are pressed by barefoot workers who tread on them in rhythm to a drum and sometimes accompanied by a singer. As soon as one steps out of line or does something the wrong way, a punishment is ordered. The offender may be lashed with a small rope or reed or lifted by hands and feet and "tossed to the four winds." Punishments are carried out amidst shouting and laughter, and afterwards the victim is cured with a drink. Naturally no one tries very hard to escape punishment.

When the work is finished, the blessing of the Lord is invoked again, and then the workers cover the general with branches and flowers and take him a prisoner to his home. The generala ransoms him with a barrel of the best wine in the house, and the music and dancing begin. Couples compete with each other in the gay *marinera*, a flirtation dance which is almost identical with the famous Chilean *cueca* just across the border. On large haciendas the introduction of machinery has done away with these colorful fiestas, but they still exist on the less extensive establishments.

CARNIVAL

THE CELEBRATION of Carnival dates back to the Middle Ages and is still popular today in most of Europe and the Americas. The word itself is said to come from the Latin *carne vale* (farewell to flesh) and quite aptly describes the last days of fleshly unrestraint before Lent. The belief seems to be that giving vent to all kinds of revelry purges the individual and makes it easier for him to appreciate the mystic qualities of the coming religious experience. Generally the celebration takes place on the three days and nights preceding Ash Wednesday, but in some places the Latin American, with his charming disregard for time, manages to begin celebrating a month or more ahead of time or to prolong the festivities for several weeks afterwards.

Though Carnival explodes with spectacular results in many parts of the Americas, the celebrations of Rio de Janeiro and those of pre-Castro Havana have always been the best known here and most often compared with our own Mardi Gras. The three celebrations were usually very similar, but in Rio the emphasis seemed to be on music, in Havana on dancing, and in New Orleans on costumes. The most important difference between the New Orleans celebration and all its Latin American counterparts, however, is the fact that the former is a carefully organized civic project in which the high society play a prominent part. From the Rio Grande on south, it is a more spontaneous festival planned by and for the common people. In places like Rio, the aristocracy are apt to head for the country or beach, preferring to sit the whole thing out somewhere else. Those who remain in town do their celebrating within the private clubs.

As early as November of the preceding year, Carnival is already the main topic of conversation in Rio. Carnival stories appear in the newspapers; tunes composed especially for the occasion are heard on the radio. Everyone is busy getting his *fantasia*, or costume, ready for the big event. Costumes range all the way from extravagant period gowns down to a silly hat above a monstrous black mustache. Many years a certain theme predominates and the city may be invaded by pirates, Turks, Egyptians, or Russian Cossacks. Usually, however, the costume is simple because even if the price were not prohibitive, the elaborate Mardi Gras costumes are not suitable for the heat of a Rio summer. As a rule, the men take a delight in dressing as women and may appear in nothing more than an abbreviated skirt and flimsy brassiere.

The heart and soul of every Rio Carnival is the music and especially that year's crop of Carnival tunes. The famous samba schools of Brazil work on their songs all year long, and the best ones are chosen at a competition in the Municipal Theater. "Come to the Mardi Gras," which was very popular in the United States at one time, was actually an old Brazilian samba called *"Não tenho lágrimas"* (I Have No Tears). The typical Carnival song, however, is not the samba but the marchinha. It is a sort of limerick set to music and is always witty and quite often naughty as well. Some of the tunes are original; others are adaptations of operas or folk songs of other countries. Every composer of popular tunes hopes to write the season's hit, but often the Carnival's most popular song turns out to be an unwritten ditty that just sprang up out of nowhere and was passed from mouth to mouth.

As the time draws near for Carnival to begin, local pickpockets and other shady characters are locked up. At noon on Saturday all business stops, and Cariocas stream jubilantly home to don their *fantasias*. At about six o'clock in the evening, the air is filled with the unmistakable beat of the samba, and waves of costumed and gyrating celebrants pour into Avenida Rio Branco from all over the city. These people are no longer tired businessmen, staid matrons, servants, politicians, or laborers. During these four days each of them is his true self or rather what he wishes he could be. In spite of what most tourists believe, the Brazilian is not essentially gay and carefree. He is the product of three "sad races"—the Portuguese, the Indian, and the Negro—and there is a melancholy background to his whole nature. But during Carnival he forgets his inhibitions, his complexes; he sings and dances in the streets without any evidence of self-consciousness or of self-display but simply because it is in him to sing and dance.

Carnival is more than just gay or exciting; it is sheer madness. It is an intoxicant more potent than any kind of alcohol. The tourist who goes to the center of town to see the spectacle finds it impossible to stand still and watch it go by. He never really knows how it happened, but there he is in the center of the avenue being swept along on the tidal wave that is slowly engulfing the center of town. The throb of the samba drums gets under his skin. He watches the others, but it is not the samba he learned at home and he struggles along awkwardly. People of every shade from jet black to pure white press against him on all sides; the rhythm seems to flow from their bodies to his, and he suddenly finds his feet doing the same step as theirs. He dodges the streams of serpentine and learns not to scream each time an icy jet of ether hits him in the face. He knows he will be back for more the next night and perhaps the next one after that.

In colonial times, the Rio Carnival was officially opened by a big bass drummer called Zé Pereira who led the crowds through the streets in Pied Piper fashion. In recent years, however, King Momus is the central personage and his arrival by ship, train, or plane is greeted with noisy tribute from his loyal subjects.

On Sunday morning people rush to the beaches attired in multihued bathing suits made of crepe paper, their faces, arms, and legs daubed with gaudy paint. Tourists gasp as they dash into the blue water and their frivolous costumes start falling to pieces. Everyone but the tourist knows, of course, that regular bathing suits are worn underneath. By Sunday afternoon the bathers are back among the milling crowds of revelers.

On Monday night there is a gala ball at the Municipal Theater where prizes are given for the best costumes and songs. It is *the* social event of Carnival and remains quite aloof from the spontaneous celebrations going on outside. After Monday night the enthusiasm begins to wane a bit, but some of the stouter souls frolic on through Tuesday.

On Tuesday evening, the Avenida Rio Branco is cleared to make way for a parade of elaborate floats. Sponsored by permanent Carnival clubs and designed by some of Brazil's leading artists and sculptors, these festive showpieces compete for worthwhile prizes and popular acclaim. In general they are of two types: true works of art representing historical or cultural subjects, and amusing though often sardonic caricatures of current events or local politics.

After the last float has passed, Carnival is officially over, and people wade wearily home through the drifts of confetti and serpentine. Actually, however, the final parade of Carnival takes place the next day when the "bull-pens" open and sheepish celebrants who got slightly out of hand file past the crowds that have gathered to see whether any local celebrities or relatives are among this year's batch of transgressors. Considering the size and exuberance of the celebration, there are very few disturbances of the peace and little evidence of drunkenness during the four days.

Rio is not the only city in Brazil that goes completely mad for three or four days. Recife, Salvador, Belem, and São Paulo are only a few of those with noteworthy celebrations. Recife, lying as it does in the economically poor but culturally rich northeastern part of the country, presents a Carnival celebration that is renowned for its folkloric representations. It was here that the two most typical Carnival dances originated—the *maracatú* and the *frêvo*. The latter is based principally on the attitudes and movements of the body and is an amazing combination of grace and virtuosity. The best *frêvo* dancers display prodigious gymnastic ability comparable only with that exhibited in certain Russian dances.

The *maracatú* is of Negro origin and goes back to colonial times when the slaves were allowed to elect their own kings, queens, ambassadors, and other officials. It was their job to settle rivalries among themselves and to act as intermediaries between slaves and masters. The Negro rulers of each district were crowned in sumptuous ceremonies to which plantation owners and their families often contributed by dressing their favorite slaves in elegant costumes and even loaning them their own jewels. With the abolition of slavery in 1888, these Negro kingdoms disappeared, but their traditions and colorful celebrations live on in the drama of the *maracatú*.

During Carnival in Recife the revelers are suddenly conscious of the sound of approaching drums and know that the *maracatús* are coming from the outskirts of the city, stopping to dance before the doors of all the churches they pass. Leading the procession is a small cart bearing the figure of some African animal such as a lion or elephant. Following it and walking under a monstrous gaudily-decorated umbrella come the king and queen in all their regal splendor. Among the members of the court which follows is a Matron of Honor carrying a small doll called *calunga* which possibly bears some relation to the African god of the same name. To the accompaniment of a band made up of primitive percussion instruments and their own chanting, the entire court takes part in a weird dance which is very reminiscent of African religious rituals.

Among other interesting folklore groups are the *caboclinhos*, who wear traditional Indian garb: red tunic-like garments with strange medals pinned on them; feather headdresses, skirts, and anklets in bright colors; necklaces of beads and animal teeth. Accompanied by their own native instruments (whose music is reminiscent of the singing of birds), the dancers spin, leap, and hop backward and forward with mathematical precision. At times they mark the rhythm by beating their arrows against their bows. The choreography attempts to portray their bitter struggle to avoid complete domination by the white man. One never knows what hour or even what day to look for them, but a Recife Carnival would not be complete without the *caboclinhos*.

Havana's Carnival is also one with a strong folklore inheritance and is definitely African in flavor. Its present form stems from the celebration of the traditional once-yearly day of freedom given to the slaves. The Day of the Kings, January 6, was chosen as their day. Wearing masks and fantastic costumes, they danced their way through the streets, collecting monetary tribute from the amused spectators. Organizing themselves into societies called *cabildos*, they began to compete with each other, and many of the Negro performances seen in later-day Carnivals were originated at this time.

Carnival as we know it today began to take shape during the first few years of the republic. In addition to the *comparsas*, or groups of Negro dancers, there were parades of distinguished persons in carriages or on horseback. In 1908 the first floats, depicting such things as Gulliver's Travels and Scenes from the Middle Ages, were brought over from New Orleans and the first "Queen of the Carnival" was elected. After that Havana began building its own floats and developed one of the most pretentious celebrations of all the Americas.

Carnival conventionally begins on the Saturday before Ash Wednesday, but it has seldom stopped after three or four days; it has usually continued on Saturday and Sunday nights for most of the Lenten period. The main attraction of the whole celebration is the dancing of the *comparsas*. There are about eighteen in all, and they come not only from different sections of the capital but from all parts of the island. Their members are not professional dancers; they are ordinary men and women of all ages, sizes, and degrees of color who dance for the sheer joy of dancing. The word "dancing" does not adequately describe their performance, however, as some of the groups have put on a series of full-scale production numbers that rival the best on Broadway. The groups go by such names as The Scorpions, The Snakes, The Marquesas, The Sultanas, The Gypsies, The Gardeners, and The Cane Cutters. Some have been in existence for nearly one hundred years, and rivalry between those groups is intense. On Carnival Saturdays, the groups start to assemble at sundown on the Malecón and begin dancing their way beneath the laurel trees of the Prado at about nine. It is one or two in the morning before the last *comparsa* passes the reviewing stand at the National Capitol. After the fourth or fifth Saturday parade, prizes are usually awarded for local color and artistry.

The approach of the *comparsas* is heralded by the dull throb of drums, and soon the *farolas* come into sight. The latter are huge multicolored lanterns of silk or paper perched on top of tall poles and carried by the leader of each group. Sometimes a bearer will twirl the lantern skillfully as he advances; occasionally one will show off his ability by balancing the long pole in its pouch and dancing down the street without touching it with his hands. Following the lantern-bearers come long files of featured dancers and chorus members, from fifty to one hundred people all gliding along in the well-known conga step. This step is said to have evolved from the shuffling walk of the chained slaves who could take but three steps in any direction and had to drag their shackles on the fourth.

Each *comparsa* brings its own native band and pauses several times along the way to present its choreographic spectacle. Oriental themes are always popular, because they make it possible to display the vivid silks, plumed turbans, and floating clouds of gauze that the Negroes adore. There is also an amazing willingness to portray the Negroes' tragic experience as slaves. Extravagant period costumes have been popular at times with the men as well as the women, and a surging conga line of brawny blacks decked out in full Louis XIV costumes is a spectacle in itself. The Scorpions once put on a savage and erotic pageant of pagan worship and human sacrifice that was almost too realistic for the spectators and left the street in stunned silence.

The *comparsas* have appeared only on Saturday night. Sunday afternoons have been dedicated to the parade of decorated floats and other vehicles and to confetti battles by masqueraders on foot.

The Carnival described in the preceding paragraphs is typical of that which existed just before and at the beginning of the Castro regime. Though Castro is apparently going to permit the continuance of the celebration, it has become only a hollow echo of the past. Also, floats and dramatic spectacles are now utilized, wherever possible, for propaganda purposes and ridicule the clergy, the aristocracy, and the country's political enemies. The future of this celebration is, without doubt, as uncertain as that of Cuba itself.

The nearby country of Haiti is another known for its exciting Carnivals. The *fête* officially occupies only the three days preceding Ash Wednesday; unofficially, however, it begins on the first Sunday after Epiphany. On that Sunday and each one from then on, groups of costumed dancers roam the city and suburbs until far into the night. Often these *bandes* carry a Maypole which they plant in someone's yard, and to the rhythm of the drums they weave a simple pattern with the colored paper streamers. Usually too they are accompanied by *marchandes* who carry rum, candy, and rolls in trays on their heads. When the show is over and the performers are rewarded with a few coins, they pack up, portable bar and all, and move on to another neighborhood.

The last three days of Carnival are gay, noisy, and colorful ones in the capital of Haiti. Almost the entire population of Port-au-Prince is in attendance wearing fanciful costumes and blowing whatever musical instruments or noisemakers they could dig up. Even the traffic cops wear masks. Floats are strikingly handsome and show great ingenuity in the use of materials. Feathers of tropical and domestic birds are combined with palm fronds, flowers, sea shells, dyed flour sacks, pop bottle tops, satins, and ribbons to create breathtaking effects. There is fun of a more subtle sort too. Feeling secure behind their masks, people have a gay time making fun of political bigwigs and local institutions. The Port-au-Prince celebration is the largest but not the only one in the country. The people of Jacmel, Cap Haitien, Cayes, and Jérémie have their own and even more uninhibited versions of Carnival.

Carnival is widely celebrated throughout Latin America except in Chile and in several of the Central American republics. In the large cities the celebrations follow much the same pattern as those of Brazil: the election of a Carnival queen, a parade of floats, groups of musicians and dancers who perform in the streets, confetti battles between masked promenaders, and general merrymaking both indoors and out. Each country, though, has something which makes its festivities a little different from all the others.

Montevideo's three days of parades feature interesting Negro *comparsas* and beautifully decorated floats, but it is the *tablados*, or tableaux, that have brought fame to the festivities. People within the same neighborhood get together and erect a huge set on one of the street corners in their section. Funds are collected ahead of time and a professional artist hired to make the sketch and direct the construction. Immense stages are put up, often reaching from sidewalk to sidewalk, and on these are constructed the gigantic figures of the tableau. The theme may be anything from pure fancy to something in local or international news. One year, for example, the First Grand Prize of eight thousand pesos went to a tableau called "For Your Love, to the Moon" which showed the hero about to take off on a rocket while his sweetheart mourned nearby. Special lighting effects dramatize the tableaux, which are usually viewed at night.

Panama City's Carnival shows an interesting blend of popular celebration and folk tradition. As in most other places it comprises the four days and nights preceding Ash Wednesday, and it is ruled by a jolly King Momus and beautiful queen. Though the floats and many beauty queens are unrivalled for their loveliness, the real beauty of the pageant is in the costumes of the people.

At Carnival time the city is literally invaded by *polleras* and *montunos*. The *pollera* is a beautifully embroidered two-piece dress which dates from colonial times. It was originally a sort of servant's livery; wealthy ladies vied with each other in dressing their children's nursemaids, and each family had a different pattern. The general pattern of the costume was Andalusian, but necklines were dropped and sleeves abbreviated to make it better suited to the climate. Nursemaids were rewarded with gold jewelry for bringing each child safely through infancy, and this jewelry became a part of the costume. For several decades the *pollera* remained a plebeian garment. Country women and lower-class city dwellers used a simple version for every day and an elaborate lace-trimmed one for special occasions. Finally upper-class Panamanians recognized the beauty of the *pollera* and it was adopted as the national costume.

To be authentic, the *pollera* which appears at fiesta time must be of white lawn, intricately embroidered with patterns featuring flowers, fruits, or birds all in one color. The handmade lace which joins the flounces on both blouse and skirt usually displays a diamond pattern in a color that matches the embroidery. An off-the-shoulder neckline is held in place by a woolen drawstring which ends in a pompon at both front and back. Several hand-embroidered petticoats and heavy gold chains around the neck complete the costume. The hair is worn in two large buns studded with glittering ornaments made of beads, dyed fish scales, sequins, and gold and silver wires. A complete costume made of fine material may cost hundreds of dollars.

The men's *montuno* costume is made of unbleached muslin embroidered in bright colors with animal motifs or cross-stitch patterns. Its long shirt hangs loose and ends in a fringe. Though these costumes are seen everywhere throughout Carnival, the largest number of them appear on Sunday, which is called Pollera Day. Monday brings Mamarrachos Night, when any kind of costume goes. Tuesday features Comparsa Night, when ten or more couples wear costumes alike and go in a group from party to party.

In addition to the *pollera* costume, there is one other thing which gives unity to the four days of festivities—the dancing of the *tamborito*. There will be a sudden beating of drums and handsome *montunos* and *polleras* quickly form into a circle, clapping hands in rhythm while one of the couples launches into the intricate steps of the dance. This happens all over—in fashionable clubs, in hotels and restaurants, and at the *toldos*, which are platforms erected on street corners for this occasion.

The *tamborito* started long ago when the Spanish conquistadores brought slaves over from Africa. During their few free moments the Negroes amused themselves by dancing, and into these dances they wove their homesickness for their native Africa and their despair at their lost liberty. Many had a primitive sense of humor which took the form

43

of mimicking their masters. The steps gradually changed during the years, and with the development of a new race known as *criollo* and the substitution of the *pollera* for the rags of the slaves, the *tamborito* acquired the grace which it has today.

The *tamborito* is performed in a circle with only one couple dancing at a time. There is no bodily contact; the man simply holds an arm protectingly over the lady's shoulder without touching her. While his partner glides gracefully around the circle waving her skirts provocatively, the man breaks into exaggerated turns, dips, and steps intended to be taken as admiration for her beauty and dancing. Music is provided by a large major drum and two minor ones with perhaps some modern instrument such as an accordion, trumpet, or flute. The women sing a sort of chant while the men shout approval to the dancers. When one couple is especially good, the men in the circle toss their hats onto the girl's head. Though the effects of the jazz age are noticeable in the dance, the *tamborito* retains the wild beat of drums, the heartbroken wail of homesick slaves, and a primitive sensuousness of movement.

Panama's Carnival comes to an end at dawn on Ash Wednesday with a ceremony known as the "Burial of the Sardine." Some man is selected from among the crowd of merrymakers in the clubs or hotels, and in a mock ceremony he pronounces a few words over a dead fish brought from the kitchen for that purpose. Making the occasion as funny as possible, he lays the fish to rest in some make-believe coffin and then buries it under a tree or ceremoniously dumps it into the sea or a swimming pool. This act symbolizes the end of Carnival and the beginning of Lent.

In the neighboring country of Colombia, it is the north coast that goes all out for Carnival. Barranquilla begins getting ready for it almost as soon as Christmas is over, and for nearly two months there are masquerades and dancing in the streets and public squares. The most colorful of all Carnival activities are the Negro dances seen in Barranquilla and throughout Guajira. They are in complete contrast to the dances of the Indians in the interior of the country and clearly indicate the differences in temperament of the two groups. The Indian usually moves quietly and slowly whereas the Negro leaps and jumps in frenzied contortions.

In the *Danza de los Pájaros* (Bird Dance), the men wear brilliant plumage and masks having distinctive bills to identify the bird represented. The dancers go through a series of turns, jumps, and pecking gestures, and beat their wings in imitation of flight. Birds are represented also in the *Coyongos* dance-drama. The *coyongo* is a large, long-beaked aquatic bird known for its fishing skill. In the dance, several *coyongos* circle around a hapless "fish" and try to eat him while the fish evades them with vigorous movements. Dialogue between the pursued and the pursuers is interspersed with the dancing.

The *Maestranza* (Household) is a comic dance in which the men dress as women and carry brooms, mops, pots and pans, and other insignia of the housekeeper. The daughters sweep, wash, iron, and cook, with grotesque movements while the mother runs about ordering them to work harder.

In Caracas, Venezuela, structures known as *templetes* are erected all over the city, and each one is provided with an orchestra. In addition to the street dancing and throwing of confetti and serpentine, there are many popular games such as sack races or others in which they carry lighted candles or eggs balanced on teaspoons. The winners receive cash prizes as well as the thrill of being carried through the crowd on the shoulders of their comrades. Even the *piñata*, which is usually thought of as a purely Mexican form of amusement, has a prominent place in these activities. Besides the parade of floats there are clever *comparsas* called The Little Burro, The Snake, The Iguana, and names of other animals. Like the fish, *El Dios Momo* is buried on Ash Wednesday, but festivities break out again the following Sunday when they celebrate the *octavita* of Carnival.

In several South American countries the throwing of serpentine and confetti was apparently thought too tame, and the revelers began hurling water, flour, and various other messy substances. These activities reached their height in Peru a few years back when the unsuspecting tourist could not walk for more than a block without finding himself covered with colored water, cheap perfume, shoe polish, flour, and anything else that fiendish minds could devise. But this was not reserved for tourists. Peruvians were just as busy sousing other Peruvians and using everything from squirt guns to fire hoses. As things got worse the number of persons killed or injured during Carnival increased, and finally in 1958, President Manuel Prado prohibited all outdoor Carnival activities. The following year, Carnival was brought back but for only one day and with all street battles strictly prohibited.

In Ecuador and Colombia, the local authorities have been doing away with the water and flour throwing but have not found it necessary to ban the festivities entirely. Paraguay still permits the throwing of water but only between one and three in the afternoon. In Argentina, water games are limited to one street in the capital and for a very short time only, but the police find it difficult to enforce the regulation.

Bolivia is the one Andean country in which Carnival has survived more or less intact in spite of water pistols and even explosive "bangers" which are hurled at buildings and humans alike. In La Paz, the celebration is officially opened at about eleven on Sunday morning with a children's procession. Long before the appointed hour, however, the city is full of small masked revelers fiercely attacking each other with "slappers" and "bangers." Apparently the bark of the latter is worse than the bite, for at times even the police become good-natured targets for the missiles. During the procession, children in every kind of costume imaginable dance down the street to the music of a band.

In the afternoon the adults have their own parade. The first part is like a Carnival procession in any other part of the world, but then come the Indians in their own costumes which are far more striking than any of the most fanciful creations. Many of the men wear peg-top trousers and short jackets of some dark material embroidered in gay colors. A brilliant scarf wound around the waist, a wool or cotton bag slung over one shoulder, and the typical knitted cap with ear flaps add additional color to the costume. The women parade in their best skirts of brocade, velvet, or plush with a bright shawl around their shoulders and the inevitable black, gray, or brown derby hat. It is customary for a woman of the Altiplano to buy a new and different colored skirt for each Carnival. Each year she wears them all to prove how many carnivals she has attended, and the older she gets the bulkier she becomes. Women from other parts prefer white embroidered petticoats to the many-colored skirts. Each group of Indians is accompanied by its own band of pan-pipes and other primitive instruments and whirls and dances as it progresses through the city.

A unique feature of the La Paz festivities is the appearance of masked clowns called *pepinos*. They wear striped costumes and are armed with a cardboard baton known as *mata-suegra* (literally, "Kill-your-mother-in-law"). Talking in falsetto voices to avoid recognition, they roam through the crowds hitting people and getting hit in retaliation. It is necessary to get a police license to wear the costume and to pin the license number in a conspicuous place so that anyone causing bodily harm or property damage can be easily identified.

Formerly Carnival ceremonies were held in every town and hamlet of Bolivia, but there has been an increasing tendency for the people to gather in the larger cities. Hundreds of Indians come into La Paz, Sucre, Cochabamba, and Oruro, lodging with relatives or camping on the outskirts of the city. Many bring a wide variety of home-manufactured items to sell. After the initial phases of Carnival are over, they retire to nearby open fields where they continue dancing and drinking for as long as a week.

Carnival seems to be of particular significance in mining towns. At this time it is customary to sacrifice a bull in front of the mine and sprinkle the warm blood all over the entrance. This is partly in thanks to Pacha-Mama (Mother Earth) for her abundance of ore but mainly to prevent any fatal accidents during the coming year. In the mining town of Oruro, Bolivia, the entire celebration of Carnival is dedicated to an image of the Virgin in a silver mine called Socovón de la Virgen. The story explaining the origin of these festivities is rather unusual.

During the latter half of the eighteenth century, a notorious bandit called Niña-Niña lived in Oruro. The authorities had tried unsuccessfully to discover his identity and did not know that he worked in a local tavern and was violently in love with his employer's daughter. In spite of his wicked ways, Niña-Niña had the pious custom of regularly going to the altar at the entrance to the Cock's Foot Silver Mine and lighting a candle before a picture of the Virgin painted on the rock. After some time he got nerve enough to ask the tavern keeper for his daughter's hand but was refused. While the couple was trying to elope, the girl's father discovered them; Niña-Niña was left lying in the street, his throat neatly slashed and streaming blood.

That night a well-bred lady knocked at the door of St. John's hospital and brought in a badly wounded man. After helping him into bed and recommending that he be well looked after, she disappeared and was never seen or heard of again. At the man's request a priest was called, and hardly had the confession been heard and the last sacraments been administered when he died. Later the priest revealed the identity of Niña-Niña and what he had told him of the circumstances leading up to his arrival at the hospital.

After the attack, Niña-Niña lost consciousness, and when he came to he was being attended to by the unknown lady who escorted him to the hospital. Just as she was leaving he recognized her as the Virgin of the mine. When curious townspeople went to the miserable room in which Niña-Niña had been living, they were astounded to find that the Virgin's image had materialized on the wall. The miners, who were touched at their patron's benevolence toward one so unworthy as Niña-Niña, changed the mine's name from Cock's Foot to The Mine of the Virgin (Socovón de la Virgen). In addition they made a vow to celebrate a feast in honor of the Virgin each year on the Saturday of Carnival, for it was on that day that the tragedy occurred.

On Carnival Saturday, old and young pour into the main street to watch the procession. Before long a string of some sixty mules and oxen files past laden with gold and silver objects of every imaginable kind. Saddles are packed high with plates, bowls, jugs, and chalices. Cloths spread over the animals' flanks gleam with closely-set rows of spoons, knives, forks, earrings, brooches, or bracelets. Mules flaunt great horsecollars of silver or bridles and reins covered with hundreds of silver coins. Each family displays its wealth in this manner, and some of the richest ride in silver-hung cars or trucks. Following them come the masqueraders in *comparsas*, each group doing its own special step.

The center of attraction is usually the Diablada, a troupe of devils who burst upon the scene in a blaze of color and spectacular choreography. Heading the group are two, more luxuriously costumed than the others, who represent Satan and Lucifer. Near them are St. Michael and the China Supay, the she-devil and only feminine figure in the group. Behind them and stretching back over fifteen blocks or more come hundreds of dancers decked out as ferocious devils. Each costume features an enormous and curiously Tibetan mask: great horns, popping eyes, monstrous jagged teeth, all in vivid reds and greens, black, white, and gold. Between the horns of each crouches an evil-looking toad, lizard, or serpent. Over the pointed, vibrating ears fall long light-colored wigs of horsehair. As blonds are more typical of a foreign race, it is logical that they should play the heavies.

Though costumes differ slightly, the majority consist of pink tights and leotard, a silk or velvet cape embroidered with dragons and serpents, a jeweled and fringed breastplate, a short four-flapped native skirt embroidered in gold and silver thread and loaded with precious stones, and heavy boots with spurs that drag. Some have a covering of silver coins like ancient coats of mail. The costume is generally inherited, and each new descendant adds to the suit what his economic condition permits.

The miners' choice of this particular representation is not a haphazard one. It is felt that there is a very close connection between miners and demons, since both spend much of their time in the center of the earth. In the miners' minds, the devil has become identified with one of their black pagan gods, Supay. They erect altars to the devil inside the mines and refer to him as El Tío (Uncle) because he is very sensitive and does not like to be called by his real name. El Tío is quick to avenge any slight but, on the other hand, will do a good turn if he feels so inclined. Originally only the Indian mineworkers dressed as devils, but in the late twenties groups of mestizo slaughterhouse workers adopted the custom. Later, around 1940, young men of the middle class joined the ranks. There are now several Diabladas in Oruro, but all maintain the same general characteristics.

While some of the spectators remain along the street watching the parading and dancing of the *comparsas*, others run ahead in order to see the procession arrive at the church of the Virgen del Socovón. The long shimmering line soon comes into sight and winds its way up the slope. After detaching itself from the rest, the first group enters the church and begins to dance, accompanied by its high-powered band. At the tinkle of a bell, all stop and the leader intones a prayer in Quechua. Alternately dancing and praying, they work their way up to the high altar where the Virgin stands above banks of flowers. As this group goes dancing out another one comes dancing in, and the performance is repeated until each group has rendered obeisance to its patron. Those outside continue their pirouetting, skipping, or swaying without pausing for a breath.

At one point, members of the Diablada interrupt their frantic leaping to perform an allegorical play depicting the rebellion of the devils in the continuous struggle between good and evil. The performance begins on the very border of Avernus with a controversy between two powerful angels: Michael, who represents harmony; and Lucifer, who symbolizes discontent and bitterness. Seven devils representing the seven cardinal sins line themselves up with Lucifer while seven angels representing the seven virtues rush to the aid of Michael. In the first battle the devils are victorious, but by the time the play ends, of course, things have gone in favor of the celestial legion.

On Carnival Sunday, the area around the church looks like a page out of Grimm's. Everything seems to be covered with a profusion of monstrous gold and silver blossoms, and the sunlight bouncing back and forth makes the whole place a pale shimmer of metal. It is actually nothing more than a display of the same silver objects seen in the opening parade. Mounting guard over the treasure sit several *cholas*, resplendent in the fierce reds, greens, and blues of their Spanish shawls.

Comparsas continue their performances throughout Carnival, some presenting plays that obviously stem from the sixteenth-century Spanish moralities. The most interesting historically is that put on by the Inca *comparsa*. The entire story of the Conquest is worked out in great detail with all the Incas speaking Quechua and the Spaniards Castilian.

In Mexico City, Carnival festivities died out soon after the 1910-1920 revolutionary period, and attempts to revive them have been unsuccessful. In most other cities and towns in the country, however, Carnival is a big event with balls, parades, rodeos, and elaborate fireworks. The gayest and most typical Mardi Gras-like celebrations are those in the port towns of Mazatlán, Acapulco, and Veracruz, and in

Mérida in Yucatán. Veracruz has probably the most elaborate costumes. Mazatlán adds a new note by opening its festivities with a solemn funeral procession during which an effigy of "Señor del Mal Humor" is laid to rest in the blue waters of the Pacific. Mazatlán is also known for its spirited battles. On shore the people bombard each other with flowers, serpentine, and confetti; on the water, fishing boats, canoes, and pleasure yachts have their own mock battle with various kinds of firearms. In Jalisco and a few other states, *cascarones* are the favorite Carnival ammunition. These are eggshells beautifully decorated and filled with whatever meets the maker's fancy. Perhaps it is a rain of confetti that descends upon the victim, but it might also be perfume, ink, chili, or just plain rotten egg. In some parts of Yucatán people throw candy and toys as well as flowers, confetti, and serpentine.

In different sections of Mexico there are special dances associated with Carnival. The Carnival dancers of Tepeyanco and other villages of Tlaxcala are called *paragüeros* (umbrella men) because of their curious headdresses. Ostrich feathers spread out in all directions like the ribs of an umbrella. An elaborate shawl embroidered with native flora and fauna, ordinary breeches, and a silly mustached mask complete the costume. Wind and string instruments play mincing nineteenth-century tunes while the men perform quadrilles with exaggerated polka and mazurka steps. This dance, of fairly recent origin, is obviously a burlesque of the superficial sumptuousness of European and particularly of French high society.

Another burlesque, this time of the bourgeois, is seen at Santa Ana Chiautempan in the state of Tlaxcala. In *Los Catrines* half of the men wear double-breasted suits, neckties, ridiculous pink masks, and carry umbrellas. The other half dress as women, covering their faces with a kerchief.

Probably the best known of Mexican Carnival dancers are the *chinelos* of the state of Morelos. Their costumes are loose-fitting, embroidered satin gowns and fantastic cup-shaped hats adorned with beads, mirrors, spangles, and ostrich plumes. They also wear black-bearded masks, often gorgeously decorated. Each afternoon during Carnival they come bouncing into town and amuse the populace for hours. They never really dance but leap with queer bouncing hops, pose in clownish postures, and cause hilarious laughter by their jokes uttered in falsetto.

Many of the village carnivals contain serious dramatic elements along with the burlesque and fun. The most elaborate performance by far is that given in Huejotzingo, just an hour's drive from Mexico City on the Puebla highway. Here several hundred inhabitants enact a three-day drama with the entire village as a stage. The story centers around the elopement of a village maiden with the famous bandit Agustín Lorenzo. The heroine, usually a stalwart Indian in chintz skirts, is quite a handful for her suitor. After several daring acrobatic feats, "she" descends from the balcony of the City Hall and leaps onto the back of Augustín's horse. The wedding takes place later in the day in a hut built of branches to represent one of the bandits' hideouts. While the bandits are celebrating the big event, soldiers arrive, capture our Huejotzingan Jesse James and set fire to his house. During the three days there are fierce battles between Indian warriors and the invading Spanish and French troops, skirmishes between soldiers and bandits who pretend to be robbing the stores, picturesque native dances, and a lively fair. The fiesta ends on a happy note when the girl's parents forgive the daring young bandit and give their blessings to the newly-wedded couple.

In Argentina, the enthusiasm for Carnival has decreased notably in the larger cities. For the people of the less densely-populated northern section of the country, however, Carnival is still the big celebration of the year. In the picturesque Quebrada de Humahuaca in the province of Jujuy, sleeping villages come to life and the faces of the taciturn Indians lose their customary inexpressiveness and wear a mask of happiness instead. The thumpity-thump of small drums reverberates along the ravine, and at times the shrill note of the Indian flute or the jangle of the ukulele-like *charango* can be distinguished. These sounds are usually emanating from some little whitewashed church in front of which a circle of blanketed men and women—some with babies on their backs—are doing the *carnavalito* around the standing musicians. In this modern version of an old collective round dance, couples continually vary a few simple figures such as the wheel, the double wheel, and the chain. Some wave a corncob or a sprig of sweet basil, though the ancient harvest significance has long since been forgotten. The leader waves a handkerchief or a ribboned stick and at times calls the changes in a high hoarse voice. The dancing goes on for hours each day and may not stop at the end of Carnival but continue for as long as a month.

In the Calchaquí Valleys of Argentina, the ripening of the algarroba beans indicates that it is time for everyone to start practicing songs and couplets for the Carnival festivities. After the algarroba harvest, the women begin mixing the starch that will be used to smear faces during the revelry. Great quantities of *aloja* (a drink made from the algarroba bean) and *chicha* (a fermented corn liquor) are prepared. The aromatic basil is gathered, for it has the ability to ward off evil and will adorn the revelers' hats and ponchos. Walls are whitewashed, stables cleaned, and horses bathed and curried.

On the Thursday before Shrove Tuesday everything is in readiness for the *tincunaco* ceremony, or meeting of the *comadres*. Though this ritual can be celebrated any time during the year, it is a very special part of the Carnival festivities. The two groups of women—mothers on one side and godmothers on the other—line up on opposite sides of an arch made of willow branches and decorated with real or paper flowers, serpentine, tiny lanterns, fruit, cheeses, or sweets of different kinds. Walking majestically to the rhythm of the music, the two groups of women approach each other and meet under the arch. As they touch their fore-heads together, the child is passed from one to the other. More often than not, the child is a candy doll prepared especially for the occasion. With this ceremony the two women are joined together in one of the most sacred ties that can unite two families and one that only death can sever. Rockets go off, starch is thrown, and the remainder of the day is spent in feasting and dancing.

By the following Sunday, Carnival has built up to a grand climax. During the morning, the women come out in their wide ruffled skirts, colorful ponchos, and white hats. By noon their faces are transformed into comical masks of starch and water. After lunch everyone comes out again, freshly scrubbed and with a new supply of starch and confetti. Mounted on horseback and singing couplets and folk songs, they wend their way to the house where they will dance in homage to Pukllay, the spirit of Carnival. Dancing barely gets under way, however, when someone opens his mouth to laugh and down goes a fistful of starch. The horseplay is resumed until the guests tire of this and begin to sing and dance again.

Carnival comes to an end with the burial of Pukllay (a rag doll dressed in native costume). The woman chosen to play the part of his widow sobs brokenly while the others beat drums and sing Carnival songs. Pukllay is carefully laid in a freshly dug grave, and flowers and sweets are heaped upon him. As each person throws in a spadeful of dirt, they all sing:

> *¡Ya se ha muerto el carnaval!*
> *Ya lo llevan a enterrar;*
> *échenle poquita tierra*
> *que se vuelve a levantar.*

> Carnival is dead now!
> They are burying him;
> Throw just a little dirt in
> So he can rise again.

MARCH-APRIL

I T IS ALMOST impossible to write out an accurate fiesta calendar for the months of March and April. So many of the celebrations during this time are scheduled to take place a certain number of days or weeks before or after Easter. Even those with fixed dates have to be changed some years, because Holy Week celebrations normally take precedence over everything else. In spite of the general confusion, however, there are several traditional fiestas of interest.

San Juan de Dios

On March 8 the town of Puno, Peru, has a charming fiesta in honor of San Juan de Dios, patron of hospitals. It really begins on the afternoon of the seventh when llamas bearing flag-bedecked loads of *ccapo* (a dry wood from the country) parade through the streets to the music of flute and drum. In the evening there are special services featuring the Sicuri dancers in the chapel of the hospital. Dancing is resumed later in the town square where boys jump and pirouette through the flames of bonfires. On the afternoon of the eighth, the image of St. John is taken out in procession, and the Sicuris perform again. The sick, though unable to participate actively, look forward to the fiesta because of the special food prepared for them and donated by the Sisters of Charity.

Fiesta del Trigo

The Wheat Festival which takes place in Leones, Argentina, on March 10 is one of the newer agricultural celebrations. In the morning there is a special mass, and the ripe wheat is blessed. In the afternoon there is a parade featuring old and modern agricultural machines and floats bearing the queens from different sections. During the fiesta the Queen of Wheat is elected and prizes are given to the producers of the best grain.

San José

March 19, the day of St. Joseph, is widely celebrated though usually with nothing more than the ordinary religious observances. One exception is Venezuela, where there are such secular elements as *piñatas*, sack races, greased pole climbing, and other games. In Haiti, the day offers a good opportunity to see a cockfight. Though a little too cruel for most of our tastes, cockfighting remains one of the most popular sports in this island country and in many parts of Mexico and Central America.

In Haiti the cockfight usually takes place within a rectangle of beaten earth enclosed by a small board fence and protected from the sun by a roof of matting. As many as two hundred Negroes, mostly of the working class, may gather in small groups around their favorite birds. Before the fight, the antagonists are carefully groomed by their seconds. Filling their own mouths with water, the men press the birds to their lips, sucking and soaking the feathers so that they will cling to the body and afford no hold for the opponent. For the same reason the lower neck feathers are always plucked and the combs cropped quite short. These birds do not use steel spurs as in so many other places, but their natural spurs are sharpened to a perfect point with penknives. Occasionally a bird whose spurs are not considered long enough will use more perfect ones clipped from some dead or retired fighter and skillfully attached with tape and wax.

When the first two birds are ready, they are placed beak to beak in the ring. They often remain motionless and silent for several seconds, glaring at each other through wary, bloodshot eyes. Then, suddenly lunging at each other, they sail into the air, claws intertwined, and hover there with beating wings like a pair of heraldic supporters. Back to earth, they roll over and over together in the dust, and at times it is difficult to distinguish the separate bundles of feathers. As the cocks shoot up into the air again, the spectators scream excitedly, working their arms up and down in a strange unconscious imitation of the contestants. Last-minute bets are placed, and after a few more excited flurries, one of the cocks falls on his back mortally wounded. He clenches and unclenches his claws once or twice and then lies still. The victor leaps on top of the dead bird and gives a long triumphant crow before he is snatched up and kissed by his exuberant owner.

Once in a while the birds will creep slowly around in a circle, stalking each other and watching for an opening like a pair of mutually respectful boxers. At other times the savage spectacle is interrupted by a bit of comic relief when one of the glaring fighters suddenly turns tail and "bicycles" away from his opponent at breakneck speed. Though it appears to be cowardice it is more likely a ruse, and the pursuer who is caught completely unawares does not have time to protect himself from the suddenly slashing spurs. The fight is usually over in a few minutes, but once in a while two evenly matched birds will become exhausted and resort to pecking each other to death.

Fiesta de la Vendimia

One of the most lavish civic fiestas of South America is the Vintage Festival of Mendoza, Argentina, which usually takes place at the end of March. For several weeks before the festivities, cities and towns throughout the province are busy selecting beauty queens to represent them. From these, one queen is chosen to represent each department, and finally one is elected to be crowned Queen of the Vintage at the climax of the festivities.

On the day of the fiesta the image of the Virgen de la Carrodilla, patroness of Mendoza, is carried through town on an oxcart preceded by the bishop. Scores of vintagers in costume arrive and present the fruits to the Bishop to be blessed. Next, the governor tries some of the new wine, and, striking a plowshare with the traditional three blows, officially opens the celebration. The parade that follows offers a graphic representation of the various stages in the history of Andean transportation. Haughty llamas are led by boys dressed as *coyos* (inhabitants of the Altiplano). These are followed by mules and burros carrying wine in their wicker baskets, ox-drawn covered wagons with huge wooden wheels and cowhide roofs, wooden carts drawn by horses, and finally modern trucks. Gauchos and *huasos* (Chilean cowboys) file by on their handsome mounts, and finally come the floats bearing the queens of each department.

In the afternoon and evening, people gather at General San Martín Park, which is artistically decorated for the occasion with colored lights. On an enormous stage and with the spectacular Andes as a backdrop, programs of Argentine music and folk dances are presented. There are usually several large-scale choreographic numbers, and from 1,000 to 2,000 artists take part in the performance.

Corn-planting Ceremonies

The Quiché Indians of Guatemala believe that the first four men created were made of corn paste into which the

Heart of Heaven breathed life. Whether or not their ancestors were made of corn, it is certain that the Indians of today cannot live without it. It is part of their every meal; it feeds their animals and chickens; it thatches the huts they live in. Nothing is more important, therefore, than to assure a bountiful harvest.

Though most of the fields bear two or more crops a year, the main corn-planting season begins in March and extends until April. Besides burning over and preparing the fields for sowing, the men must purify themselves for the event. For almost two weeks before the big day, they must remain apart from their wives. On the Sunday before the planting begins, the Indians bring their seeds to be blessed at a special mass. In Chichicastenango, each family places lighted candles, incense, and flower petals on the floor and then kneels around them in a circle to pray. Sometimes they make mosaics with the red, white, and yellow corn, embodying the candles in the design.

The night before the planting, the women pray at home before lighted candles while the men burn incense in the fields and sprinkle the ground with *aguardiente*, a local brandy. At daybreak the women carry candles and food to the fields. After tapers are placed in the directions of the four winds, the fields are sown and everyone joins in the big feast.

San Isidro

In Río Frío, Colombia, St. Isidore is saddled with the very special obligation of bringing rain. The beginning of April is supposed to mark the end of the dry season, so on April 4 the image of the saint is carried through town with everyone following and chanting his praises. The need for rain is carefully explained, and he is expected to produce at least a shower before the observances are over. To give him plenty of time, the procession proceeds slowly, taking two steps forward and one backward each time. If there is still no shower after several turns through town, the chanting changes from praises to reproaches. After several more times around, this becomes hearty abuse interspersed with variegated profanity. If the skies remain unmoved, poor San Isidro is angrily shoved back into his niche and left there for another year.

Sealing the Frost

Each year around the beginning of April, the Cuchumatan Indians of Santa Eulalia, Guatemala, take part in a ceremony to protect their corn from the frost. As everyone in that part of the world knows, the frost lives in a crack in the mountain not far from Santa Eulalia. Each spring this must be carefully sealed so that the young shoots of corn will not be frostbitten. The prayermakers, who are believed to have special power over the weather, lead the procession to the cliff where one of them ties a rope around his waist and lets himself be lowered over the edge. Dangling perilously, he continues the descent until he is opposite the frost-crack and then signals his helpers to fasten the rope. After he has sealed the crack with mortar he is hauled up again, and then he has the honor of leading the procession back to the village. Occasionally the tender shoots of corn get nipped anyway, and that particular prayermaker is unceremoniously dismissed from office.

San Marcos

The day of St. Mark, April 25, initiates a ten-day spring festival in Aguascalientes, Mexico. Instituted in 1604, this was for a long time one of Mexico's most brilliant and important fiestas. People would travel clear across the country to take part in the festivities and to buy rare silks and other things from the Orient. Even today there is something going on day and night: early morning serenades, parades, flower battles, the coronation of a queen, athletic events, art exhibits, regional dances, cockfights, bullfights, and formal balls. There is an opportunity to try the many savory national dishes and a specialty of the fair known as *chara-musca* (a taffy candy made in the shape of animals and people and decorated with nuts). In the background of all the activities is the lively music of the *mariachis*. These strolling folk ensembles are composed of various stringed instruments and usually a cornet. They were extremely popular during the reign of Maximilian and often played for weddings of members of the French court. It has been said that the name *mariachi* is nothing more than a corruption of the French *mariage*.

In Peru the day of St. Mark is a time for the marking of livestock. There are different methods in different places, but it is always done with great ceremony and followed by gay fiestas. In the vicinity of Puno, the owner of the cattle initiates the ceremony with an offering to Pacha-Mama (Mother Earth) on the eve of the marking. The offering is repeated the next day in the corral in front of the animals and to the music of flute and drum. Afterward, men and women carrying a large sea shell full of corn gruel and a bouquet of wild flowers add their prayers to Pacha-Mama for abundant reproduction of the animals and throw the flowers and the contents of the shell in offering.

Before marking the cattle, a fat specimen of each sex is chosen and painted with red earth. Around the horns of the male and the neck of the female are hung wreathes of wild flowers. Next the two animals are tied together, belly to belly, and made to lie on the ground while the owner throws silver filings over them so that they will bring him money. Finally the ears of all the cattle are marked with special slits and the tails cut off. The blood is saved and mixed with *chicha*, which everyone drinks to assure an abundance of meat. After the marking, everyone goes to the ranch house, where gay singing, dancing, and feasting begin.

Santo Toribio

On April 27 a dramatic fiesta in la Villa de Macate, Peru, reconstructs a miracle performed there by St. Toribio. A long time ago, the stream which supplies the town with water went dry, and the inhabitants were about to pack their belongings and go in search of a new place to live. Santo Toribio happened to be passing by. Feeling sorry for the people, he struck the rocks near the spring three times with his staff, thus causing the water to flow again. On the day of the fiesta his image is taken in procession, along with musicians, dancers, and fireworks, to the place of the miracle, about a mile from the church. At the end of the religious service, the priest strikes the same rocks three times with a staff; the water, which had previously been diverted, again floods the stream.

Fiesta de las Cruces

In late April the Mayas of Quintana Roo, Mexico, celebrate their Fiesta of the Patron Crosses. At this time a strange celebration known as *okoztah-pol* takes place. At dawn on the second day of the fiesta, a pig is sacrificed, cooked, and eaten. Its decorated head is placed on the altar, and early the next day a dance burlesquing the selling of a pig takes place in the atrium of the church. To the tune of a Spanish song, *"La Carbonerita,"* nine girls carrying bowls of *pinole* (a powder of toasted corn) and agave leaves for spoons make a circle around a table. A man with a gourd rattle enters leading the pig (the decorated head borne by a second man) and offers it for sale. While the bartering goes on, the girls circle nine times against the sun and nine times sunwise, keeping track by cigarettes laid on the table. The pig-impersonator pretends to escape and is recaptured. Finally he is sold to the organizer of the fiesta for a hundred cigarettes, and the *pinole* is served to the guests.

Fiesta del Mar

At the end of summer, sometime during March or April, the people along the coast of Uruguay pay homage to the sea with their very colorful Fiesta del Mar. The curving shoreline between the two peninsulas of Punta del Este and Punta Ballena is illuminated with huge torches placed close to the ground and about fifteen feet apart. The fiesta begins with a parade of boats, large and small and specially decorated for the occasion. Soon after this all attention is focused on the coronation of the Queen of the Sea, which usually takes place on the pier of the Club de Pesca at Punta del Este. A man representing Neptune emerges from the water dressed in a gilded suit, and, holding the traditional trident in one hand, he goes to the chosen queen and places the crown upon her head. She then rides through the city on a float accompanied by her royal court and followed by a long caravan of automobiles. Often there is a floating stage where choreographic numbers depict such things as the mythical realm of Neptune or events in the history of Punta del Este. An aquatic ballet adds variety to the program. The fiesta ends with a fantastic display of fireworks that lasts for almost an hour.

El Señor de los Temblores

Early in the seventeenth century, according to legend, some fishermen in the South American port of Callao found a strange-looking box floating in the water. Because of its shape they believed it contained a crucifix and informed the church authorities in Lima. The authorities ordered that it be brought to them, but the box became so heavy that it was impossible to move it. The same thing happened when they decided to send it to Ayacucho. When Cuzco was suggested, however, the box became very light as a sign that the image wanted to go there. It was installed in a chapel of the unfinished cathedral in Cuzco and called the Señor de Carlos V, because it was believed that the image had come from Spain. Shortly afterward, this Peruvian city was hit by the terrible earthquakes of 1650. The earth shook for three days until scarcely a building remained standing. Finally, when the crucifix was taken from the still undamaged church and carried in procession, the trembling stopped. From that time on the image was called el Señor de los Temblores (Lord of the Earthquakes), and for nearly 300 years Cuzco remained free of earthquakes.

Every year on the Monday before Easter, the Lord of Earthquakes is taken out in procession. During the morning his chapel is the scene of great activity. To the accompaniment of violins, harp, and women singing Quechua hymns, the *mayordomos* of the fiesta carefully wipe the image and dress it in white, lace-trimmed panties. Over those go a white loin cloth and finally one of black velvet, embroidered in gold and set with precious jewels. The image is left bare above the waist, but a magnificent curly wig is substituted for the everyday one, and a gold crown set on that.

At about five in the afternoon, a military band and a group of acolytes carrying silver crosses and censers line up at the cathedral to escort the Señor. The image comes through the door on a heavy litter of solid silver borne on the shoulders of thirty men. Followed by church dignitaries in elegant robes, the group completes a tour of the city, making courtesy calls at various churches where the litter is taken inside. Each time there is much disputing as to who should have the honor of carrying it to the next stop, for it is believed that those who do will be rewarded by eternal salvation. Indians carrying lighted candles strew the route with *ñujchu* petals, making a red carpet for the Señor to pass over. When the procession returns to the cathedral, the bearers make the sign of the cross with the figure in the direction of the four cardinal points. Everyone kneels weeping and asking for favors, but no one dares look at the face of the image, for it is believed that the glance of the Señor singles out those doomed to die during the coming year. A mournful wail fills the air as they beg: "Lord, if this year the choice falls on me, grant me the grace of a happy death."

The Indians' fanatical veneration of this image is evidenced by the following story. In 1875 Monseñor Ochoa, then Bishop of Cuzco, arranged to have the image repainted, because time and the smoke of countless candles had turned it almost black. When the Indians heard of the indignity that was about to be perpetrated upon their Lord, discontent brewed like a coming thunderstorm. Scarcely had the painter set up his ladder in front of the altar when hundreds of indignant Indians stormed the cathedral door demanding that no impious hand be laid upon the Señor. To try to calm them, the bishop had the painter's ladder thrown to the crowd. This was promptly broken to pieces but failed to stem the tide of fury that was racing through the mob. The Indians hurled stones at the windows, tried to break the doors down, and shrieked: "Tonight we'll drink chicha in the bishop's skull." Fortunately, before they finally smashed their way into the cathedral, the painter and the bishop managed to escape by a secret door which led to the episcopal palace. Cheated of their revenge, the Indians raged through town ravaging and sacking everything they could lay hands on. It was several days before they finally calmed down.

Although Cuzco was convulsed by a serious earthquake in 1941, the Indians have never lost faith in the efficacy of the Señor de los Temblores. He had permitted an earthquake, it was true, but he had spared their lives. Without his protection, the damage would have been a thousand times greater.

São Benedito

In Brazil, St. Benedict is the patron saint of the Negroes, and celebrations in his honor are among the most colorful in the country. At Aparecida do Norte, halfway between Rio and São Paulo, the yearly festivities are held on the Monday after Easter. Pilgrims come from all over the state to keep promises made to the miraculous saint. Many of them are ancient Negroes who still remember the horrors of slavery.

The two most important figures of the whole celebration

are the king and the queen, chosen each year by the Negro brotherhoods. Usually there is a white king and a Negro queen one year, and the following year it is reversed. The parish priest is not forgotten on this day, for besides presiding over the mass he has the sacred duty of blessing the royal crowns, a silver one for the king and a gold one for the queen.

After the mass a procession forms outside the church led by young boys who have just completed their first communion. Following them are members of the Brotherhood of St. Benedict wearing white hats and blue chest ribbons. Finally come the monarchs themselves, carrying their crowns on cushions and flanked by drummers. The crowd follows behind them, eager to arrive at the king's home, where they will be served the special St. Benedict's sweets. These are made of such things as citron, pumpkin, potato, or oranges. The town dignitaries are usually given custard or gelatin and soft drinks in addition.

In the meantime the air is filled with primitive music as fantastic dance groups called *congadas* and *moçambiques* perform in front of the host's house, in the square opposite St. Benedict's church, and in other parts of town. Besides the local *moçambiques*, several groups come from other towns to take part. Colorful silk banners proclaim their place of origin and the name of the brotherhood to which they belong.

The Negroes believe that St. Benedict was a farmer who invented the *moçambique* dance for the benefit of other farmers. Thus, every dancer must be a farmer though he need not necessarily be Negro. Actually, the dances have evolved from old war dances which the early missionaries altered and used to add color to the religious processions. One is an adaptation of a fifteenth-century sword dance and offers a skillful display of fencing. Sometimes dancers wear bells tied to their legs or test their skill by dancing over wooden rods placed crosswise on the ground. The *moçambique* dances are purely gymnastic feats characterized by grace of movement and agility. In contrast, the dances of the *congadas* act out old African stories. The dancing goes on for hours on end until superseded by the display of fireworks at the end of the evening. After the last rocket has gone up, the drums begin again but this time the rhythm is slower, for what they are playing now are songs of farewell.

Cuasimodo

Cuasimodo, or the Sunday following Easter, has a special significance in Peru. It is a time for visiting the homes of the sick to cheer them up and to bring consolation to their families. In Ayacucho there are services in the church on Saturday night and the square is lighted with bonfires. The next morning the procession, headed by a band and priests carrying the Sacred Host under a pallium, makes its way from house to house. Indian women carrying lighted candles scatter golden *retama* petals along the way.

Semana Criolla

Uruguay, which is today one of the most cosmopolitan of the Latin American countries, used to be the domain of the arrogant gaucho. This man of the plains, molded by the endless struggle with rigorous nature, spirited cattle, and hostile Indians, was completely distinct from the peasant, who is the normal bearer of folk culture. In manner, dress, and often in blood, the old-time gaucho was as much Indian as Spanish. He was tough, cruel, restless, a man whose wealth was his horse and whose argument was his *façon* (a knife as long as a bayonet). For over 150 years he was master of the plains, but with the establishment of law and economic order he rapidly faded away. People of Uruguay, however, are determined that the gaucho shall never be forgotten.

Throughout the country are numerous clubs with such names as "Los Cimarrones" (The Wild Ones), "El Pericón" (a native dance, or "Vivaró" (an indigenous tree). The club buildings themselves are veritable museums adorned with such objects as *façones*, *rastras* (wide metal belts), intricately braided lassos, and *boleadoras* (leather thongs with balls at one end which were thrown around the legs of fleeing animals). Here rich landowners, businessmen and professional men gather to partake of *asados con cuero* (whole animals barbecued over an open fire with the hide left on), *mazamorra* (a dish of ground corn and milk), *empanadas* (meat turnovers), sausages made of capybara, and other foods. They amuse themselves with *payadas* (the gaucho's popular vocal duels), regional dances, and horseback games.

This cult of the gaucho reaches its climax during a week-long celebration known as Semana Criolla. Coinciding with the religious observance of Holy Week, the activities take place on a stretch of turf called La Rural in the Prado, a Montevideo park. Men in typical gaucho dress—high boots, baggy trousers, *chiripá* (a length of cloth draped diaper-fashion), *rastro*, *poncho*, and cowboy hat—watch or take part in the various contests. There are prizes for the best costume, riding equipment, dancing, singing, lassoing, and bronco-busting. The latter, of course, monopolizes most of the attention. Applicants from all over the country are carefully screened, for no more than thirty men may participate. Sometimes women take part, and people still talk about the beautiful Nieves Mira, who was the major attraction for several years. They also remember the Negro, Diego Rodríguez, nicknamed "El Fantasma" (The Ghost), who used to perform with his poncho drawn over his eyes. Though competition is keen, the most important thing is not who is the best bronco-buster, whose costume is most elegant, or which horse has the best saddle. What matters most to everyone is that the gaucho shall not die out.

HOLY WEEK

S EMANA SANTA, or Holy Week, is celebrated in every
part of Latin America. It is a time of almost continual
religious observances, of colorful processions, of vivid
passion plays. Churches are beautifully decorated for
the occasion with green growing things and golden fruit.
Scenes depicting events leading up to the crucifixion and
resurrection are erected in many of them. During the days of
mourning, the church bells are silenced and *matracas,* or
wooden rattles, are used to announce the services. Altars and
saints are covered in many of the churches during this time.

As in our own country, there is a definite shift of population during Easter Week. Many city dwellers take advantage
of the holidays to go to seaside or mountain resorts, thus
avoiding the crowds of countryfolk who invade cities and
towns for the religious festivities. Tourists lucky enough to
be in Panama at this time have an unequaled opportunity
to meet the shy *cholos,* who spend the rest of the year in in-
accessible villages in the mountains or on the plains.

Holy Week begins on Palm Sunday with the blessing of

palms in the churches. Some of the people carry simple palm branches, but many have attractively woven and decorated figures. Banners, crosses, spears, and letters are among the many unusual forms. In Salvador, Brazil, the streets are filled with palm vendors offering such things as sabres, hats, and various articles of clothing made out of palm fibres.

Some of the smaller towns have processions every day during Holy Week, but in most places nothing much happens between Palm Sunday and Maundy Thursday. On Thursday special altars known as *monumentos* are decorated with flowers and lighted candles. People go from church to church to view the *monumentos* until they have visited seven different churches. On this day also, priests wash the feet of twelve of their altar boys or members of the parish to commemorate the washing of the feet of the twelve disciples by Christ. Small villages love to dramatize the Last Supper and the betrayal and arrest of Christ.

Events on Good Friday center around the sentence and procession of the three falls in the morning and the crucifixion and descent from the cross in the afternoon. It is a time of universal mourning. In Costa Rica, people dress in black and there are no busses, trains, or other means of public transportation all day. There is only one day of mourning, however, for in Catholic Latin America the resurrection is celebrated the next day.

On Saturday morning the Mass of Glory takes place, and the sombre part of Holy Week is over. Church bells once again ring with a deafening clamor; firecrackers go off in happy bursts. In some places effigies of Judas are hanged or burned. There is general rejoicing and merrymaking of all kinds. People rush through the streets beating on tin cans or drums and shouting. Factory whistles, boat whistles, and automobile horns add to the deafening uproar.

In most places Easter is just another Sunday. There are very few religious processions and no profane parade of new clothes either inside or outside the church.

One town that vividly relives the past for an entire week is Taxco, Mexico. At six o'clock on the morning of Palm Sunday, people of the neighboring village of Tehuilotepec set out toward Taxco with an image of Christ mounted on a donkey. Almost the entire village is in attendance carrying arches and bouquets of flowers and palm fronds. At the Plazuela de la Garita, which is the entrance to Taxco, the procession is joined by twelve men representing the apostles and dressed more or less in Biblical fashion. This procession, commemorating the triumphant entry of Christ into Jerusalem, arrives at the ornate church of Santa Prisca at about ten o'clock, and the local inhabitants join the pilgrims for the Blessing of the Palms.

On Monday evening at nine, the images of San Miguel and La Natividad are joined by other images from nearby towns and carried on beautifully decorated litters between a double line of men, women, and children carrying lighted candles. Each image has its own group of musicians. Many of the followers carry staffs trimmed with gay tissue paper streamers and colored gourds.

On Tuesday evening there is another candlelight procession, this time featuring three images of Christ that are taken from local churches. Heading the procession are an impressive choir singing sacred music and groups of musicians playing drums and *chirimías* (small flute-like instruments). Also forming a part of the procession is a group of persons dressed in deep mourning and dragging chains which are fastened to their ankles. These people, called *almas encadenadas* (souls in chains), symbolize the souls in purgatory.

At three o'clock on Wednesday afternoon the huge bronze bells of Santa Prisca softly toll, calling the faithful to Las Tinieblas (Darkness). This ceremony, held in the church, recalls the darkness and dreariness that the Lord went through during His days of travail and His prayer in the Garden of Olives. There is again a procession at nine o'clock at night bearing the Blessed Trinity, the Virgen de Fatima,

Señor del Calvario, Señor de la Portada, and two figures representing Adam and Eve.

On Thursday the courtyard of Santa Prisca church is turned into a veritable bower with fresh green boughs and singing birds in cages. Little girls dressed as angels in white satin and silver wings keep vigil, for this is supposed to represent the Garden of Gethsemane. At five in the afternoon the faithful are called to church by the *matraca*, and the rites of the Washing of the Feet and the Last Supper are enacted.

Soon the streets of town are filled with Sayones, groups of men dressed as Roman soldiers or centurions, their brilliantly colored satin costumes adding gay flashes of color to the crowd. Most of these men play the same role every year in fulfillment of a vow. At seven o'clock the man chosen to play the part of Jesus appears in the Garden, and an unkempt, long-haired Judas approaches and kisses him on the cheek. Jesus is immediately seized by the Sayones and taken to prison where He remains in chains throughout the night. At eleven o'clock the sentence dictated by Pontius Pilate is read, and Pilate washes his hands, signifying that he cleanses himself of the blood of Jesus.

While all this has been going on, processions from the surrounding villages, bearing huge images of the crucified Christ on wooden litters decorated with lanterns and flowers, have been entering the town on all sides. Groups of pilgrims, all carrying candles, follow each image. During these processions the *encruzados* make their first appearance. These penitents wear only a long black skirt and a black hood which completely hides their head. Their arms are extended in the form of a cross, and across their back and arms is tied a huge bundle of thorny branches with the thorns pressing down on their bare flesh. The bundles are enormous, and it is claimed that some weigh as much as one hundred pounds. A few of the penitents also wear wide horsehair belts which further add to their torture. Often the penitents faint along the way and have to be revived.

On Friday morning the Adoration of the Cross takes place. A large group of children comes down the street, bending under the weight of a huge cross which is later transferred to Christ to carry on the Road to Calvary. The latter, with the historic three falls, is portrayed by images. So also are the crucifixion and descent from the cross, which take place at about four in the afternoon. The image of the crucified Christ is placed in a coffin, and an impressive funeral procession accompanies His remains to the place that represents the tomb. The *encruzados*, still carrying their brambles, stagger along.

On Saturday morning the bells ring out in joy and gladness, and the Sayones fall in varying postures of dismay. On Sunday there is a final procession with an image of Christ resurrected.

The preceding are merely the religious ceremonies which take place. Holy Week in Taxco is also known for the variety and beauty of the regional dances performed there and for unusual fireworks such as the daylight *castillos*. The typical *castillo*, which is a part of fiestas in almost all parts of the country, is a reed structure thirty to one hundred feet high consisting of a series of complicated fireworks made to represent animals, flowers, birds, crosses, saints, and other forms. The various sections set each other off in sequence, and the resulting symphony of color lasts from twenty minutes to a half hour. The daylight *castillos* have humorous scenes of animals and people similar to those on European clock towers, but instead of being set in motion by a clock mechanism, they are animated by the fireworks.

Popayán, Colombia, is another place famous for the beauty of its Holy Week celebrations. The whole town begins to get ready long before Palm Sunday. Most of the houses are freshly calcimined in pleasing shades of green, pink, yellow, or blue. Gardens are given special attention to assure a blaze of color for Holy Week. Interiors of churches are redecorated, and the fabulous gold and silver objects given to the churches years ago by rich men of the colony are put on display.

On the Saturday before Palm Sunday a group of men gathers at the little Chapel of Bethlehem overlooking the city to prepare the two images that will be carried in the night processions. These men, who are also the *cargueros* (bearers), provide the money for the conservation and decoration of the images. Ability to pay does not necessarily guarantee one a position, however, for the honor is usually passed from father to son.

On Palm Sunday the traditional blessing of the palms takes place in the morning, and in the afternoon the two images are brought down from the Bethlehem Chapel between rows of waving palm branches to join the police drum corps, the army band, and schoolgirls dressed in their blue-and-white uniforms.

Tuesday afternoon is dedicated to a unique ceremony called the Feast of the Prisoners. A procession of litters covered with huge bowls of soup, salad, fruit, beans, meat, gelatin pudding, and cases of soft drinks sets out for the prison accompanied by the archbishop in full regalia, government officials, schoolgirls with bags of food, and the inevitable army band. When the procession arrives at the prison, the prisoners are brought out into the courtyard to listen to speeches and to be served their feast. From among the prisoners, one who is nearing the end of his sentence is selected, and on Thursday afternoon he sits, manacled and guarded, at a table in front of the bank. He is supposed to represent Barrabas whom the crowd chose to free instead of Christ. During the afternoon people pass by his table and leave donations of food or money for him to claim at the end of the day when he is set free.

Tuesday night brings forth the first of the beautiful candlelight processions in which large decorated litters bear the beloved saints or depict scenes from the Passion of Christ. On Friday, for example, there are life-size figures of men carrying hammers and pliers used to take Christ's body from the cross, and on another litter an angel and grinning skeleton carrying a scythe. The shimmering light of the candles, the slow tolling of a small bell carried by one of the acolytes, and the murmuring of the candlebearers reciting the rosary create a spine-tingling sensation in the spectators.

It is said that Popayán's impressive candlelight processions can be credited with having saved the town from invasion. At one time fierce mountain tribes, who had been driven back but never subdued by the Spaniards, began gathering their forces in the hills at the edge of town, planning to attack in the still of the night. Suddenly strange funereal music rose from the town, and the startled warriors noticed a fiery serpent winding slowly toward the hills where they lay hidden. Dropping their weapons, they fled in panic and from then on left the peaceful little town alone.

No one knows when Popayán's first procession took place, but a reference dated 1558 indicates that Easter ceremonies were being held there more than half a century before the Pilgrims landed at Plymouth. Since then the processions have been held every year, even during independence uprisings or civil wars. Many times truces were called just to allow the traditional processions to pass through the streets.

Along with those of Taxco and Popayán, the processions of Antigua, Guatemala, rank high on the list of outstanding ones. Starting on Palm Sunday the processions are held throughout Easter Week, sometimes beginning at eight in the morning and lasting all day. Probably the most impressive is the one on Good Friday during which a life-size figure of Christ carrying a huge cross is carried high above the heads of the crowd. Every few blocks the purple-robed, white-gloved bearers relinquish the heavy platform to fresh contingents so that as many as possible can express their piety by taking an active part in the colorful rite.

At three o'clock in the afternoon (the hour of Christ's death) the bearers all change to black robes. Accompanying the litter through the streets are groups of men armored and helmeted to represent the Roman soldiers, some mounted and some on foot. All along the route are elaborate carpets fashioned of dyed sawdust, sand, flowers, and pine needles. Marchers carefully side-step these as only the litter bearing Christ and His cross are permitted to pass over them. Before leaving each carpet the bearers pause for a moment and carefully erase the picture with their feet.

In Sonsonate, El Salvador, the Good Friday procession passes over similar multicolored sawdust mats which are made to represent Biblical scenes, birds, flowers, or fruits. This awesome procession leaves the church at three in the afternoon and does not return until three the next morning.

In Costa Rica, a touch of drama and real-life "angels" add originality to the Friday processions. In the morning the procession bearing the cross-burdened image of Christ sets out on its predetermined route. At the first stop, a lovely girl representing the Samaritan woman at Jacob's well steps out from the crowd and raises a jug of water to the painted face of the image. At the second stop, Mary Magdalene comes forward and anoints the Saviour's feet with oil from a little crystal flask. The next stop reveals a lovely Veronica eagerly waiting to wipe His brow with a sparkling white cloth. Finally an image or picture of Mary, Mother of Jesus, joins the procession.

In the afternoon the image of Christ is taken from the cross and carried through the streets in an elaborate casket. Borne aloft on small platforms are precious little "angels," girls from two to seven years of age, several of them holding mottoes bearing the last words of Christ. The vacant cross, Veronica, Mary Magdalene, and the Samaritan women are also borne on platforms.

Though many towns dramatize portions of Holy Week events, the most complete and elaborate passion plays are those of three small towns in Mexico—Malinalco, Tzintzuntzan, and Ixtapalapa. In Malinalco it is a week-long affair with everyone in town taking part. The well-to-do men dress as Romans and decorate their horses with wonderful ribbons, feathers, bells, and other things. The less fortunate ones represent the Christians, who had no horses. Their costumes, however, are gorgeous satin creations combining such colors as lime green and magenta. The little girls all dress as angels with glittering silver wings attached to their white garments.

In Tzintzuntzan the play begins at noon on Thursday and ends at midnight on Good Friday. It is held outdoors under the olive trees near the church, and the beauty of the setting and the fine acting of the main characters make it a truly outstanding performance. The Ixtapalapa pageant takes place on the same two days and in a variety of settings throughout the town. The costumes, which are usually rented from some theatrical company in the capital, are among the most elaborate to be found anywhere.

A less professional but nonetheless interesting passion play is that seen in Paleca, near the capital of El Salvador. Though economic conditions permit only the simplest of settings and costumes, the enthusiasm of both actors and spectators is as great as in the Mexican versions.

In contrast to the solemnity of the religious processions and passion plays is the horseplay involving Judas which most Latin American countries enjoy on the Saturday before Easter. In Panama, Costa Rica, and Guatemala an effigy of Judas is paraded through the streets, and there is a dramatic reading of his last will and testament in which local writers have a chance to air the town scandals or poke fun at local celebrities. Following this the effigy is hanged or burned with much merriment.

In some parts of Paraguay, firecrackers are concealed in the straw body of Judas, and after he is hanged people have the fun of shooting at him to try to hit a firecracker. This provides great excitement for the crowds until Judas has completely exploded and burned. In Tobatí, Paraguay, small animals such as toads or kittens are sometimes substituted for the firecrackers, and these come scrambling out when the effigy is set afire.

In Mexico the original purpose of avenging the betrayal of Christ developed into a general manifestation of rather violent political and social opinion. Though some of the papier-mâché Judas effigies were made to represent such things as clowns, skeletons, cowboys, devils, and pirates, the majority clearly portrayed disliked politicians or other unpopular citizens.

Until a few years ago, traffic in the center of Mexico City was rerouted for several hours on Saturday morning to provide space for the Judas games. All along Tacuba Street were hung enormous figures, many contributed by local merchants and strung with gifts of merchandise. As their fuses were lighted, the firecrackers inside went off with loud explosions blowing the figure to bits. The crowd, mostly boys, fought furiously over each part of the figure that fell off, and especially over the gifts. Often the victor lost his shirt in the struggle. Though the government has outlawed the firecrackers, the figures are still being made and are displayed in the markets and in front of the San Pablo church as early as a week before Easter. Ranging anywhere from ten inches to ten feet high, they have an enormous sale as they are one of the strongest expressions of Mexican folk art.

All over Haiti, effigies of Judas, dressed in a weird assortment of costumes, appear early in Holy Week. "Monsieur Judas" first goes to visit a peasant family as one of the twelve apostles and an honored guest. As soon as the death of Christ is announced on Good Friday, the symbolic traitor flees, aided by some conspirator who hides him in a ravine or other secluded spot on the edge of town. On Saturday morning the hunt begins, and the whole town—including stiff-jointed ancients and bare-bottomed small fry—takes part. Some of the bloodthirsty participants become almost hysterical in their efforts to find the villain. Shouting *"Qui bo' li?"* (Where is he?) and brandishing clubs, machetes, old colonial swords, and knives, they thrash through the ravines and canebrakes. If by chance they first find someone else's Judas, so much the better; they whack it up with glee. By noon the countryside of Haiti is strewn with dismembered dummies, bleeding sawdust and rags.

Though fervent Catholics attend special masses in the churches, the general tone of Holy Week celebrations in Haiti is more profane than religious. Carnival celebrations, which do not end with the beginning of Lent but continue to break out again every Saturday and Sunday night, reach a peak on the Friday, Saturday, and Sunday of Easter Week. Hundreds of Rara bands that have been dancing ecstatically through the countryside for weeks now convene in the larger cities and towns, especially in the south in the town of Léogane.

Each Rara band has a leader known as the *Roi Lwalwadi* (the King of Lwalwadi) who is a dancer of very special talents. His elegant costume is often of expensive satin or velvet and may be covered with tiny mirrors or bits of colored glass. With this goes a towering headdress of papier-mâché in imitation of the headdresses used in West Africa. Each king has his own type of dance; it may be a belly dance, a graceful ballet-like performance, or a dance involving complicated footwork and semiacrobatics such as the imitation of a pair of scissors at work.

When two bands come face to face on the road, the leaders challenge each other to a competitive dance, for the function of the king is to outdance any other king whom the band happens to meet. They dance to the beat of drums or to the music of *vaccines* (long bamboo flutes which the musician both blows and beats). When it becomes dark the band lights its way with wooden torches or candelabra of tiny oil lamps.

In addition to the *Roi Lwalwadi*, there are other traditional personalities such as the *major jonc*, a baton twirler, and the *jongleur*, a juggler or strong man who performs such feats as dancing while holding a fully set table off the ground with his teeth. In the southwest, near Jérémie, there are wrestling exhibitions known as *pingé* during Easter Week. Some wrestlers take their own musicians with them as they wander about looking for an opponent. When a challenge is made and accepted, the spectators form a circle around the wrestlers, and the performance takes place against a background of excited drumming.

In Indian countries such as Guatemala, Easter observances are often so mixed with pagan rites that it is difficult to tell where one ends and another begins. Coming as it does in March or April, Holy Week coincides in time with the fertility rites held in ancient times to bring rain and good crops. In the picturesque little church of Santo Tomás in Chichicastenango, Indians can be seen all during the week kneeling in prayer over parti-colored ears of seed corn. In many villages arches of fruit, vegetables, and flowers are erected. Stuffed squirrels, raccoons, rabbits, and other small animals of tribal significance are featured on them, and sometimes even live animals are used.

The town of Atitlán, Guatemala, sometimes stages a peculiar race on Maundy Thursday between two arches erected near the church. Two teams of four runners each dash from one arch to the other carrying an image of St. John. In front of one arch stands the Virgin and at the other, Christ Crucified. Each time the runners touch an image it is moved a step forward so that the race gets shorter each time. Nevertheless, the men may run as many as a hundred lengths and end stumbling with fatigue. It is said that the race is a part of the training or testing of neophyte shamans.

In some Guatemalan towns ceremonial burlesque goes hand in hand with solemn religious observances. In Chiantla the apostles often escape from the Good Friday procession and hide in the ravines. Men and boys dressed in purple robes and peaked headdresses take off in pursuit, and eventually all the apostles are dragged back to the procession. In a few villages it is believed that Mary and John enjoyed a passionate interlude on the night before the Crucifixion.

Therefore the two images are forced to spend Thursday night locked in separate cells in the village jail.

Andean countries also exhibit this familiar mélange of pagan and religious observance during Holy Week. In addition to taking part in the traditional processions, the Altiplano Indians set aside one day for a ceremony dedicated to Pacha-Mama in which herbs and fetal parts of a lamb or goat are burned as offerings. In Puno, Peru, Good Friday celebrations include a solemn procession of the Holy Sepulcher and a lively fair featuring the sale of miniature houses, ranches, and other objects. Undoubtedly it is believed that wishes will come true if objectified on this day.

In several villages of Mexico, Easter observances are also combined with some more primitive rite. In Cherán a young unmarried couple is chosen in each section of town to take a large decorated cross to church on Palm Sunday. While the boys selected for this honor make a trip to the hot country to obtain palm leaves, their girl friends remain at home grinding white corn for *pinole*. This is mixed with brown sugar and rolled into large balls that are wrapped in cornhusks and painted with colored designs. The balls are fastened to the cross along with attractive fibre bags and napkins given to the girl by her relatives. Green palm leaves are added to the top and to the ends of the arms of the cross. On Palm Sunday the boy carries this cross to church while the girl carries a long pole hung with every kind of fruit imaginable; sometimes a whole bunch of bananas or a watermelon is included. At times it is almost more than she can carry, but to be the most popular girl she must not only have the best decorated pinole balls and the greatest number of bags and napkins but must also carry the heaviest load of fruit.

In the interior of Panama, Holy Week festivities are accompanied by devil dancers wearing wild animals' heads and bells for tails. They pass through the villages on Saturday to cleanse the houses of evil spirits for the coming year. Devils appear in many of the larger towns also and fight

mock battles on street corners with people dressed as angels.
Almost every part of Mexico contributes some colorful
dance to the Holy Week festivities. Tepoztlán, near Cuernavaca, has a three-day diversion known as Fiesta del Brinco
(Festival of Hops or Jumps). Men wearing long silk robes of
brilliant hues and imposing feather headdresses dance for
three whole days without interruption. Relays of dancers
relieve each other so that the hopping never stops.

Among the most exciting dances seen during Easter Week
are those of the Yaqui Indians in Sonora. On the Saturday
before Easter three dancers called *pascolas* appear in the
thatched arbor erected especially for the festival. Their
heads and torsos are bare. Their trousers are formed from a
checked blanket cleverly draped and held up by a brightly
colored belt. Around their legs are dried cocoons filled with
gravel, and in their hands wooden rattles. Two musicians
begin to play a lively tune on the harp and violin. The *pascolas* tuck their rattles in their belts and dance, one at a time,
with fast steps which at times resemble the European clog
and at others the Spanish zapateado. The continual rustling
of the cocoons makes a subtle undertone to the notes of the
instruments.

After each dancer has had his turn, the music becomes
more primitive. One musician beats on half of a gourd floating in a bowl of water; two others have gourds placed flat on
the ground to give resonance to the sound of a straight stick
drawn across a notched stick laid upon them. Using their
rattles this time, the dancers begin slowly and gradually
work up to a fast and furious rhythm with more movement
of the upper body and more vigorous footwork.

While waiting their turn, the *pascolas* amuse the spectators, for they are also clowns. These comic interludes savor
of lusty but amiable obscenity, and the men in the audience
do not seem to mind even the passes at their womenfolk.
They laugh good-naturedly, because "that's the way the
pascolas are!"

After a while a handsome youth appears, also stripped to

the waist, with a tiny deer head strapped to the top of his head. Deer claws hang from the leather belt that secures his draped trousers, and cocoons rustle softly at his ankles. In each hand he carries a large gourd rattle. He enters, stepping lightly, stopping now and then to paw the ground nervously and sniff about with quivering nostrils. When he is convinced that no danger is lurking, he becomes calmer. He nibbles daintily at make-believe plants; he takes a drink by wetting his nose in the musician's bowl of water; he rubs against one of the men whom he pretends is a tree. All the while, he moves his feet rhythmically and shakes his gourd rattles without losing a beat. Sometimes one or more of the *pascolas* join him, burlesquing his movements or pretending to pursue him. With short intervals of rest and mezcal drinking, this continues all night.

Toward dawn of Easter Sunday the hunt becomes more realistic. The *pascolas*, who represent coyotes, pursue the deer until they trap him. After he is symbolically killed and skinned, his "carcass" is presented to the man in charge of the fiesta, who is obliged to purchase it with a specified number of bottles of liquor.

Though perhaps at their best during the Holy Week festivities, the *pascolas* also perform at other religious fiestas during the year.

MAY

SINCE THE END of the eighteenth century, the month of May has been set apart by the Roman Catholic Church as the "Month of Mary." In most Latin American countries special devotions are offered to the Blessed Virgin all through the month. In Mexico this month has a special significance for little girls under ten years of age. Every day after school tiny "brides" in long white dresses, veiled and with wreaths of white flowers on their heads, are seen carrying blossoms to the church. While the adults sing hymns, the children parade through the church to the altar where they lay their offerings at the feet of the Virgin.

In El Salvador the religious ceremonies during this month in honor of the Virgin Mary are called Flores de Mayo, probably because there is an abundance of wild flowers at this time. The ceremonies are especially colorful in San Vicente. Early in the morning, men and women pass through the streets playing guitars and marimbas; often they carry large drums and strange metal boxes which provide a rhythmic background. At six o'clock the Salvadorian flag is raised at

85

the house of the *capitana*, or woman in charge of the fiesta, and the town band presents a concert. Sometime during the morning a masked clown rides through the town on horseback passing out programs of the coming events. At midday there is a parade of decorated vehicles with ridiculously masked people on foot. Finally between four and five in the afternoon "la Flor" takes place.

Starting at the house of the *capitana*, the fiesta organizers and their women friends go through the streets throwing great quantities of anise seeds, candies, and sweetmeats. Men posted along the way respond with a hailstorm of flowers, corn, and other grains. This continues until they arrive at the atrium of the church. At six the Virgin is carried from the house of the *capitana* to the church in a showy procession, and a second and even showier procession takes place later that night. This continues throughout the month of May but with a different *capitana* each day.

In Brazil too the "Month of Mary" receives special significance. Church altars are blanketed in white flowers, and religious processions take place almost every day. Taking a conspicuous part in the latter are the members of the Daughters of Mary religious society, robed in white with filmy veils and blue sashes.

In some parts of Brazil, however, the month of May is devoted to certain saints. In Poços de Caldas the *festa* of St. Benedict goes on for thirty-one days with special processions on Sundays. In Belém various saints are honored by their most fervent devotees on days the worshipers choose. Rich in folklore, these neighborhood celebrations are highlighted by raising of a votive mast, or flagpole. The mast, laden with streamers, flowers, and fruit, is first carried through the streets in a procession and then raised in front of the devotee's house. Chanting of prayers and beating of drums accompany the ceremony, which is followed by a feast and frequently by fireworks.

Día de la Cruz

The most important day in the whole month of May is the third, or Day of the Holy Cross. This commemorates the discovery by St. Helena, in 326, of the cross on which the Lord was crucified. Throughout Latin America, roadside and village crosses are adorned with flowers, and the most famous miraculous crosses are honored by special fiestas.

At the foot of the sierra in the Argentine provinces of La Rioja and Santiago del Estero stand several large crosses representing each of the nearby villages. On May 3, the villagers bring their cross to town in a picturesque procession and place it on a table covered with a white cloth. Great quantities of flowers are brought and heaped around it, and the crowd prays in front of it. Afterward the festivities begin with eating, drinking, and dancing. On the last day of the fiesta the cross is again carried in a procession and then returned to the edge of the sierra so that it may continue to protect the cultivated fields.

In Peru the Indians are busy for days ahead of time taking down all the wooden crosses near the churches, along the roads, and on mountaintops. These are carefully repaired, repainted, and adorned with streamers and flowers. The Indians watch over them the entire night of the second in a ceremony called Cruzvelacuy, a fiesta-like vigil in which food, drink, and music play a prominent part. Household crosses are also cleaned and adorned, and on the third all crosses are taken to church for the priest's blessing. Exceptionally interesting crosses are found around Huaylas Pass, where they are made of reed in fanciful forms and adorned with bright, multicolored wax flowers.

The small port of Eten, Peru, offers a charming procession in honor of its miraculous cross. The cross, with a silver crown on top and wide silk bands hanging over the arms to form a robe, is carried on a litter hung with silver ex-votos representing parts of the body or fish, all of which have been given in gratitude for the miracles performed by the cross.

On the streets where the fishermen live, artistically adorned arches are erected. Some years special balloons shower confetti, flowers, or verses praising the cross as the procession passes through the arches. In Puno a fiesta and market of miniature objects similar to the Bolivian Alacitas Fair are held on the Calvario Chico Hill.

The Day of the Cross is of special importance throughout the Andes for it has replaced the Inca ceremonies called Aymuray, or "harvest month." The Quechua Indians, however, still observe their ancient festival for the beginning of the harvest on this day. A tree is erected and laden with fruits and gifts of various sorts. Around this the Indians dance the Ayriwa, a dance of the young maize. After the dance the gifts and fruit are shaken out of the tree and divided, and the Aymuray (triumphal song of the harvest) is sung.

In Guatemala too the Day of the Cross is a reminder of the past. Before the Conquest, thousands of Indians flocked to the shores of Lake Amatitlán at this time of year to pray to their most powerful god and to carry out elaborate fertility rites. During these rites children were often thrown into the lake as sacrifices, and the stone figures of lesser gods were brought from distant villages to pay homage to their chief. The Spanish priests, taking advantage of the multitude which began to arrive the first week of May, quickly set up a strong counter-attraction to these pagan ceremonies in the village of Amatitlán which they established across the lake. Today the fiesta, which takes place on May 2 and 3, features Indian dances, music, water sports, and an animated fair. Indians and ladinos alike congregate to pray and play and to buy the gaily decorated boxes, *cajetas de Amatitlán*, filled with sweets of the season.

In El Salvador, the Día de la Cruz is celebrated in people's homes. A cross is set up in the patio or garden and adorned with all kinds of bright paper decorations and appetizing fruits which visitors may feel free to take. The belief exists among the lower classes that in houses where no altar is erected to the cross the devil will come and dance there until midnight. Besides the delicious native foods and drinks, music, dances, and fireworks, each celebration includes three rosaries beginning early in the evening and ending at dawn. At the last rosary a long imprecation against the devil is recited in unison, and in an endless murmur the name of the son of God is pronounced 1,000 times—Jesús, Jesús, Jesús, Jesús . . . — while a count is kept with grains of cereal or small stones.

In Caracas and most other parts of Venezuela the celebration is known as Velorio de Cruz. One special room of the house is chosen and decorated with hanging cloths of various colors. An altar is formed by covering a table with a white sheet, and over this a blue cloth is hung horizontally to represent the sky. Crosses sheathed in tissue paper and images of saints are much in evidence, and lighted candles cover the altar. The highlight of the fiesta, which takes place in front of the altar, is the performance of the troubadours who come from various parts of the country. Playing their instruments, they improvise couplets and a great variety of poetic forms. Guests often contribute their own lively verses which add to the general merriment.

May 3 is celebrated in Mexico mainly by masons and builders. On all buildings under construction, a cross is erected at the highest point and decorated with colored streamers, paper flags, and flowers. Firecrackers and rockets burst all day long, and music is sometimes supplied by a small group of musicians or a radio. Workers have their own fiesta in each building, often as guests of the owner, and enjoy a special repast of *atole* (corn-meal gruel), tamales, or *mole de guajalote* (turkey with a hot sauce). The gaiety of the fiesta depends upon the amount of tequila or pulque available.

The village of Italaque, Bolivia, is one of the centers for the training of the Sicuris who appear at so many of the Andean fiestas. On May 3, as part of the fiesta of the Holy Cross, the students must undergo a special test. First they are given a heavy meal and plenty of chicha to drink. Then, while playing their instruments, they must run up to the Calvary on a hill about 1500 feet high and back without resting. Almost always a few fall by the wayside, and once in a while one will die from overeating and drinking or a bad heart. If nothing happens to any of the contestants it is considered a bad omen, and the group does not continue studying together.

El Cux de Lerma

In Campeche, Mexico, the three-day celebration beginning on May 3 is called El Cux de Lerma. As in so many fiestas in this region, everything centers around the lowly pig. The men in charge of the fiesta make great sport of hunting for the pigs that will be killed for the feast. After decorating them with ribbons and little flags, they parade them through town to the accompaniment of music and rockets to let everyone know that things are getting under way.

Men and women work together the first night preparing the tamales which are served at a special feast on the third. In addition to the religious observances on the fourth and the preparation of a second meal, *chilmole de pavo* (turkey with a rich chili sauce), to be consumed in the afternoon, there is a special pig's head ceremony. Adorned with colored papers and resting on a platter, the head is escorted through the streets by a group of musicians and finally delivered to the house of a man selected to provide a pig for the following year's fiesta. There is dancing all that night, and on the fifth another feast and another dance. During this last dance a man with a *petaca* (straw mat) on his back and a chicken tied to that makes his appearance. In both hands he carries branches of laurel. With him are two girls wearing large red handkerchiefs on their heads; in their right hands they hold a gourd filled with chocolate and in their left another red kerchief. The three do a dance together in which they frighten the chicken with the branches and the handkerchiefs. After this performance is over, the man dances the *torito* with one of the girls and the fiesta comes to an end.

Cinco de Mayo

One of Mexico's most important national holidays is the Fifth of May, which commemorates the victory of the Mexican forces over the French army at Puebla in 1862. Since that famous fifth of May, the city has been called "Puebla la heroíca," and on this date a sham battle is staged there to commemorate the event.

At Peñón, near the great central airport of Mexico City, an elaborate folk play takes place; it not only depicts the historical battle but also some of the events leading up to it. The village plaza is the main stage, while the nearby peñón (big rock), from which the place derives its name, represents the Puebla forts. The act of treaties usually takes place in a nearby schoolyard.

The play begins at eleven o'clock in the morning with a parade of all the forces accompanied by bands and native musicians. General Zaragoza, the leader of the Mexican army, is dressed in an elegant *charro* suit and rides a magnificent horse. From the back of his hat hangs a cloth with "¡Viva México!" embroidered on it. Porfirio Díaz, another famous general, wears a plumed hat and lavishly embroidered uniform hung with many medals. Also recognizable are General Negrete, General Berriozabal, General Doblado, and General Prim. On the back of the French leader, Marshal Lorencz, hangs a cloth embroidered with "¡Viva Francia!" The Zacapoaxtlas from the Sierra de Puebla are present with their Indian leader, Lucas. There are large numbers of Chinacos divided into cavalry and infantry. Groups of common soldiers wearing uniforms of all periods surge through the crowd. Not even the *soldaderas* have been left out. These are the women who follow their men to cook for them and often fight at their side. Each one carries on her back a doll, to represent a baby, and a small basket with food and water. The French Zouaves are dressed in red or blue trousers, a small blue sack coat, white canvas leggings, and a red or blue fez.

At the end of the parade the order to break ranks is given, and the soldiers go to eat in small groups. For the next hour they play their own little game of trying to steal food, ammunition, and arms from the enemy. Adding comedy to the situation is the clipping of the "wild" Zacapoaxtlas who have arrived from the sierra with long hair. They pretend to be afraid of the scissors and weep bitterly over the loss of their hair.

During the first scene of the actual drama the diplomats seat themselves around a table to present their claims before the Juárez government for injuries to persons and property during the Three Year War. Gesticulating expressively and trying to speak in the manner of the country they represent, the diplomats repeat verbatim long sections of the real treaties. The English and Spanish representatives, finally realizing the injustice of their claims, agree to withdraw and leave the country with their troops. Only France declares war.

When the envoy reaches Zaragoza with the declaration of war, the latter tears it up angrily and tells his soldiers to prepare for battle. The Mexican army takes possession of the hill, and the French rush up in a sweeping circle. Three times they attack the fort and are repulsed. At one point the Mexican army drives them down to the village. The fighting goes on for several hours. There is continuous noise from the rifles and cannons, loaded with powder only. There are shouted dialogues—some memorized, others extemporaneous. Over it all can be heard the bugles sounding orders. There is hand-to-hand fighting and at times the spectators, carried away by the reality of the scene, rush in to the aid of the Mexicans, beating the enemy with their fists or throwing dirt in their faces. When a soldier's powder gives out, he is "dead" and must leave the battlefield.

As night begins to fall, Zaragoza and Lorencez meet face

to face, showing off their skill in fencing and riding. They both fight valiantly, but the Mexican leader wins. While the French flag is lowered, he reads aloud the report sent by the real Zaragoza to President Juárez: "The arms of the Republic have been covered with glory. The French soldiers behaved with courage and their generals blunderingly." But the play is not over yet, for the "dead" must be buried. Soldiers from both sides are placed on cots or stretchers or in coffins. Led by bands playing funeral marches, the procession leaves the plaza and is soon lost in the darkness.

San Isidro

St. Isidore, patron of agriculture, has his own special day on May 15, but in Moche, Peru, the entire first two weeks of May are given over to a celebration in his honor. Each night San Isidro, dressed in a straw hat and humble clothes, goes to stay at a different farm in the community. Late each afternoon a lively procession headed by a band escorts the saint to the house of his next host. There his litter is placed on an improvised outdoor altar hung with apples, bananas, oranges, figs, and every other kind of fruit produced on that farm. Each altar is decorated in a different way, and each host tries to outdo the previous one. It would be impolite to sleep while San Isidro is a guest, so the night is spent in vigil at his altar. Every saint enjoys a fiesta, however, so there are food, drinks, music, and dancing. The next afternoon, as the saint is preparing to leave, the altar is dismantled and the fruit distributed among the guests.

On the afternoon of the fourteenth San Isidro is returned to the church in Moche. His straw hat is replaced with a silver one and his ordinary cape with a velvet one embroidered with gold and set with precious stones. After the procession on the fifteenth the streets are invaded by devil dancers wearing vivid costumes with horned masks. On the nights of the fourteenth and fifteenth they roam through the countryside stealing whatever they can from small farms. They are not punished, because they are the "devils of San Isidro."

Small villages near the city of Mérida in Venezuela also make much of the fiesta of San Isidro, which they celebrate on May 15. Groups of peasants come down from the hills into Mérida leading yokes of oxen elaborately decorated with real flowers, fruit, and tiny flags of various colors. An outdoor mass, the blessing of the oxen and fruits, and a procession with the saint highlight the day's activities. In the town of Lagunillas, also in Venezuela, the saint's procession is accompanied by people disguised as old men, devils, bears, and monkeys, and by other masked individuals who perform an interesting ribbon dance.

In Mexico the most interesting fiesta on the fifteenth of May is probably that which takes place in Acapazingo near Cuernavaca. Besides the blessing of the seeds and a procession led by oxen, there is an outdoor play depicting the favors expected from the saint during the coming year. Masked dances of different kinds are also performed. In Metepec, in the state of Mexico, the yokes of the oxen are decorated with unusual pictures made with different seeds.

Santa Rita

May 22 is the day of Santa Rita, and in the village of Apastepeque in El Salvador the saint is honored with a performance of the *Tunco de Monte*, or Dance of the Mountain Pig. The principal character in this dance-drama is covered by a large pigskin, and after many hours of monotonous recitals and pursuit by the other dancers he is cornered and "killed." The victorious hunter, who is dressed in a Spanish costume of the sixteenth century, figuratively cuts the pig to pieces and gives each of the bystanders a portion. The person chosen for this is always adept at repartee, and as he divides the meat he makes clever remarks or shady jokes about the villagers to the delight of everyone. Interspersed with the jokes are pleas to the saint for propitious weather and abundant crops.

94

Festa do Divino

For the fishermen living in and around Tietê, Brazil, Whitsunday is the big day of the year. Coming fifty days after Easter and usually during the month of May, it is the occasion for their Festa do Divino, or Feast of the Holy Ghost. The celebration carries on a tradition started several centuries ago in Portugal to commemorate the Descent of the Holy Ghost upon the Apostles.

On this day all the fishermen dress in white outfits with sashes and long stocking caps and carry an oar in one hand. During the procession they form a double line, and the symbol of the Holy Ghost (a dove set on a beribboned crown) is carried beneath their crossed oars. The townspeople follow the musicians and fishermen to the river's edge where the latter climb into their large fishing canoes which have been decked out in gay bunting for the occasion. Lining up in the middle of the stream, they begin a floating regatta. As they glide with the current, the fishermen stand holding their oars upright. The celebration ends in the parish church where the men present their oars so that their work may be blessed for the coming year.

JUNE

UNE IS A GOOD month for fiestas in the town of Tehuantepec, Mexico, for one neighborhood after another honors its patron saint for an entire week with feasting,
dancing, and parades. Though the fiestas are similar to
those found in many other parts of the country, nowhere
else are there Indian women even remotely resembling the
fabulous Tehuanas of this region. Tall, willowy and graceful,
they look like bronzed Greek goddesses, and their beautiful
carriage is the envy of many an aspiring fashion model. In
the matriarchal society over which these proud beauties
preside, the men are practically useless individuals; they
are relegated to performing the menial chores around the
house, acting as messengers, and siring the offspring. They
are seldom entrusted with money and are never permitted to
run any of the business establishments or to handle the
family finances.

The dress of the Tehuanas is one of the most awe-inspir-
ing to be found anywhere and may be instrumental in keeping the men in a place of secondary importance. The skirts
are long and full and of brightly colored cotton print. At

the bottom of each skirt is a white ruffle, twelve to sixteen inches long, starched and pleated with thousands of minute creases that would drive the most exacting laundress mad. The short, square blouses or huipils are of vivid red, purple, yellow, or blue decorated with elaborate geometric designs. For ornaments they use necklaces, bracelets, and earrings of gold coins, and it is not unusual to see a Tehuana walking down the street decked out in a thousand dollars' worth of gold pieces.

For fiestas the Tehuanas wear skirts of silk, satin, or velvet embroidered with bright-colored flowers copied from Chinese shawls and ending in the same pleated ruffle. They use matching huipils and wear a white lace headdress which is the most enchantingly becoming of feminine adornments. Actually it is a child's dress with a large ruffled collar and wide pleated border at the bottom of the skirt and sleeves. When attending mass it is pulled completely over the head and shoulders so that the face is tightly framed in the neck of the dress with the ruffled collar standing out like the white petals of a daisy. The rest of the time it is worn bottom side up with the wide pleated border sweeping back from the face. Either way it is lovely, and the costume lives up to its reputation as the most beautiful regional dress in Mexico.

At fiesta time a bamboo or palm-thatched pavilion is erected near the house of the *mayordomo* and decorated with banana trees, bunches of green coconuts, branches of weeping willow, and rows of little tissue paper flags. Usually there is a marimba orchestra and also a dance band, and modern dances are mixed with those typical of the region such as the *sandunga*, *llorona*, and *tortuga*. The *sandunga*, which is the one most often associated with the Tehuanas, is a traditional courtship mime in which the partners face each other in two lines and weave back and forth in front of each other. At times the man follows the woman around, and she is always demure yet provocative.

Near the end of each afternoon, dancing stops and everyone parades through town to the church. Sometimes oxen are decorated and join the parade. Many of the fiestas end with a *tirada de fruta*, or fruit-throwing. The Tehuanas carry on their heads huge lacquered gourds full of fruit topped by an artistic arrangement of tissue paper flags cut into lacy patterns. When they reach the church they climb to the roof and to a war theme played on flute and drum begin to hurl bananas, mangos, papayas, and other tropical fruit at the crowd below. An occasional coconut or pineapple adds a touch of danger to the game.

Día de San Juan

On the eve of St. John's Day, June 24, people in many parts of South America gather around bonfires for one of their biggest celebrations of the year. Couples dance around the fires or leap through them in daring games. In parts of Paraguay, people walk through the live coals barefoot as proof of their faith. These bonfires have both a religious and a pagan significance. Some people believe that they are to warm up St. John, for the twenty-fourth of June is the coldest day of winter. For many people, however, the celebration is really dedicated to the winter solstice, and the fires are a plea to the sun to return.

St. John's Day is one of those that tried to replace an old pagan festival and almost got lost in the process. For centuries June 24, or Midsummer Eve, was probably the most important of the annual festivals of Europe. Various forms of pagan sun worship and purification rites took place at this time. When Christmas Day was set as December 25, St. John the Baptist's Day was placed on June 24, because according to the New Testament, John was just six months older than Jesus. The date had to be put ahead one day, because it was obvious that any saint's day following a day and night of wild heathen revelry wouldn't have a chance. The Church attempted to substitute water rites for the pagan purification ones, but although ritual baths were added to the observances, the fire worship and belief in certain magical practices continued and were brought to America by the Spanish and Portuguese colonizers.

There are a great many superstitions connected with St. John's Day. In parts of Mexico and Paraguay, women of the poorer classes cut their hair on this day, for it is believed that if they do not, their hair will stop growing during the rest of the year. In Paraguay also the ears of corn from which seed is taken must be thrown into a stream so that the new crop will produce large ears. Indians in the valley of Andahuaylas, Peru, burn their old clothes on St. John's Eve, believing that with them goes their poverty.

In many countries a person's future can be foretold by breaking an egg into a glass of water and leaving it behind the bedroom door. If, on the morning of the twenty-fourth, the egg white looks like a church, there will be a wedding; if a ship, a voyage; if a coffin, death. In some places hot molten lead is dropped into a basin of cold water. If it takes the form of pearls or sea shells, it means much money; if it looks like an altar with flowers, the future will be filled with happiness; if the surface is flat as in a cemetery, the person whose fortune is being told will soon die.

There are many devices available to lovers. A cross of laurel leaves placed under the pillow on St. John's Eve will bring dreams of a future sweetheart. If a blindfolded girl plucks a green lime from a tree she will marry a young man; a ripe lime indicates an older man. Corn and beans may be planted at this time and if the corn comes up first, the girl who planted it will marry a foreigner, since corn is blond; if the beans appear first, she will marry one of her own race, for beans are dark. To find the name of her future mate a girl can drive a knife into a banana stalk that has not yet produced and leave it there from midnight until six o'clock in the morning. During this time the sap is supposed to inscribe the name of some man on the blade. If no banana plant is handy, the names of all possible candidates may be written on separate pieces of paper, each one folded several times and put in a bowl of water. The next morning, the paper telling the name of the girl's future husband should be found floating open on the water.

Early on the morning of St. John's Day it is the custom of the poorer class to rush to the nearest stream or lake for their ritual bath. This will not only cure them of certain physical and spiritual ills but will bring them luck for the whole year to come. This ritual is most spectacular in the coastal regions of Venezuela where the aquatic rites have almost completely supplanted the fire rites. Thousands of Negroes join in the collective bath, and many of them dip their farming tools or machetes to assure themselves of success in their work. It is believed that on this morning the Dove of the Holy Ghost flies swiftly by, and when its passing is felt by someone in the crowd, a unanimous and profound cry rises from the water. A statue of St. John is carried into the water too to give the saint who was so busy baptizing others the same service himself. Afterward he is given a drink of rum to ward off the cold.

Although fire and aquatic rites and divinations are fairly widespread, some places have their own special celebrations for the Day of St. John. In Chambo, Ecuador, the day brings forth large groups of *diablitos* (devils) in glittering costumes. Accompanied by other groups of dancers they go through town whipping everyone who tries to molest them. It is said that anyone who dresses as a devil and participates in the festivities for twelve consecutive years will receive eternal glory. Some of today's *diablitos* have been participating for fifteen years or more.

In many parts of Brazil votive masts are erected. These tall poles, crowned with images or pictures of the saint, flowers, fruits, and gay floating streamers, are often carried in procession through the town before being placed in front of homes where special *festas* are to take place. In the large cities fireworks are gradually being substituted for all other activities, and residence streets on St. John's Eve look very much like those of American cities during the good old Fourth of July days.

The rural sections of Paraguay look forward to St. John's Day as the time of the *Toro Candil*, a game involving a make-believe bull whose horns and tail have been covered with kerosene-soaked rags and then lighted. The *toro* dashes through the crowds scattering people in every direction and finally is challenged in the public square by a man called *cheolo*. During the heat of the fight when all eyes are on the bull, men disguised as Guaicurú Indians burst in with wild shouts and abduct the girls. The young men, forgetting the bullfight, dash off in pursuit of the abductors and eventually bring back all the girls and return them to their parents.

Among the Negroes of Venezuela, this saint's day is celebrated by drum dances which may continue for several days. In this country there is no cohesive religious system of African origin comparable with voodoo, *macumba*, or *candomblé*. When the drums resound, however, the frenzy of the dancing, the surrender of the individual soul to a group feeling that completely absorbs and transforms it, and the unconscious seeking of the state of possession clearly bring to mind the African heritage of these people. The shape and sound of the drums vary according to the region. The dances may be done by groups or by one couple at a time performing within a circle formed by the musicians and onlookers. The theme of the dances may be erotic or something connected with their work such as hunting, felling trees, or washing clothes. Negroes in the Dominican Republic also dance to drums on the eve of St. John's Day, and the *Sarandunga* dance done in Baní is especially interesting.

Though most of Mexico considers June 24 the Day of St. John and celebrates with more or less religious observances, in some places the holiday remains entirely a pagan one. In the mountain village of Jesús María de Alica, near Tepic, the celebration is called Gran Fiesta del Sol (Great Sun Festival) and is in honor of the summer solstice. People visiting the little town on this day have the feeling of being transported back in time to the glorious pre-Conquest days.

Soon after sunrise a regal procession begins to wend its way through the village. Leading it is the High Priest, magnificent in a white chamois skin cape, a short skirt adorned with feathers of tropical birds, white chamois boots, and a monstrous feather headdress. In one hand he holds a lance and in the other a round leather shield with a sun painted on it which he twirls as he walks. The warriors who escort him are clothed in skins of wolves and wear crude helmets on their heads. Next come the Chief Justice and the lesser justices attired in red chamois skin, the Military Chief in a tiger skin and gorgeous feather headdress. Everywhere are almost naked warriors carrying bows and arrows, workers in animal skins carrying the implements of their trade, maidens in knee-length skirts and low-necked embroidered blouses carrying garlands of wild flowers. A corpulent Indian carries the big pre-Conquest drum known as *teponaxtle*, and the sound produced as he hits it with a large stick can be heard for miles around. Chamois-clad musicians beat on other drums of various sizes and shapes, play *chirimías* and strange instruments such as the *trompa*. The latter, made of a strong hollow reed about a yard and a half long, has a string attached along its entire length. The musician puts the instrument to his lips and while blowing makes the string vibrate with one finger.

Accompanying the musicians are thirty dancers in chamois costumes and feather headdresses adorned with small mirrors, little bells, and rattles. Shouting and striking the ground, a little old man with long white hair indicates the change of figures to the dancers. When the procession arrives at the main square, everyone takes his prearranged place; the long pageant, which involves war chants, battle pantomimes, dances, and prayers to the sun, begins to unfold. At noon the *teponaxtle* sounds and all stand up and offer one last fervent prayer to the sun. The music then breaks forth with renewed frenzy, and the various groups begin to disperse.

Some of the Guatemalan Indian towns, notably Camotán and San Juan Sacatepéquez, have a ritual dance known as *Los Gigantes* (The Giants) which they perform on this day. Its complicated plot is taken from the Popol Vuh (the sacred book of the Quichés), but two Biblical incidents— the fight between David and Goliath and the beheading of St. John—are rather clumsily superimposed. The costumes of the dancers are red, blue, yellow, and white to signify the four directions and are covered with motifs representing the days of the sacred month. Further symbolism is noted in the veils worn by several dancers to indicate that early legendary period when the faces of the sun and moon were still covered. The dance both begins and ends with an elaborate homage to the sun in which the dancers salute the points of its rising and setting and trace its course with their swords.

Día del Indio

In Peru, June 24 is officially called Día del Indio (Day of the Indian). A full-scale fiesta takes place just outside of Lima on the Pampas de Amancaes, so named from the yellow flowers which carpet the plains and hillsides at this time of the year. To this spot come thousands of Indians from all over the country dressed in their most showy costumes. To the plaintive and aboriginal music of the native harps, flutes, panpipes, guitars, and drums, each group performs its own regional dances. Though once a completely spontaneous affair, it is now organized with grandstands for the spectators and even a horse show thrown in for good measure. Hundreds of booths are erected from which come the exotic aromas of such native foods as *escabeche* (meat or fish rolled in meal, cooked with various spices and covered with a sour sauce), *huevos a la huancaina* (eggs cooked in native style), *pato a la chiclayana* (a highly seasoned duck dish), and *mazamorra* (a corn-meal dish similar to our own spoon pudding). To quench the thirst there is an adequate supply of such native drinks as *pisco* and *chicha*.

In Cuzco a reconstruction of the ancient Inca *Inti Raymi* fiesta to the sun takes place at the old Inca fortress on Sacsahuamán Hill. Hundreds of Inca warriors march about. There are masked dancers, plumed dancers, and troupes leading reluctant llamas. The High Priest is there, dressed in black and surrounded by kneeling vestal virgins. The Inca himself delivers a long ovation to the sun in Quechua. After the performance, the fiesta center changes to the main square, or Plaza de Armas. In the center of the square, looking down at the crowded scene, is a statue of a featherdecked North American Indian—the victim of a mixup in shipments from a stateside statue maker. Somewhere in the United States there stands a statue of the last emperor of the Incas posing as a North American.

San Pedro y San Pablo

Because of the tradition that Peter and Paul were martyred on the same day, both saints are honored on the same day of the church calendar—June 29. St. Peter gets most of the attention, however, as he is the most popular of the patron saints of fishermen. In fishing villages and port towns throughout Latin America, boats are decorated with flowers and flags; to the accompaniment of singing or native music they glide across the water in solemn procession bearing the image of St. Peter. Often they stop at some altar decorated with shells, seaweed, or fish that has been specially erected on shore or on a barge or other floating object. Usually the saint is honored by a procession through town too. In Callao, Peru, the *mayordomos* of the fiesta fish feverishly during the fluvial procession, and everything they catch is used to adorn the saint's litter.

Fishing villages are not the only ones paying homage to St. Peter on this day. A quick glance at a map will reveal numerous towns named after this popular saint, and his day is often feted whether he happens to be the patron saint or not. The Negroes of Venezuela take advantage of the proximity of this date to that of St. John's Day to continue their drum dances and make one long celebration. Paraguayans repeat the same games enjoyed at the previous festival, and the flaming *Toro Candil* again dashes through the screaming crowds. Guatemalan Indians make much of the day with their usual exotic processions during which neither rockets, drums, shrill *chirimías*, nor clouds of copal incense can detract from the beauty of the Indians' hand-woven garments.

Corpus Christi

Corpus Christi, which was officially instituted in 1246 and extended to the entire Christian world in 1264, honors the sacrament of the Eucharist, or the presence of Christ in the form of bread. It is celebrated on the Thursday after Trinity Sunday and thus nearly always falls within the month of June. Established in Spanish America by royal decree in the second half of the sixteenth century, the festival was supposed to feature performances and parades of people representing dragons, little devils, and giants, as had been the custom in Spain. Giants and dragons have disappeared through the years, but devils still persist in a few places. In small towns of Panama the day features the dance of the "Dirty Little Devils" and a longer dramatization of the struggle between good and evil in which Lucifer and his devils are confronted by St. Michael.

The most famous Corpus Christi devils are those of San Francisco de Yare in Venezuela, a highly organized group of citizens who dance annually in fulfillment of some vow. At nine o'clock on Thursday morning a burst of fireworks announces the arrival of the devil dancers, and people gather in the Plaza Bolívar and adjacent streets. The drumbeats and demoniacal din become louder and louder, and soon from eighty to one hundred masked devils are leaping frenetically through the crowd. Dressed in red and wearing a grotesque horned mask with the snout of an ox or pig, each dancer carries in his right hand one or two maracas and in his left a stick with a small bag tied on the end—a receptacle for the donations of the faithful. Around each dancer's waist are cowbells and rattles made of pop bottle tops which, together with the drums and maracas, create a truly infernal din.

Arriving at the entrance to the church, the devils continue dancing until the service begins and then kneel in concentrated silence. As soon as the mass is over they jump, shout, and gesticulate with renewed vigor. Suddenly they fall to their knees in two long lines leading up to the door of the church. The head devil, distinguishable by a four-horned mask, and his assistant in a three-horned version dance together up this path; they try unsuccessfully to enter the church and return to their places in line. Immediately another pair comes forward, and the ritual is repeated until each pair of kneeling figures has had a turn to dance. This part over, the devils dance together once again and tirelessly cavort through town until early afternoon when the church bells announce that the procession is about to begin. Returning to the church, they rest briefly until the Sacred Host appears in the doorway.

Heading the procession is a man armed with a whip with which he pretends to beat the devils. The latter, dancing like possessed, begin to fall back without ever turning their backs on the holy symbol. After a short tour around the square, the Sacred Host is returned to its sanctuary. The devils burst out in heart-rending wails and try frantically to get into the church, but their efforts are in vain. The dance becomes more hysterical until finally all the devils drop to their knees and throw their horned masks in front of them in sign of submission. Getting up again they resume the dance while making their way to El Calvario where a special altar has been erected in front of the three crosses. To reach the crosses they have to go up a path outlined by branches of trees and shrubs which have recently been stuck in the ground. After kneeling in front of the crosses, they savagely yank out all the branches and throw them in the air as in some ancient rite of spring. This ends the dance, and the devils then go to the house of their leader where everyone dances the *bamba*, an old dance of Spanish origin which has nothing to do with the earlier ceremony.

The day of Corpus Christi is celebrated with religious processions of one kind or another in all parts of Latin America. In Colombia it is the custom to erect special altars on street corners and in the main square. Each altar is presented by a certain group: the sisters of a convent, religious societies, or just groups of neighbors. Each vies with the other to produce something original and spectacular. Working with nothing more than cheap colored cottons, silver paper, cellophane, and flowers, they produce really lovely creations: a great silver lyre, a golden chalice by an open book, a series of fountains cascading one into the other, and numerous scenes from the Bible. The procession, which includes school children and members of the various religious societies, stops along the way at each of the altars. Diminutive flower girls, often dressed as angels, carry baskets of petals which they strew in the path of the priest carrying the Host. In some of the mountain villages young trees are planted in the plazas and all kinds of animals paraded through the streets to symbolize the earthly paradise.

In Cuzco, Peru, Corpus Christi is one of the big celebrations of the year, and festivities are extended for nearly two and a half weeks. On Wednesday morning, just before the big day, everyone in town is awakened at four o'clock by the pealing of church bells reminding them that there is much to be done. The streets through which the procession will pass have to be cleaned, fruit stands installed, and temporary altars erected around the main square. There is even greater activity in the outlying parishes where images have to be readied for their entrance into Cuzco.

One of the first saints to begin the journey is Jerome, who comes from his church in San Jerónimo some five or six miles away. As Doctor of the Church and translator of the Bible he carries in his right hand the plume of Wisdom and in his left a heavy book. His beautiful scarlet robes are protected on the long walk by a linen duster. While the men take turns carrying the image, the women walk alongside carrying food and drink wrapped in their shawls. The musicians accompanying them play on brass instruments, native flutes, and conch shells. When this group reaches the parish of San Sebastián they are met by a priest and other dignitaries, and after a short ceremony the image of St. Sebastian joins them in the walk to Cuzco. They arrive at the city at about eleven o'clock and first go to the church of Santa Clara to pay their respects to the Virgin of Bethlehem, patroness of Cuzco. Lined up outside the church are other images awaiting their turn: St. Christopher, who has come down the hill from San Cristóbal; St. Blaise, from the parish of San Blas; St. Barbara, who has journeyed from Poroy, nearly eight miles away; and many others.

After the images are blessed they go to the cathedral to spend the night. There is much folkloric gossip about these saints and virgins whom the Indians love and consider human. Once left alone they will enjoy themselves just like anyone else. For several years one of the virgins had a tear in her dress which the *mayordomos* would not permit to be mended because it had been made by the holy spur of Santiago when he was dancing with her.

On Thursday the big procession takes place in Cuzco, and the city swarms with the color of the native dress of various regions and of the shawls and fine carpets which are draped over the balconies as in colonial times. From the Avenida del Sol, near the Plaza de Armas, come tempting aromas of the special holiday foods being sold there: *achira* (a white, slightly sweet root), *uchu* (cold guinea pig), a certain kind of fish, sea leaves, and popcorn.

On the Sunday following Corpus Christi the Merced

church celebrates with a special procession, and on the next Thursday, or *octava*, all the saints are again taken out in procession from the cathedral where they have remained all this time. The last of the celebrations takes place on the Sunday following the *octava* and is called Corpus-Christi-de-Belén. A more pagan and more colorful procession than the original, this one honors the patroness of Cuzco, who is taken from her temporary residence in the Santa Clara church and returned to her own home in the parish church of Belén.

In Mexico City, Corpus Christi is eagerly awaited by the children, many of whom dress in special costumes for the occasion. Little boys in native garb carry on their backs crates filled with pottery, live chickens, or anything else that one is likely to carry to market; little girls are bewitching in China Poblana or other regional dresses. There are special services for them in the cathedral and processions around the main square in which they take part. Tiny mules made of matchsticks or cornhusks and adorned with miniature baskets of candy, fruit, or flowers are sold in the streets, markets, and plazas on this day.

The most exciting Corpus Christi celebrations in Mexico are those of Papantla and Pahuatlán where the *Danza de los Voladores*, or Flying Pole Dance, is performed. About a week before the fiesta a group of men from Papantla goes into the jungle to look for the finest tree available. When one is selected, they dance around it and ask forgiveness for cutting it. As they carry it through the jungle they are careful not to let it touch the ground, and every once in a while they give it a little brandy to refresh it. When they reach Papantla an impressive ceremony takes place around the deep hole into which the tree is to be placed. Incense is burned to scare away evil spirits, and into the hole are thrown chickens, turkeys, corn, brandy, and cigarettes to nourish the pole and keep it happy so that it will not claim the life of one of the dancers.

On the day of the fiesta the five Totonac Indians who are

to perform this ancient Aztec dance march into town in single file with their captain leading the way and parade around the square to the music of flute and drum. Then, after weaving a dancing chain seven times around the pole, the dancers and their captain quickly climb to the top. There, on a platform about a foot and a half square and seventy or more feet above the ground, the captain bows to each of the cardinal points and performs special acrobatics while playing his flute. The four *voladores* tie ropes around their feet and with wild cries leap out into space. The ropes are suspended from a revolving scaffold and arranged in such a way that they unwind as the fliers descend. Each *volador*, with arms outstretched to simulate the flight of a bird, makes thirteen spirals around the pole and just as his head is about to touch the ground leaps gracefully to his feet. The magic number thirteen multiplied by the four dancers makes fifty-two, the sacred pre-Conquest cycle or century. The *Danza de los Voladores* is usually performed several times during the fiesta, which lasts until the Sunday following Corpus Christi.

Pahuatlán has increased the number of its fliers to six, which they feel is more elegant. As in Papantla all are men, but one is dressed in billowing skirts to represent Malinche, the Indian girl who befriended Cortés.

The Flying Pole Dance is often preceded by another colorful Indian dance called *Los Quetzales*. The dance itself is simple but the costumes, inspired by the regal Quetzal bird, are spectacular, especially the headdress which consists of a gigantic wheel set on top of a conical hat. This wheel, which is made of reeds, has brilliantly colored paper ribbons woven through it ending in a border of feathers. In some places the dancers themselves form a wheel of color as they rotate on a crude wooden contraption.

In the Tarascan villages of Michoacán, Mexico, Corpus Christi fiestas take the form of mock markets. Everyone offers for sale miniatures of something representing his occupation. House builders have tiny houses, weavers tiny blankets or belts, bakers tiny loaves of bread. Farmers exhibit seeds of the things they grow. Restaurant owners set up small tables and serve bite-size portions of food in tiny dishes. Everything is paid for with mock money—chewing gum, candy, or almost any small object at hand.

In Paracho there is a special parade featuring more than 1000 people divided into groups representing each of the manual arts: carpenters, blacksmiths, bricklayers, bakers, and many others. Each group carries something representative of its trade. Bakers make enormous loaves of bread decorated with interesting figures; the makers of musical instruments may show off a collection of violins and guitars ranging in size from one inch to six feet long; undertakers may have gigantic coffins decorated with amusing figures.

At Tzintzuntzan the spotlight is on the muleteers, crate carriers, and plowboys who parade through town with a group of musicians. First come the horses, mules, and burros loaded with make-believe merchandise. Following them are plows drawn by oxen decorated with colored papers and small wheat cakes which hang from their horns and backs. Last come children with small crates on their backs filled with a great variety of objects. When they reach the atrium of the church the plowboys begin to plow a piece of ground set aside for them. Following the plow are women who make a pretense of planting. As the women in this town do not do this kind of work, the performance is intended as a burlesque of their neighbors who do. In the *octava* of this fiesta the play centers around a miniature cornfield. A man representing a watchman wears an old coat, straw hat, wooden mask, and carries a musket. After making a great show of loading his gun, he stalks about the cornfield in search of a stuffed opossum and fox that have been planted there. When he finds them he shoots and runs, holding up the animals for everyone to see.

Mexican villages are known for the originality of their festivities and nearly everyone has some peculiar feature for Corpus Christi, depending upon its products and interests.

JULY

SANTA ISABEL

FROM JULY 6 TO 8 residents of the Callejón de Huaylas, Peru, hold an interesting fiesta in honor of St. Elizabeth to commemorate the visit paid her by her cousin the Virgin Mary. The first part of the celebration, which takes place on the night of the sixth, makes no reference to the saint but recalls instead the war between Peru and Chile in 1879 when that section of the country was occupied by Chileans. Two fairly large wooden boats, their chimneys emitting smoke, are brought into the main square by rival wards. They are hung with lanterns and garlands of flowers and piloted by "sailors" with grotesquely painted faces. Couples dancing to the music of a band follow each boat, and the whole scene is surrounded by a hilarious crowd. The delirium reaches a climax when the two boats meet and the skirmishes begin. The finale represents the heroic sinking of the Chilean war vessel La Esmeralda by the Peruvian ship Huáscar during the Battle of Iquique.

Virgen del Carmen

July 16 is an important day in many of the Latin American countries but goes by different names. In Peru it is the day of the Virgen del Carmen, and nearly every church in the country that has an image of her stages a big procession. In the small town of Pucará the day features a lively sale of sturdy mountain-bred horses from Chumbivilcas. The qualifying races afford great amusement as the riders clash and fall. In the little white colonial town of Paucartambo the festival takes on the aspects of Carnival with an endless jumble of strange dances and even stranger costumes. At times Indians in gay *chullos* with knitted masks cavort with stuffed animals on canes; men disguised as women whirl around in their full skirts and petticoats; or, a comic "doctor" in top hat, black frock, and trousers gives humorous answers to the "patients" who consult him. There are Huaca Huaca dancers who perform a bullfight farce, dancers masquerading as monkeys, Kollas representing warriors of Lake Titicaca Basin, Chunchos or jungle "savages," Tercianos who pretend to be striken with malarial fever and chills and beat each other with small white cloth bags. The fiesta is very typical of the Andean ten-ring circus type, and one never knows quite what to expect.

Nuestra Señora de Itatí

In Argentina, the most famous festival on the sixteenth of July takes place in the town of Itatí, situated on the banks of the Paraná River. Activities begin on the fourteenth when everyone goes to the edge of town to welcome the thousands of pilgrims from San Luis del Palmar who come in a long parade of horsemen, carts, and marchers carrying flags and an image of St. Louis. Pilgrims come from other parts of Argentina too and take part at night in the dancing, drinking, and games of chance. Religious services are held in the monumental basilica which houses the image of the Virgin, a copper statue over twenty-four feet high. Visitors can climb inside the statue up to the crown.

Virgen de la Tirana

In Chile, where truly picturesque fiestas and indigenous dances are often hard to find, the small town of La Tirana honors its virgin each year on the sixteenth of July. Dancers in bizarre costumes and grotesque masks perform the *tipicasque* dances which go on for hours without stopping. The villagers identify the Virgen de la Tirana with both an Inca princess, la ñusta Huillao, and the Virgen del Carmen, and the fiesta itself is both pagan and religious.

According to legend, the Inca princess was the supreme ruler of her realm for four years after her father's death. During this time she fell in love with a Spaniard who educated her in the Catholic religion. Upon learning that she had renounced her own gods, the other Incas killed both the princess and her lover. Later a missionary arrived and succeeded in converting them all to Catholicism.

Pilgrimage of Saut d'eau

Every year around the middle of July, people of Haiti make a pilgrimage to the church in Ville-Bonheur and to a nearby waterfall. Although this is really a church holiday honoring Our Lady of Mt. Carmel on July 16, it is usually known by the more popular name of pilgrimage of Saut d'eau (waterfall).

Ville-Bonheur, about sixty miles north of the capital, is reached by a winding mountain road which leads past tiny hamlets and cemeteries with heavy monuments built in the shape of doll houses two or three stories high. The town of Ville-Bonheur is at its liveliest at this time of year. Everywhere are peasants dancing to the sound of jazz orchestras, buying things to eat or drink from hastily-erected booths, or standing in thick clusters around the lively dice games.

There are women selling candles and small heart-shaped amulets made of printed cotton. Others are selling colored cords to hang as offerings upon the sacred trees at the falls. Penitents in different colored garb wander through the crowds distributing food to the poor, hoping by this act of Christian charity to appease the African *loa* (deities) whom they have offended.

Just outside of Ville-Bonheur is a sacred grove which at night is aglow from the light of thousands of candles. Many of the peasants ecstatically anoint themselves with the candle grease that collects on the rocks. Many years ago, it seems, a lovely luminous virgin suddenly appeared on top of a palm tree in this grove. After singing a beautiful song and being seen by many of the country people, she disappeared just as suddenly. People came from all over to worship the tree and were miraculously cured. The church was neglected, and the priest ordered that the palm tree be chopped down; but he could find no one willing to do this. Finally he became so incensed at the adoration of the people for the tree that he himself cut it down. When the faithful merely transferred their veneration to the roots, these were torn out until nothing but a gaping hole remained. Not long afterward the priest died of a stroke, a circumstance which convinced his parishioners of the authenticity of the vision.

Early in the morning large groups of peasants set out along the trail that leads to the waterfall where the votaries of voodoo have a ceremony of baptism. Several times they cross the stream on shaky logs and finally have to remove their shoes and walk on the pebbly stream bottom for at least 500 yards. After passing through a cavern-like place with huge igneous cliffs, the trail descends rapidly in hairpin turns through dense tropical growth to the falls themselves.

It is easy to see why this awesome site is believed to be the home of spirits. Two great streams fall from the lip of the precipice, more than 100 feet above the cool green depths of the ravine, breaking up near the bottom into spray which doesn't quite hide the luxuriant ferns and mosses under-neath. The tall trees and high cliff walls permit only stray shafts of sunlight to enter, and striking the rising spray they convert it into an iridescent mist crossed by tiny rainbows. This place, which is a natural cathedral, mysterious and almost unreal, is the home of Damballah-wèdo, Grande-Bossine, and other aquatic deities.

Some of the worshipers are busy tying their colored cord offerings to the sacred trees at the foot of the falls. Others are already in the pool or exposing their bodies to the violence of the cascade itself. They frolic about excited and happy yet a little afraid at being in the presence of spirits. Suddenly a bather is shaken by tremblings and begins to stagger drunkenly. The others help him to the bank. His eyes are upturned and he mutters strange words in a voice which those present recognize as belonging to Damballah-wèdo. They crowd around him in adoration, squeezing his hand and asking those small favors which the *loa* dispense among those they love. When Damballah returns to his resting place in the huge fig tree at the very edge of the falls, the pilgrims take pinches of earth from around the tree, carefully wrap them in their handkerchiefs and start out on the trail back to town. Later in the day these pilgrims are seen in the church in Ville-Bonheur paying their respects to the Virgin, for "to serve the *loa* you have to be a Catholic!" These words, spoken by a Haitian peasant, express precisely the paradoxical ties between voodoo and Christianity which are so much in evidence during this pilgrimage in July.

Muerte del Señor San José

The townspeople of San Vicente in El Salvador make quite a dramatic event out of the death *(muerte)* of Joseph which they celebrate from July 17 to 19. Masses begin nine days before that, and the saint is placed in a small canopied bed with his holy wife and divine son at his side appearing to assist him. Beside the bed is a small table with medicine bottles, glasses, and a bowl of broth. Each day fresh broth is brought by some of the pious ladies of the church who inquire of the sexton: "How is the sick one today?" He answers: "He is better, or worse, or the same," whatever he feels like saying at the moment.

As the days go on, the faithful notice from the posture of the saint that he is becoming weaker. Finally, on the afternoon of the seventeenth, he dies. The church fills with people who kneel beside the sorrowing Jesus and Mary and weep real tears of affliction. One group of musicians plays and sings near the bed of the saint while another answers with celestial music from a platform that is supposed to represent the abode of the Almighty. Suddenly from the bed rises the soul of the saint in the form of a white dove which flutters about for a moment and then goes up to the sky through a small window made for that purpose. On the eighteenth the image is laid out in state, and after an early mass an orchestra begins to play well-known classical works and continues until nine that night. The next day they do the same until four or five in the afternoon when the burial takes place.

Lunes del Cerro

Since ancient times a fiesta of fantastic beauty has taken place on a hillside just outside the city of Oaxaca in southern Mexico. Originally its purpose was to sacrifice a beautiful maiden to one of the gods. People came from all over bearing gifts of flowers, fruits, silks, and embroideries, and groups of dancers performed graceful gyrations before the bloody altar. The ceremony was called Guelaguetza, which in the Zapotecan language means an offering or gift. The Spanish priests permitted and encouraged the Guelaguetza, forbidding only the human sacrifice, and the gifts and dances metamorphosed into acts of gratitude to the true God.

Today the ceremony, which is called Lunes del Cerro (Monday on the Hill), begins on the Monday after the day of Our Lady of Mount Carmel (July 16) and lasts for a week. Groups of dancers in breathtaking costumes come from nearly every village in the state of Oaxaca bearing gifts typical of the products and handicrafts of the region. Dancers from Cuatla are distinguished by their beautifully embroidered blouses; those from along the coast sport blouses flashing with beadwork. Women from Yalalag are striking in full dresses of woven white wool with towering black turbans made from their own hair twined with black yarn. Tehuanas from Tehuantepec glide about in their exotic and unusual costumes. The most popular of all the dancers who perform during the week, however, are the Plume Dancers from Teotitlán del Valle in their monstrous feather headdresses dyed all colors of the rainbow and decorated with mirrors, colored stones, and tinsel.

The *Danza de las Plumas*, which is performed several times a year in Teotitlán del Valle, is often simplified and uses only a few plumed dancers. When done in its entirety, it is a complicated dance-drama two or three hours long recounting the conquest of Mexico. The fifteen to twenty plumed dancers, of course, represent Montezuma and his men. Small boys dressed in hideous blue uniforms and caps play the parts of the Spanish soldiers. Only Hernán Cortés and Pedro de Alvarado are permitted to wear fine plumed hats. One child represents Malinche, the Indian interpreter who helped Cortés. The dancing, interspersed with passages of narrative, depicts the arrival of Cortés, the alerting of Montezuma and his men, several fierce battles, and the eventual submission of the Indians to the Cross.

Santiago

Santiago (St. James) is the patron saint of Spain and his day, July 25, is one of the most important feast days in Latin America. Before sunrise on this day a group of Ayarachi dancers from Paratía, Peru, sets out for the small town of Lampa, near Juliaca. When they come to the river along the way, they lie down on their stomachs with their arms behind their heads and imitate a condor washing its face. The condors are believed to be their ancestors and, though humorous to observe, this ritual is taken very seriously. As the first rays of the sun appear, they weep copiously and then proceed on their way. When they reach Lampa they join with other groups of Indians who are invading the town from every direction. Riding around the plaza on spirited horses are small groups of *Ccaperos* (firemakers) dressed as colonial or republican generals with many colorful ribbons hanging from under their Napoleon hats. The Ayarachi dancers, who are dressed in dark homespun suits with white woolen shawls, wear a distinctive white brocaded silk band —the white symbolizing the condor. Donning a headdress of ostrich feathers, which falls down over his head and opens like a fan at the top, each dancer begins to blow a double-rowed panpipe which he holds in his left hand. In his other hand is a stick decorated with colored wool which he uses to beat a small drum hanging from around his neck. *Ayarachi* means funeral music in the Aymará language, and the lugubrious little tune they play is believed to be the same one that was played for the funeral of Manco Cápac. Dancing in a circle, they move with great solemnity and are at times joined by their women, who keep step with them inside the circle.

Guatemala is also the scene of many colorful Indian dances on the twenty-fifth of July. In Chimaltenango, dancers are busy for months ahead rehearsing an interesting dance-drama which takes six hours to tell the story of a sixteenth-century Spaniard who lost his herd of bulls.

Santiago Atitlán, another Guatemalan town, offers an unusually good performance of the country's best known dance—*La Conquista*. Strangely enough, the theme of this dance—the defeat of the Quichés by the Spanish invaders and the death of the native leader, Tecum Umán—has never aroused any resentment among the Indian population. About twenty dancers, decked out in bright cottons and velvets, take part. Those representing Spaniards wear pink wooden masks with yellow hair and beards; those who take the part of Indians use brown masks with black hair; the few who represent sorcerers wear false faces of brilliant red sometimes embellished with toads or serpents. The dialogue of this dance-drama runs to more than forty typewritten pages. Performers recite their parts in high singsong voices while shaking rattles and moving to the music of drum and *chirimía*.

The action begins at the Quiché court, where scouts have just brought word of the Spaniards' impending arrival. Two Spanish spies are captured and brought before the native king, whom they try to persuade to become a vassal of Spain. Though sorcerers predict that his refusal will bring disaster, the king orders Tecum Umán to prepare his warriors for battle. The invaders arrive—on horseback, whenever possible—and the battle begins. Twice the Indians are able to drive back the Spaniards, but during the third clash the Quichés begin to weaken. Tecum Umán suggests that the outcome be decided by single combat between himself and the Spanish leader Alvarado. After a long and valiant fight, the Indian chieftain is finally pierced through the heart by his adversary's sword. The dying man delivers a flowery oration, then carefully removes his headdress as he is placed into a waiting coffin to be carried in a funeral procession to the church.

Processions in Santiago Atitlán are among the most colorful in the country, and the one honoring their patron at about noon on July 25 is no exception. First to come down the high, white semicircle of the church steps are the members of the *cofradía* with their glittering staffs of office. Their white, red, and purple striped trousers, dark coats, and scarlet *tzutes* (head coverings) stand out sharply against the white background. Following them is a large group of women just as striking in their bright red skirts, white blouses, and many-colored headdresses which stand out around their heads like halos. A small native band comes next and finally the saints. St. James, gorgeous in blue velvet and carrying a streamer-decorated sword, is mounted on a horse and is obviously the hero of the day. Alongside march the dancers, who have hardly had a chance to rest since their morning performance. The strings of beads and little mirrors decorating the Indians' costumes reflect the rays of the sun, and their feather plumes bob gently as they walk. Alvarado and Tecum Umán walk side by side, on the best of terms after their "fight to the finish." The sorcerer shakes his blood-red mask frighteningly from side to side as he holds out a symbolic hatchet and crimson idol-doll.

Through the crowded streets the procession moves, accompanied by clouds of incense and bursting rockets. Several times along the way it stops at some small open-front shelter strewn with pine needles. Here the saints rest while prayers are said and dances performed.

In the Dominican Republic, towns often stage a *corrida de sortija*, or tournament of the ring, on St. James' Day. For this game, which dates back to the Crusades and is still popular today in many parts of Europe, a wire is stretched between two tall posts and strung with varicolored wooden rings. The contestants, on horseback, ride at full speed between the posts and attempt to spear a ring. In the old days the Spaniards carried swords or daggers, but today's riders use a small stick instead. It is a difficult feat, and when someone manages to spear a ring a roar of applause bursts from the crowd. Each success merits a ribbon, and when the tournament is concluded the winner is the man with the most trophies.

Though most Guatemalan towns honor St. James on the twenty-fifth of July, Momostenango, which also claims this saint as its patron, does not begin its festivities until the twenty-eighth. For three whole days this white-walled, red-roofed village is the scene of bustling activity. From the hill country above and the valleys below people stream in by a dozen different roads and paths—women in figure-striped green-and-blue skirts from Totonicapán, in voluminous blue skirts and purple-and-yellow blouses from Quezaltenango, in yellow-and-orange wrap-arounds from San Marcos. Each locality, and usually each Indian village in Guatemala, has its own distinctive hand-woven costume, which makes it easy to determine a person's origin. It is said that an expert can even tell a woman's approximate age, marital status, number of children, and the size of her husband's cornfield from the design of her blouse.

During the morning the Indians fill the church making the rounds of the various brightly-painted saints, kissing the glass cases in which they are kept and placing little candles before them. Others kneel on the floor, praying aloud in a confusing murmur of Quiché and Spanish. Many scatter red and white rose petals on the floor around them— red to indicate a desire for more children, white in honor of their dead.

Outside, the market place begins to come to life. Indians are busy arranging their fruits and vegetables in neat, colorful piles. There are clusters of handmade pottery decorated with simple designs in green and yellow; blankets of black, white, and purple, many with highly conventionalized deer, rabbits, or birds. Every kind of local handicraft is represented as well as cheap imported items such as combs, hair ribbons, and even chewing gum.

Long before noon the plaza is packed solidly with people clustered around the various dancing groups. In one clearing, velvet-clad dancers are surging back and forth clashing their tin swords. It is the dance of the Moors and Christians, and the former are resplendent in three-tiered gold and silver crowns resembling papal tiaras. As in all countries where this dance is performed, the infidels are definitely the favorites, have the most luxurious costumes and the majority of the speaking parts.

In the center of another group are dancers called *Mexicanos* in hideous yellow masks and khaki suits fringed to represent buckskin. They step about, shaking gourd rattles and yelling wildly. From time to time they stop to tell an obviously off-color story and to make a pass at La Margarita, a dancer decked out in a gaily flowered dress with a simpering, red-cheeked mask and bobbing brown curls.

Nearby, in a third ring, the Dance of the Bulls takes place. Men in typical velvet costumes, some with elegant plumed hats, represent the owner of a cattle ranch and his cowboys. Each does a short solo dance and then they join forces in a peculiar sort of jig. Small boys in bull masks dance to one side and from time to time make unexpected dashes at the men. At the end of the day there is a glorious fight in which the owner of the ranch and all the bulls are killed.

At noon the ringing of the church bell announces the beginning of the procession. Marchers and saints file slowly out of the church at the head of the big plaza. Women in bright red blouses and blue wrap-around skirts carry flower-wrapped candles as they follow behind the saints. As usual, men walk alongside incensing the saints with spicy copal and setting off rockets in deafening succession. Masked dancers leave their circles and cavort in and out among the marchers. Several marimbas are carried along to keep everyone in step, and they bob up and down as lightly as if they were made of feathers instead of heavy wood. Through the narrow streets of town they go, stopping occasionally while dancers perform a short impromptu number. Finally the procession, which includes more dancing than any other in Guatemala, winds slowly back to the church where the saints are reinstalled in their niches.

After lunch the tempo of the celebration quickens. Salomón roars fiercely in defiance of the Christians and brandishes his sword with renewed vigor. The little bulls run about excitedly attacking their masters. Around the corner from the plaza the Quichés are lined up ready to defend their homeland. At the top of the sloping street are the Spaniards mounted bareback on unbridled ponies. The opposing armies rush at each other, brandish their weapons, and then beat a disorderly retreat to their original positions. After several repetitions of this, the Spaniards dismount and come down on foot, their staggering gait probably due more to *aguardiente* than to battle fatigue. Finally, when Alvarado finishes off the Indian leader, Tecum Umán, and the latter is carried to the church in his coffin, the dancing comes to a stop for the day.

Independence in Peru

From July 28 to August 1, Independence celebrations of one kind or another take place all over Peru. It is a time for expositions of national products, street fairs, bullfights, parades of elaborate floats, fireworks. In Curahuasi the Mistis often stage a fight between a condor and a bull. The condor, who is given a good stiff drink ahead of time, defends himself with his immense wings and usually does very well for himself. At the same fiesta there are numerous games such as greased pole climbing and magical jars, the latter similar to the Mexican piñata. Several jars which may contain food, various prizes, or just dirt, ashes, or colored water, are hung on poles in the town square. Contestants are blindfolded and given a stick with which to break the jar. When successful, they are allowed to keep the contents which pour down upon them.

AUGUST

TRANSFIGURACION DEL SALVADOR

As both the country of El Salvador and its capital, San Salvador, were named for the Saviour and share Him as their patron, it is not surprising that the August fiesta commemorating the Transfiguration of Christ is the most important one of the year. Activities begin on the first and continue for six days, taking place in the capital itself.

The simple religious ceremony of colonial times gained in significance in the year 1777 when Silvestre García, a deeply religious man and painter by trade, carved and painted a beautiful statue of the Holy Saviour for the people of his country to venerate and to bear in public procession on this special feast day. In 1821, when independence was declared from Spain, many of the more popular elements were added and it became a civic as well as a religious celebration.

Today there is almost no let-up in the activities from the morning of the first day until after the final religious serv-

125

ices on the sixth. Each day there are parades of allegorical floats including the one bearing the queen and her lovely court. There are special football and baseball games with teams from other countries, boxing matches, ribbon races on motorcycles, bicycles, or on foot, parades and contests for decorated motorcycles and bicycles, parades of masked and costumed people, Indian dances in Libertad Park, and social dancing in many of the parks. Children too share in the fun, and there are special races for tricycle riders and skaters, outdoor games and *piñatas* in many parts of the city. An elaborate party is given for the children in the national orphanage with special games, food, and toys. Even the prisoners in the penitentiary are entertained with special movies.

On the afternoon of the fifth the traditional *bajada* (descent) takes place, and it has been estimated that nearly two hundred thousand people join in this procession. The statue of the Divine Saviour is carried on an enormous float with a large globe at the top. Also on the float is a man representing Christ who is dressed in red and blue and who sits on a throne surrounded by angels and clouds. The procession stops when the float is opposite the cathedral, and Christ disappears into the globe. He comes out, dressed in white this time, between the prophets Moses and Elijah, symbolizing the Transfiguration of Jesus on Mount Tabor. At this moment people applaud and shout, the band strikes up the national anthem, and artillery salvos split the air. It is interesting to note that, although this is the middle of the rainy season in El Salvador, it has almost never rained during the *bajada*. Also, every time the statue has fallen during the *bajada*, the government has been overthrown or there has been a bad earthquake soon afterward.

Señor de la Capilla

The first week of August is also celebrated in Saltillo, Mexico, where a lavish fair honors an image of Christ in a small chapel (*capilla*) of the cathedral. Indians of the surrounding hills and villages come down to join in the festivities and to sell the serapes for which the region is noted. *Matachín* dancers appear on the first and again on the sixth. The *matachines* are organized groups of dancers who call themselves "Soldiers of the Virgin" and who in most places are a part of the church organization. There are also professional groups who hire themselves out as entertainers to enliven parties or civic celebrations. The dance itself is a form of the morisca dance, or battle mime, which was extremely popular in Renaissance Europe. Through the years swords have been exchanged for sham weapons and the dance has degenerated into a mere display of vigorous steps and varied patterns.

The *matachines* dance in two long lines and are directed by a leader, called a *monarca*, and two assistants. Some of the patterns are of European type—cross-overs, dos-à-dos, and heys; most of the steps, however, are purely indigenous. They dance to the music of violins, drums, and sometimes guitars or a harp. Though the costume varies slightly in different parts of Mexico, most dancers wear vivid costumes and headdresses decorated with ribbons, feathers, and bits of mirror or glass. In the right hand they carry a wooden rattle and in the left a sort of trident adorned with feathers.

Nuestra Señora de los Angeles

August 2 is the day of Costa Rica's patron saint, Our Lady of the Angels. Though celebrated throughout the country, it is of special significance in Cartago, where the image is enshrined in the Basilica. The church is built on the very spot where the saint is said to have appeared about 300 years ago.

According to legend, a poor Indian girl went out to the edge of town one day to gather firewood. There, on a rock next to a spring, was a small black stone image of the Virgin which glowed brightly even in the daylight. Wrapping it up in her shawl, the girl took it to the hut where she lived and hid it in a box. In the morning the image was gone. The next time the girl went into the woods, she felt drawn by a strange attraction to the rock where she had found the little statue. There, in the same place and glowing with the same strange brilliant light, was the tiny black image. Quickly seizing her treasure, she again hid it in her house. Again it disappeared during the night.

After this happened several times, the girl told her friends about it, and the news soon reached the ears of the parish priest. When he went to the rock with the girl, he found the image just as she had described it. He was convinced that it was a miracle and that the Virgin wanted a sanctuary built on that particular spot.

Each year thousands of pilgrims visit the shrine. In the courtyard behind the Basilica is a fountain where worshipers can partake of the miraculous spring water. Some merely drink of it; others wash in it; still others carry it away in bottles. Inside the church the little eight-inch statue, which has been affectionately nicknamed "La Negrita" (Little Black One), stands encased in a mantle of gold and precious stones worth over half a million dollars. When the image was stolen in May 1950 the entire country went into mourning. The statue itself was found hidden in the church a week later, but it took much longer to apprehend the thieves and recover the jewels.

On August 2 each year the Virgin is taken in solemn procession from the Basilica to the parochial church of St. Nicholas in the same city. It remains there until the first Saturday of September, when it is returned in a much more elaborate procession. The streets are well scrubbed hours ahead of time and the entire route decorated with carpets of artistically arranged flowers and colored sand. The procession is led by the military band of Cartago, and following it are the Virgin and various floats with costumed people depicting religious scenes and events. Many worshipers used to appear dressed as Indians with weird designs painted on their faces in fulfillment of some special vow to the Virgin. In 1958, however, this was prohibited by the ecclesiastical authorities as being a pagan diversion. The penitents now must content themselves with going barefoot along the route carrying huge rocks on their shoulders or heads.

Assumption

Though belief in the Assumption of the Virgin Mary has been required of Roman Catholics only since 1950, this feast day, August 15, has been celebrated since the sixth century. The dogma is simply that the body of Mary, instead of being subjected to the usual earthly disintegrating processes, was united with her soul in heaven.

In the state of Oaxaca, Mexico, church festivals are particularly interesting because of the natives' habit of taking the mysteries literally. Many villages celebrate the Assumption with complete piety by sending a fireworks-rigged effigy of the Virgin Mary to heaven on a skyrocket.

In most Latin American countries there is nothing more on this day than a rather colorless parade, but the Guatemalan villages, as usual, can be counted on for intriguing ritual dances and colorful processions. In Santa Cruz del Quiché, where this holiday runs into the Fiestas Elenas (August 16-20), the celebrating is prolonged for nearly a week and is usually highlighted by the famous Snake Dance and Deer Dance.

The Snake Dance (*La Culebra*), which also goes by the name of Dance of the Jesters (*Los Gracejos*), was one of the early pagan dances which Spanish priests worked so hard to suppress or else adapted to their own purposes. Performed by secret societies in caves and other hidden places, the dance managed to survive the period of persecution and thus has remained virtually unchanged.

A day or two before the fiesta several men, accompanied by a sorcerer, go into the mountains to find the snakes. They burn copal and candles and chant prayers to their ancient gods. The snakes, poisonous and non-poisonous alike, are soon captured and carried back to town in jars. To avoid possible accidents, the venom is extracted or the mouths of the snakes are sewn shut.

The first part of the dance is pure slapstick. The dancers appear in ragged clothes and masks of various colors and designs—black masks with huge eyes and curling lips, red ones with gold mustaches, brown ones with ribald features, deathlike faces of grayish white. All carry whips with which they clownishly lash each other. One of the dancers is distinguished by a fur-trimmed suit and carries a stuffed fox. While he makes frightening lunges at the audience, children try to sneak up behind and pull the fox's tail. There is always one dancer disguised as a woman, and the others take turns dancing with her. Each time one makes a suggestive or an obscene gesture he is severely lashed by his companions. It is said that often these dancers are men who have actually sinned and are seeking just punishment.

Just before dusk the dance reaches its climax with the appearance of the serpents. The music of the marimbas, which has been going on all day, becomes more agitated. For a while the snakes are allowed to wriggle about on the ground, and then they are picked up by each dancer in turn. The snake twines about his neck and arms as he dances. Sometimes it is thrust down the neck of his blouse or jacket and is greeted by howls from the audience when it slips out of a trouser leg. When the fiesta is over, the snakes are returned to the mountains.

The following legend attempts to explain the origin of this unusual dance. One day God was very worried and those who surrounded Him tried in every way possible to cheer him up. They donned their most elaborate costumes and danced all their best dances, but He seemed not even to notice them. Finally they put on their oldest clothes and their ugliest masks and began to crack jokes and play tricks on one another. Great was their relief when God burst into roars of mirth.

The second half of the dance is said to have evolved as a ritualistic appeal for good crops. The stuffed fox is supposed to symbolize the fertility of the soil, and the serpent—plumed in the widespread ancient cult—represents life-giving rain.

The Deer Dance *(Baile del Venado)* is also symbolic and represents the struggle between mankind and animals. Though smaller villages have to be content with a simplified version, a few of the larger ones are able to present the dance in its entirety as described here.

Several days before the fiesta, men from the village go to the forest to select a tree. It must be straight as a rod for at least 75 feet, and when the proper one is found it is stripped and carried back to the village to the accompaniment of music and fireworks. It if should make any sound while drying out, a new tree must be selected, for the sound is the voice of the tree saying that it does not wish to take part in the fiesta.

When the tree is ready, a ceremony of tribal significance takes place beside the hole in which it is to be placed. The *shaman* (witch doctor or sorcerer) places lighted candles, burning incense and pine needles around the hole and nine jars of incense on the tree trunk itself. After a round of fireworks and long prayers, men disguised as animals step forward and strike the pole nine times, making each time the Maya cross—symbol of the four directions. With more prayers and incense, the pole is fitted into place and a rope stretched from the top of it to the peak of the church. Guards are set up to make sure that no one walks underneath the rope, for that is certain to bring bad luck to the dancers performing on it.

On the day of the fiesta, dancers line up in two lines beside the pole. With the *shaman* are a dancer dressed as a monkey and others in the skins and masks of various wild animals. Dancers in the other line are dressed as old men and old women and represent mankind. After embracing each other briefly, the monkey climbs to the peak of the church and the *shaman* to the top of the pole. The *shaman* waits with open arms as the monkey crosses the rope, performing prodigious gymnastic feats and ludicrous antics en route. Then, while the monkey descends the pole with the same silly antics, dancers dressed as dogs howl dismally below. As soon as the monkey reaches the ground, animals and mankind begin dancing solemnly around him. Though simple and extremely monotonous, the dance has been known to go on for as long as fifteen days before the animals yield to the domination of man. When the dance finally ends, the pole is chopped to bits so that each villager may have a piece as an amulet.

An entirely different type of dance, also presented in Santa Cruz Quiché around the fifteenth of August, is that known as *El Convite* (The Invitation). It is performed by the *ladinos* (whites or mixed) for pure entertainment and has no underlying religious significance. It is obviously of Spanish origin with steps like those of the courtly minuet. The costumes are elaborate creations like those seen at any fancy-dress ball anywhere.

Nossa Senhora dos Navegantes

In the southern part of the state of São Paulo, Brazil, August 15 is known as the day of Our Lady of the Navigators and is celebrated with water pageants of one kind or another. In many small communities canoes are decorated with flowers and colored paper. A captain, a purser, three musicians, and two rowers are selected for each one. The canoes go from place to place providing out-of-the-way settlements with entertainment and receiving in turn gifts of food, money, and sometimes a night's lodging. On shore there is usually an allegorical parade before or in the church with the musicians representing the Three Wise Men. Songs used for these festivities are genuine folk music and suffer no seasonal change as happens with Carnival music.

Homage to Cuauhtemoc

Each year on August 21 there is an impressive ceremony in front of the statue to Cuauhtemoc on the Paseo de la Reforma in Mexico City. For more than four centuries the natives have honored this brave Indian chieftain who led the last defense of the Aztec capital, Tenochtitlán, against Cortés. Usually two or three groups of *concheros* dance and sing, and then an Indian steps forth and reads in his native tongue an account of the life of Cuauhtemoc. Another one reads the same thing in Spanish, and then they all sing impressive songs of many stanzas commemorating the various chieftains.

The *conchero* dancers are probably the most extraordinary of all Mexican dance groups and the most numerous also. The number of *concheros* in the states of Guanajuato, Querétaro, Tlaxcala, Hidalgo, and the Federal District has been estimated at about fifty thousand. Each individual group has between fifty and one hundred members and is called a *mesa* (table) from the altar around which it is organized. The officials of each *mesa* are called first and second captain, sergeant of the mesa, field sergeant, and standard-bearers. The rest of the *concheros* are ranked according to their ability as dancers.

A person becomes a *conchero* for one of two reasons: it is quite often a tradition in his family; or, it may be part of a vow to a saint for past or future favors. Each member has the moral obligation of treating everyone he meets with respect and consideration and of helping fellow members in case of sickness, death, or financial misfortune. Whoever fails in his duty is subject to the punishment decreed by the superior officers, usually a certain number of lashes.

On the road the *concheros* march in military formation and only the leader, who is dressed as a devil, can run about as he pleases. It is his duty to clear the way for the dancers and to keep people from crowding too close during the performance. The *concheros* are always easily distinguished by their large banners or flags bearing pictures of Christ and various saints. Their feather headdresses trimmed with mirrors and beads are also distinctive. In some places the men wear brown chamois-skin suits adorned with beads and leather fringe, and in other places a long fringed skirt is the typical costume. The men always wear wigs of long hair, because the Chichimecas, who originated this dance, wore theirs long.

The name *conchero* (those of the shell) comes from the musical instrument which the men carry—a *concha*, or shell of the armadillo strung and played like a guitar. Each dancer dances for himself, in his own place, and to his own accompaniment. The steps consist of nimble springs, skips, *pas de basques*, and rockings back and forth, all punctuated with vigorous stamping on the ground. The dance starts off slowly, increasing in speed and volume until a climax is reached, and then everything stops. Soon the dancers begin again with new steps done to different melodies, and the strenuous performance continues at intervals all day.

Though the *concheros* have as their symbol the Holy Cross, they also worship the four cardinal points and the four winds as in ancient times. Of the numerous fiestas at which they perform the four most important are those at the sanctuaries situated in the four directions from Mexico City—the Basilica of Guadalupe, Chalma, Los Remedios, and Amecameca.

Santa Rosa

August 30 is an important day for Peruvians, for it is the day of their own special saint, Rose of Lima. Born Isabel de Flores in 1586, she was never called anything but Rosa or Rosita because of her flower-like complexion and gentle ways. From childhood on she devoted herself to the ill and unfortunate. Though her parents refused to let her enter a convent, she donned the Dominican robes and lived the life of a nun in her own home. Even before her untimely death at the age of 31, Rosa had come to be regarded as a saint by the residents of Lima. In 1671 she was canonized by Pope Clement X, who not only declared her a saint but also "principal and universal patron not only of Lima and Peru, but of all and every province, kingdom, island and region of terra firma in all America, the Philippines, and the Indies."

Each year on August 30, the silver statue of Santa Rosa is taken from her shrine in the church of Santo Domingo and carried in state through the streets of Lima to the great cathedral. The platform bearing the statue and other relics of the saint is a veritable garden of roses. White-robed children sing hymns along the way while adults in purple robes march with lighted candles. Every side street along the route is filled with stalls offering native delicacies, for here, as in all fiestas, the saint is feasted in the most literal sense of the word.

Venezuelan Harvest Festival

The descendants of the Ayama and Gayo Indians in the state of Lara, Venezuela, have an interesting harvest ceremony called *Baile de las Turas*, or Dance of the Flutes. When the corn begins to show signs of ripening, usually near the end of August, the villagers of San Miguel and Bobare know that it is time to express their gratitude to Nature for the rains which made the harvest abundant. It is also time to elect the new overseers whose term of office extends from harvest to harvest. Thus, the ceremony of the flutes is of a politico-religious character.

Everything is done to the music of *turas* (reed flutes), *maracas*, and *cachos* (deerskulls, from which the sound emerges by blowing through the occipital hole). The ceremony is divided into two parts: the Dance of the Small Flute, which is performed in the courtyard of the overseer and lasts a whole day and night, and the Dance of the Big Flute, which is performed when the corn is ready for preparation of the *carato* (a refreshing drink) and which lasts for four days and four nights.

The Dance of the Big Flute is the more important, and in it participate all those specified in an old document which is used as a guide: one superintendent, eight overseers (half men and half women), 64 hunters, 128 assistants (half men and half women), and 32 musicians. The dance is of collective character. Men and women are alternated in two long rows facing each other. In the middle, under a canopy of fruit offerings, sits the *cacique*, or mayor. The overseers begin and, with a *maraca* in one hand, dance up and down the long rows of dancers, who remain motionless. They bow and execute some fanciful gestures, pretending to drive out the devil, and do a final dance sequence in front of the *cacique*. Then the long rows of dancers begin to move slowly in time with the music, winding their way in graceful arabesques which, viewed from above, resemble the patterns decorating primitive pottery. In complete contrast to the majority of Indian celebrations, the consumption of alcoholic drink is strictly prohibited during the ceremony of the flutes.

SEPTEMBER

NATIVITY OF THE BLESSED VIRGIN MARY

ASIDE FROM CHRISTMAS, there are only two other birth-
days celebrated by the Church: John the Baptist's
and that of the Virgin Mary. The latter, on September 8, is one of the big fiestas of the year, especially in the Andean countries and in Mexico. Festivities
usually begin on the first and last for the entire week.

In Chumbivilcas, Peru, two of the days are devoted to
colorful bullfights. The night before these begin, there is a
great feast with the owners of the bulls supplying everyone
with *chicha*. On the two special days, the bulls are decked
out in gay cloths—homespun wool for the Indians' bulls and
fancy embroidered silk ones for the Mistis' bulls. Both men
and women take part in baiting the bulls, and many use colored Manila silk shawls as bullfighter's capes. If the men
have been able to catch a condor, it is tied to the back of one
of the bulls. Background music is provided by a group of

men in handsome capes with gold inwoven designs of the Inca sun and animals. Tropical bird feathers decorate the crowns of their hats. Usually they are accompanied by a clown who goes about striking people with a stick. When an Indian fighter gets wounded, the panpipes give forth with the lugubrious *ayarachi* or Inca funeral hymn.

September 8 is the biggest feast day of the year for the town of Cajamarca, Peru, and the celebration which takes place at the Baños del Inca is attended by thousands of people, mostly Indian. Several groups of dancers and musicians take part in the procession, and young girls dressed as brides dance in front of the litter bearing the Virgin.

The two sleepy little Peruvian villages of Sapallanga and Chavín de Pariarca also come awake with a bang during the first week of September. The former presents, in addition to the usual processions, fireworks and dances, an elaborate historical dance-drama called La Pandilla de los Incas. About one hundred elegantly costumed dancers represent the Incas and the important Spaniards at the time of the Conquest. The other town, Chavín de Pariarca, stages a dance during which there is a spirited battle on horseback. As in similar dances elsewhere, history is slightly garbled with the Spaniards fighting both Moors and Indians in the New World.

Virgen de los Remedios

In Mexico, nearly all celebrations on the eighth of September are dedicated to a foot-high, roughly-hewn wooden image known as the Virgin of the Remedies. Though the least attractive of Mexico's famous virgins, she has one of the most interesting histories.

When Cortés conquered Mexico he ordered the destruction of all the natives' heathen idols, but he could find only one Christian image with which to replace them—a little homemade Virgin-and-Child with simple round holes for eyes and mouth. When the Spaniards were driven out of the Aztec capital on the famous "Sad Night" of July 20, 1520, one of the men managed to rescue the image, but it disappeared soon afterward.

Twenty years later, it is said, the Virgin appeared to an old Indian hunting on a hillside and told him to look among the maguey plants for the little lost image. He found it and took it home with him where he built an altar for it. The next morning the statue was gone, and he found it back on the hillside again. Several times he brought the image home and even tried locking it in a box and sleeping on the lid, but each morning it was back on the same maguey plant. When the bewildered old man told the priests about it, they quickly concluded that the Virgin wanted to remain in that particular place. A church was erected there and in time became the wealthiest shrine in all Mexico.

Though the Virgin of Guadalupe was the official Patroness of New Spain, Our Lady of the Remedies was always the favorite of the Spaniards, and they conferred upon her the title of La Conquistadora for her help during the Conquest of Mexico. In the Mexican Revolution of 1810 her picture was on the banners of the Royalists, but this time she and her supporters were defeated by the Insurgents and the Virgin of Guadalupe who graced their banners. The revolutionists quickly despoiled the shrine and appropriated the fabulous treasures that had been heaped upon the Virgin. The little image, however, was forgiven for having been on the side of the enemy and still has a devoted following. In fact, her yearly fiesta is next in importance to that of the Virgin of Guadalupe. It begins on the first and goes on for a week, the last day being the most important. Since the sanctuary, which stands on the edge of the village of San Bartolo Naucálpam, is but a few miles from Mexico City, all the usual amusements are brought out. The fiesta also attracts a large number of *conchero* groups. Here, as at other places where they appear, they set up their freshly painted crosses, pray, blow incense, and dance around them.

During the week-long celebration in the town of Tepoztlán, the Virgin has to share the spotlight with an Aztec deity called Tepoztecatl. The inhabitants of this region are largely of Aztec descent and many preserve their old language and traditions. On a cliff several hundred feet above the town rises an ancient temple, called Tepozteco, which was dedicated to the Aztec god of pulque and agriculture. He has always been the mythical hero of the village, and tales are told about how he fought singlehanded and won victories over all the surrounding villages. On the last day of the fiesta, Tepoztecatl appears on a platform in vivid Indian attire and dances to the beat of an Indian drum. Several horsemen appear, attack the old Aztec and try to dislodge the supports of the tower. The dance-drama is supposed to symbolize both the prowess of Tepoztecatl and the Christians' attack on the pagan gods.

San Roque

On the first Sunday in September the town of Tarija, Bolivia, initiates a celebration in honor of its patron saint, San Roque. Natives of Tarija are very different from the Aymará and Quechua Indians who predominate at most of the Bolivian fiestas mentioned in this book. A mixture of Tomata Indians and Spaniards, they are called *chapacos* and look more like southern Europeans than like the rest of the Bolivians. Also, they speak Spanish with very few Indian words mixed in.

During the first day of their big fiesta all the townspeople turn out to greet the saint as he is carried through the streets in a procession. The women in their layers of brightly colored silk and rayon skirts, their violently polychromatic blouses trimmed with laces and ribbons, and their flowered silk shawls make even a peacock look pale by comparison. The men wear thick flannel trousers, dark red ponchos, silver-buckled sandals, broad-brimmed hats, and silk kerchiefs around their necks. Even the dogs are all decked out for the big day in colorful ribbons.

For the procession, San Roque is dressed in silk garments

richly embroidered with gold thread. In his right hand he carries a small stick and in his left a pilgrim's staff; at his feet is a dog with a piece of bread in its mouth which it is offering to the saint. Dancers called *chunchos* (not the same as the *chunchos* of the Altiplano) accompany the flower-strewn litter of the saint. They too are dressed in lively colors and wear feathered headdresses and cloth veils. Strumming on crude four-stringed instruments, they mark each step by alternately putting their chins down on their chests and throwing their heads back. As the procession passes through the streets, women throw flowers from the balconies.

On Monday and Tuesday the saint is usually paraded again, and on the second Sunday in September the *octava* begins with more processions. During the fiesta there are elaborate fireworks and various competitive games. The main difference between this and most other Bolivian fiestas is that it is strictly a Catholic celebration. None of the activities, not even the dancing of the *chunchos*, is offered in homage to Inca or pre-Inca deities under pretext of fulfilling a promise to a Christian saint.

Día de los Charros

Among the things that always come to mind when one thinks of Mexico are the charros. These handsome horsemen are frequently seen riding through Chapultepec Park in Mexico City or at the head of parades on some holiday. The charro is more or less the national hero and has his own special day, September 14. On this day many of the charro associations stage a parade and *jaripeo* (rodeo).

The charros, of course, date from shortly after the Conquest, because there were no horses in the New World until the arrival of the Spaniards. When the Spanish settlers began raising horses they had to employ native *vaqueros* or herdsmen to handle them, and these men quickly became excellent riders. By the middle of the seventeenth century a new social class had emerged—the *mestizo rancheros* (ranchers or small landholders of mixed Spanish and Indian blood). They took pride in owning good horses, and their chief amusement was riding them. Since there was little to spend their money on in the country, they adorned their horses' harnesses with silver and wore suits of rich materials with much embroidery. It is said that people of good taste began calling them *charros*, which means "loud" or "flashy." The rancheros of Salamanca, whose costume they adopted and then changed somewhat, were also called *charros*, however, so the name may have originated in either or both ways.

The Mexican charro of today is really a sportsman in spite of the fact that his name implies a rustic environment. He belongs to one of the many charro associations, each of which has its own ranch and arena for rodeos. In addition to participating in their own events, the charros willingly accept invitations to take part in popular celebrations, and their appearance is always greeted by thunderous applause from the public.

The charro's costume consists of long, tight-fitting trousers, a long-sleeved shirt called *guayabera*, a flowing bow tie, a short cloth jacket reserved for gala occasions, and a felt or woven palm sombrero. The costume worn at rodeos is fairly simple whereas the formal version is lavishly embroidered. The charro always wears a gun but even in olden times it was not used to settle arguments as among the cowboys in this country. The gun is a symbol of the charro's willingness to defend his country, and charros have always participated in Mexico's struggles to win or maintain independence.

Though the charro takes pride in his costume, he is most concerned with the choosing and care of his horse. The charros' horses are generally short and broad with thin legs and always perfect physical specimens. A great many superstitions enter into the selection. The horse must be of a dark color, for light colors bring bad luck. A black horse must have at least one white spot, preferably a star on his forehead. The star must be clearly defined, and if there is the slightest blur the horse is quickly rejected. The favorite horse is one without any white on its legs, but white socks are all right on any of the legs except the right foreleg. All cowlicks must also be examined, for there are certain bad luck cowlicks found just above the brow, at the point of the shoulders, above the cheek, on one side of the tail, or on the inside of the upper leg. Cowlicks on the ears, by the side of the neck, and on one side of the belly are all good luck cowlicks.

The *jaripeo*, sometimes called Fiesta Charra, usually has at least ten different events, and the charros participate in those of their preference. Naturally every charro must be able to perform all the tricks. During the first event, participating charros put their mounts through their paces and are given points for the way they handle their horses. The horses must be able to walk backward gracefully and in a straight line, come to a sudden stop in a prescribed manner, and obey various instructions without the slightest hesitation or protest. Following this are exhibitions of various skills or tricks such as the *manganas*, *peales*, *colas*, and *paso de la muerte*.

A *mangana* is the difficult skill of lassoing a running horse by the front feet. It is done on foot and on horseback, and the running animal must be brought to a dead stop with its front feet tied together. To make the trick even more difficult, the rope is given several twirls before it is thrown. A *peal* is the same as a *mangana* except that the running horse must be stopped by lassoing the hind legs.

In the *cola*, which means "tail," a running steer is released from the corrals. The charro must take off at the precise instant the steer enters the arena and keep right beside it. If he should fall behind there is always the danger that the steer might cross the path of the running horse and upset the rider. As he rides, the charro leans over and slaps the hindquarters of the steer. This is to make certain that the animal will not kick or jump to one side or spring any other unsuspected maneuver when it feels the hand of the charro upon its body. The charro's hand must then jump to the neck and glide back along the full length of the animal to the very tail.

Horse and steer are still running at full speed when the charro grabs the tail of the steer and twists it around his own right leg as near the stirrup as possible. If done correctly, the steer will fall on its back and do a complete roll.

Another difficult trick, the *paso de la muerte* (death's pass), consists of chasing a running wild horse and changing mounts on the run. The charro must then stay on the wild horse's back, wide-brimmed hat and all.

Somewhere in the middle of the program there is a break; animals are removed from the arena and the charras come into their own. These girls, dressed in the striking China Poblana costume, dance the famous *Jarabe Tapatío* with the charros. This dance is probably the best known of all Latin American folk dances and is often called the Mexican Hat Dance from the step in which the girl dances around the brim of her partner's sombrero. The traditional China Poblana costume consists of a full red flannel skirt with a wide band of green at the top, trimmed all over with sparkling sequins; a white short-sleeved, embroidered blouse; a *rebozo*, or scarf, folded over the shoulders and tucked in at the waist; red or green high-heeled shoes; and several strings of beads, bracelets, and earrings.

There are several legends explaining the origin of this costume. The word *china* means Chinese or a Chinese girl; *poblana* means "from or of the city of Puebla." According to the most popular legend, sometime in the middle of the seventeenth century English pirates captured a Chinese boat on which there was a lovely princess. She was taken to Manila and sold to a merchant who in turn took her to Acapulco and sold her as a slave to Captain Miguel Sosa, a well-to-do resident of Puebla. The girl was baptized, became a devout Christian and led an exemplary life. She was much loved by the people of Puebla, and girls there began to copy her beautiful red-and-green costume. Today it is seen all over Mexico on gala occasions and especially in the state of Jalisco. The *Jarabe Tapatío* belongs very definitely to Jalisco, and the word *tapatío* itself is the adjective used to describe anything from that state.

Mexican Independence

On the night of the fifteenth of September in the year 1810 Father Miguel Hidalgo y Costilla stood on the balcony of the town hall in Dolores, Guanajuato, and called upon the townfolks to rise up against the Spanish government. Early the following morning, the Independence Revolution was launched. In 1822—a year after independence had been won —September 16 was established as National Independence Day and a custom inaugurated which has been repeated every year since that time.

Each year at 11:00 p.m. on the night of the fifteenth, Hidalgo's call to arms, known as the Grito de Dolores, is re-enacted in every city and town of Mexico. In the capital, it is the president himself who gives the thrilling cry from the balcony of the National Palace. The crowds below in the *zócalo* (main square) echo the *grito* as the president rings the liberty bell which is said to be the one used by Padre Hidalgo. Immediately all of the great bells of the Metropolitan Cathedral, which flanks the *zócalo* on the north side, burst into a deafening clamor; factory whistles, automobile horns, and a wide variety of noisemakers add to the din. In the state capitals the governors do the honors, and in other cities, towns, and villages the municipal president officiates. Everywhere the *grito* is followed by fireworks and general merrymaking.

In the towns of Querétaro, San Miguel de Allende, and Dolores Hidalgo the entire historical episode is re-enacted beginning in Querétaro, where Doñ Josefa (the wife of the corregidor and herself a plotter) was held prisoner. A runner carries a scroll with the message that the plot has been discovered to San Miguel, where it was delivered to Captain Ignacio Allende, and then on to Dolores, where it was given to Padre Hidalgo.

On the sixteenth there are military parades in the larger

cities and parades of school children in the smaller places. Often a boy is selected and dressed as a priest to represent Hidalgo and a young girl chosen as *la Patria*, or the Fatherland. In San Miguel de Allende the independence holidays become a full-fledged production which lasts for about two weeks. There are parades of elaborate floats with historical tableaux, rodeos, bullfights, fireworks, and both native and popular dances. *Concheros* come from all parts, and sometimes three or four hundred gyrate for days and nights without rest in front of Allende's house.

Chilean Independence

Two days after the Mexican celebrations, the country of Chile celebrates its independence. On the morning of the eighteenth, there are parades, and in the afternoon people dance in the *ramadas*—temporary thatched stands where food and refreshments are served. Young people like to do the *cueca*, the national dance and only true Chilean folk dance. In the cities no typical costume is worn for this, but in smaller places the man dresses as a *huaso*, or Chilean cowboy, and the girl wears a full calico skirt. The one requisite is a handkerchief for each of them.

Like many other folk dances, the theme of the *cueca* is a flirtation which moves through courtship to as suggestive a conquest and surrender as the dancers care or dare to give it. It is always done as a couple dance, but several pairs may be on the floor together. Some of the steps of the dance show Spanish influence whereas the loose-legged clogging and general easy laxness of the *cueca* seem to derive from the dancing of the Negroes that were brought to Chile in colonial times. Neither the steps nor the figures are arbitrary, and improvisations are constantly made which add to the interest and the beauty of the dance. Some of the expert dancers go through the most amazing gyrations with their feet while balancing a glassful of water on their heads. In all versions the handkerchief plays a major part in the courtship with both the man and the woman waving it provocatively and gracefully. The music of the *cueca*, like Chilean folk music in general, is light, gay, and very Spanish in feeling. It is played on guitar, tambourine, and harp, softly at first and then with fire. The spectators clap their hands in time to the music, shouting encouragement, taunting the male for his timidity, or complimenting the woman.

Many of the towns near big cattle ranches also stage a rodeo for the Independence holidays. The Chilean rodeo, however, is nothing like that of Mexico or the United States and is completely lacking in both violence and excitement. The arena, which is called *media luna* (half moon), is oval shaped and divided in half the long way by a log fence or other barricade. Two sections of the wall are padded thickly with bulrushes. The horsemen, who stand ready in the center, work in pairs, and as soon as the first steer enters two of them dash after it. The lead horseman must bring the steer to a stop by pinning it against the bulrush pad, release him, haze him in the opposite direction and pin him against the other pad of rushes. This complicated maneuver is calculated to reveal every fault of performance in both man and mount and must be completed within a specified number of seconds if the horseman is even to score. The spectators will occasionally shout *"¡Bueno!"* or *"¡Bravo!"* when an expert rider has made a good run, but generally only the judges show keen interest.

Though the performance may be lacking in color, the performers certainly are not. With the exception of the Mexican charro, the Chilean huaso is the most colorfully costumed horseman in Latin America. Above his high-heeled boots and oversized spurs that huaso wears long, fringed, quilted leggings of soft black leather. Over his bolero-like jacket is a short silk or wool cape covered with vivid contrasting stripes an inch wide. His dark-colored hat is broad-brimmed, flat-crowned, and held on by a chin strap. He uses a V-shaped saddle hidden between piles of colorful pads and surmounted by a deep, cushiony sheepskin. It seems incredible that anyone sitting high on this oriental pile could be such an expert horseman.

The huaso is not a sportsman like the charro and does not belong to a special club. He may be a working cowboy or a small rancher or farmer. Sometimes even the owner of a large ranch becomes a first-class huaso. Whatever his station in life, the huaso adds a colorful note to Chile's rather unspectacular celebrations.

Apparition of the Infant Jesus in Eten

One of the most interesting places in Peru is the ancient Villa de Eten, which has many descendants of the Mochicas and is the only place where that language is still spoken. There are many fiestas, of which the two most important are on June 2 and September 18 and celebrate the apparitions of the Infant Jesus in the Sacred Host. These took place in the year 1649, and soon after the second one a tidal wave wiped out the village. The chapel where the apparitions took place, however, was unharmed and from that time on it has been called La Capilla de los Milagros (Chapel of the Miracles).

The September 18th fiesta lasts for three days, though festivities really begin weeks in advance with the candle-making and other preparations. On the eve of the first day of the fiesta, there is a special mass attended by all the *mayordomos*, musicians, dancers, and townspeople and followed by fireworks and lighted balloons. The next day there is a procession to the Capilla de los Milagros, about a mile away. The first image to appear is the Magdalena, and she is followed by St. Peter with the silver keys of heaven in one hand and a silver fish in the other. Next comes the Señor del Mar (Lord of the Sea) and last the litter bearing the Custodia under a pallium. The latter is accompanied by the priest and twenty-four *mayordomos* who take turns bearing the litter and drinking to the Sacred Host. On the return trip the Magdalena rides backward following the Señor del Mar and facing the Host. This time the procession winds through the arches erected by the villagers and stops at improvised altars along the way. Accompanying the procession are many dancing groups: *pastores* (shepherds), *serranitos* (little Indians from the Sierra), *faroles* (a group which dances with lighted lanterns at street corners after dark), and bullfighters. Each group wears its own typical costume and dances to its own music. When they reach the church again, a large fireworks wheel is set off. The women of this town, called *chinas*, present a pretty picture in their full black skirts and white blouses embroidered with purple borders.

San Miguel

September 29 is the day of St. Michael, and as this is one of the most popular names given to towns and villages, there are celebrations in his honor in many parts of Latin America. One of the most lavish is that of San Miguel de Allende in Mexico, where people are still in a gay mood from the long Independence Day celebrations earlier in the month. The fiesta of the town's patron saint is usually a four-day spree much like the famous pre-Lenten carnivals. There is one continuous round of parades, street dancing, and parties. Hundreds of costumed native dancers come from various parts of Mexico and gyrate tirelessly through the streets and plaza. On the last day there is usually a bullfight with some of Mexico's top *toreros*, and festivities end in the evening with street dancing, band concerts, and a breathtaking fireworks display.

In many Mexican Indian villages the saint is honored with indigenous dances. In Jesús María in the state of Nayarit, the Coras perform a dance called *Los Maromeros* (The Acrobats). The dancers wear their regular clothes but adorn their hats with ribbons and carry stout canes. From their shoulders hang the typical cross-stitched Cora bags. The dance is performed inside the church to the music of a small drum and flute played by the same musician. Dancers weave slowly toward the altar with symbolic gestures in the four directions and perform various acrobatic feats such as dancing under their cane with one end held on the floor. The dance of *Las Palmas* (The Palms) is also done on St. Michael's Day. The dancers, still in white suits, have red bandannas hanging down in front from under their shirts. They use a headdress of flowers and feathers and suspended from it a fine net of blue and white beads which hangs down to about the middle of the chest. Each dancer carries a painted tin rattle and a fan-shaped bamboo palm adorned with artificial blue and yellow flowers. The leader is called *el viejo* (old man), though he is not necessarily old, and wears a wooden mask with a horsehair mustache. He carries a whip and is the clown of the group. There is also a Malinche, the female figure which appears in so many native dances and is named after the Indian mistress of Cortés. The music for the dance is unusually lovely and played on violin and flute. The dancers perform elaborate figures, frequently spreading their feet apart and bending backward. In one part, the men take turns dancing with the Malinche.

In Tuxtla Gutiérrez, the capital of Chiapas, the Zoques stage a performance for St. Michael in which the principal characters are three Lucifers and three angels, all wearing masks. Anyone who wishes and who owns a devil's mask may join in. The first angel represents St. Michael and carries a scale in one hand and a sword in the other. The other angels carry swords and flowers instead of scales. The steps are very simple and done to the music of stringed instruments. For the finale, one of the Lucifers is seated in a chair rigged with fireworks, and his hasty exit as they are set off causes great merriment among the spectators.

Villagers of Acapazingo (state of Morelos) regard the twenty-ninth of September with great awe, for they believe that the devil runs around loose on that date and tries to get into people's homes. Crosses are hung in front of huts and on nearby trees, and special ones are woven with flowers gathered the day before. Often the women perform a special dance with great bundles of flowers in their arms.

Aguas de Oxalá

Members of the Apô Afonjá *candomblé* group in Salvador, Brazil, reserve the last Friday of September each year for the purification rite called Aguas de Oxalá (Waters of Oxalá). Oxalá is one of the principal gods or saints of the African religion, and many of the groups in the state of Salvador consider him the father of all the others. His pre-eminence in Salvador is probably due to the fact that he has become identified in the minds of his worshipers—who are also Roman Catholics—with Our Lord of Bomfin (Good Fortune), patron saint of the favorite church of the Negroes.

The ceremony of the sacred waters takes place at the ridgetop headquarters of the Apô Afonjá *candomblé* at São Gonçalo do Retiro on the outskirts of the city of Salvador and begins at about three o'clock in the morning. At first all is darkness and silence, then suddenly a *candomblé* dignitary emerges from the shadows tinkling a tiny bell. Immediately the place comes alive as ghostly figures silently approach from all directions. Ever so quietly, with only a slight rustling of skirts and a shuffling of bare feet, the white-clad participants form a single line facing the dirt road. Most of them are women, but there are a few old men in the group. Each one carries an earthen jar or vase on top of the head or on one shoulder.

At a given signal the procession, slowly and with great dignity, begins to descend a steep hillside at the base of which lies a sacred spring. One by one the solemn participants fill their jars with water, replace them on their heads or shoulders, and return to the top of the hill. From here they proceed to a special hut where each person in turn empties his jar into a large receptacle made especially to receive the sacred waters of Oxalá. It is almost light by the time the last member of the group finishes his ritual task.

Almost immediately the stillness is broken by the unmistakable sound of African drums and gongs.

Several of the *filhas de santo*, or daughters of the saint, now begin to dance outside the water hut while others give forth with the weird, shrill chants that are an integral part of ceremonial dances. The throbbing of the drums and the insistent clanging of the gongs go on . . . and on . . . and on. The dancing becomes more frenzied until nearly all of the holy daughters have become possessed. Their violent seizures and convulsive trembling are followed by the trancelike performance of the special dances of the gods they represent.

The *candomblé of* Engenho Velho, the oldest in Salvador, has a similar ceremony for the Aguas de Oxalá on the last Friday of August.

OCTOBER

SAN FRANCISCO DE ASIS

ONE OF THE MOST beloved of all saints is St. Francis of Assisi. His day is the fourth of October, and fiestas are offered to him in many parts of Latin America. In Uruapan, Mexico, there is an interesting parade of decorated oxen, and several regional dances such as the *Viejitos*, *Moros y Cristianos*, and *Canacuas* are performed. *Canacuas*, which has not yet been described, is the Tarascan word for "crowns." Only young, unmarried girls may take part in the dance. Though the girls are actually of the mestizo class, they wear the costume of the Tarascan women—full, dark-colored skirts pleated in back, gaily embroidered white blouses, long white aprons, rebozos crossed and tucked in at the waist, and several strings of colorful beads. Each girl carries a large painted gourd bowl, called *xicapextli*, filled with flowers and fruit. The dance steps are simple but graceful, many of them done with the bowls on the dancers' heads. A small orchestra of stringed instruments accompanies the dancing and the sev-

153

eral songs which are a part of the dance. Toward the end, a man dressed as an Indian and carrying a live chicken or turkey joins the group. He dances with one girl at a time doing both the Jarabe of the Bottle and the Jarabe of the Knot. In the former the couple dance around a bottle placed on the floor taking care not to knock off the silver coin balanced on the stopper. In the second dance, a knot is tied and untied with the feet while dancing. There is always much enthusiastic clapping from those not participating.

In Arequipa, Peru, San Francisco shares the spotlight on this day with Santo Domingo. Simultaneous processions set out from their respective churches, each with music, fireworks, and a large following. They meet at the Plaza de Armas under a specially decorated triumphal arch. Here the two images are made to greet each other in a majestic reverence to symbolize the historical meeting of the two saints. After more fireworks, the images are returned and the day is spent in feasting, dancing, or watching the bullfights. On August 4, the day of Santo Domingo, the processions also take place in the very same manner.

For the residents of Quibdó, Colombia, the fiesta of San Francisco is one of the biggest of the year and begins on the twenty-sixth of September. The whole town is divided into eight parts, and each section must put up its own altars, arches, and decorate the streets for the procession on the fourth. In addition, each section is responsible for one of the days of the fiesta and must take charge of the popular sports such as boxing, horse and bicycle racing, and contests such as greased-pig-catching. People dress up in various disguises, and the streets are filled with devils, savages, alligators, and great cats. At times there are floats pulled by men, women, and children, and always there is street dancing, fireworks, and bullfighting with the *vacalocas* (crazy cows). Like the *torito* of other countries, this is the wooden framework of a cow or bull with flaming horns propelled by a man. On the last day the afternoon is given over to a long procession in which the local police, school children, religious organizations, and general public accompany St. Francis on his long trek through town.

Virgen de Zapopan

In Guadalajara, Mexico, St. Francis has had to give up his day to the more popular Virgin of Zapopan, whose fiesta is celebrated October 4 and 5. This image first put in an appearance during a battle between the Spaniards and the Chimalhuacano Indians in the early part of the sixteenth century. The natives were about to be annihilated when the Franciscan Friar Antonio Segovia entered the battlefield with the image of the Virgin in his hand. As soon as the Indians saw it, they surrendered and were spared by the Spaniards. In 1541 when many of these same Indians settled in the village of Zapopan, the padre made them a present of the image.

In 1734 this Virgin was made patroness of rains by the civil and ecclesiastical councils, and it was decreed that she spend from June 13 to October 4 of each year visiting the churches of Guadalajara. There are so many that she is not able to spend more than two or three days in each one, except for the cathedral, where she remains for a week. On her last day in the city, all the congregations unite for a formal leave-taking, and the Virgin is showered with prayers and offerings of candles and flowers.

On the morning of the fourth, the image of the Virgin is dressed in a dark traveling suit and taken in state to the town of Zapopan. On the flower-covered arches erected along the route are fireworks carefully set to go off as the Virgin passes underneath. Flower girls strew petals in her path, and exotically clad dancers perform for her pleasure. None of this, however, seems to cheer up the marchers from Guadalajara who, clad in black and solemn-faced, are mourning the loss of their favorite saint. When the Virgin reaches her home, an elaborately adorned seventeenth century church and monastery, she changes into her fiesta robes of white satin, dons her diamonds, and assumes her place on the altar.

Festa da Luz

The second Sunday in October marks the beginning of Belém's lovely Festival of Light which honors Our Lady of Nazareth. The accompanying pilgrimage, which dates back to the year 1700, is one of the most impressive in Brazil and often draws as many as one hundred thousand participants.

A preliminary procession is held Saturday evening when the image, dressed in satin and escorted by a large group of penitents, rides through the streets to the cathedral in a *berlinda*—a glass-enclosed case mounted on wheels. The most important procession, however, is the one on Sunday morning when the image is returned to its own altar. Again it rides in the *berlinda*, this time escorted by ecclesiastic and civil dignitaries. Following it is the so-called Miracle Car borne on the backs of staggering penitents. This "car" is actually a heavy dais bearing representations of the Virgin's major miracles and takes the place of the twelve canoes filled with children that once commemorated disasters at sea averted by her intervention. The Miracle Car is followed by men, women, and children of all ages and economic conditions. Many of them walk barefoot; some wear hair shirts or girdles or carry heavy objects in penitence. Often there are children dressed as angels fulfilling vows made in their behalf by their parents while they were seriously ill.

The square in front of the church is decorated with lights in beautiful designs of flowers, birds, or stylized themes, and the building itself is outlined in lights. Every inch of available space is given over to booths where wares of all kinds are sold, and different instrumental groups supply the crowds with continuous music. It is one of the gayest fairs in Brazil and lasts for two full weeks.

Día de la Raza

October 12, which we have labeled Columbus Day, is called Day of the Race in Latin American countries to signify the origin of their present population. Usually there is nothing more than speeches or parades of school children to mark the day, however.

In the capital of the Dominican Republic, there is usually an impressive ceremony at the Cathedral of Santo Domingo where the ancient casket which reportedly holds the remains of Columbus is put on display. The tomb is unlocked only once a year on this date and requires the presence of the bishop, the governor, and the mayor of the city, each of whom holds one of the three necessary keys. At one time in the past there was an interesting historical pageant in addition to the usual parades. The admiral's ships landed once more and the founding of Santo Domingo by Columbus' brother Bartholomew was acted out by troops in armor bearing the banners of old Spain. It is hoped that this pageant will be reinstated in the future.

Señor de los Milagros

Every year on the 18th and 19th of October, people of Lima turn out by the thousands to honor the image of Our Lord of Miracles. The devotion to this image began back in the seventeenth century when devastating earthquakes nearly destroyed the city of Lima. In spite of the prayers of the faithful and the intercession of saints who were taken out in procession, the quaking continued week after week and thousands of lives were lost. During one particularly heavy jolt all of the buildings in one of the Negro sections were demolished. Only a small piece of adobe wall was left standing, and on this piece was a picture of Christ which an unknown Negro artist had painted there several years before. A group of Negroes who had been standing near the wall and were miraculously saved carried the wall with its sacred painting through the streets. They were soon followed by hysterical mobs, screaming, confessing their sins, and flagellating themselves. The earth stopped trembling at last.

The original painting, still on a fragment of the wall, has been set in a gorgeous silver mounting and is housed in the church of Las Nazarenas in the center of the city. A replica of it has been made for use in the processions and is kept in a small adjacent chapel.

To this day Our Lord of Miracles, as the painting was named, is the favorite image of the Negroes. It is the Negro brotherhood, now several thousand strong, that organizes the procession and above all carries the heavy litter of ornately worked silver. Hundreds of them, in their purple robes, surround the litter carrying lighted candles and censers. Many walk backward in order not to turn their backs to the Señor. But this celebration is not only for the Negroes. Thousands of white people also join the procession as it moves slowly through town. Balconies of houses along the route are hung with embroidered banners, and women toss flowers in the path of the marchers. Often white doves are seen ascending from paper cages carried by devout participants. The procession stops at each of the churches along the way and leaves some of the flowers that spectators have showered upon the litter.

On the 28th of October the Lord of Miracles is again taken out in procession, this time for only one day. Whereas the first two processions are clearly dominated by the poorer classes, this one is more for the upper classes and consequently of smaller proportions.

Black Christ of Portobelo

Residents of Portobelo, Panama, also have a miraculous Christ which they ceremoniously fete on the 21st of October. This life-size image is made of very dark wood and thus is always referred to as the Black Christ.

The story goes that in 1658 the image was being sent from Spain to the Colombian port of Cartagena. The ship carrying it stopped briefly at Portobelo for fresh supplies and provisions. When the captain put out to sea again, a severe storm came up unexpectedly and forced him to return to port. The captain made four more attempts to continue his journey and each time was thwarted by similar storms. By this time the crew was convinced that the image wished to remain in Portobelo, and they tossed it overboard before setting sail again.

The residents of Portobelo fished the Black Christ out of the bay and installed it in a place of honor in their church. Shortly afterward an epidemic of cholera raced across the isthmus, miraculously sparing this one community. Credited with having saved the town, the Black Christ thus became the patron saint of Portobelo.

At 6:00 p.m. on October 21, religious ceremonies are held in the church, and the procession starts out from there at about eight o'clock. The platform bearing the statue is profusely decorated with flowers and lighted candles and is carried on the shoulders of eight men. Keeping time to the music of the local band, the bearers proceed through town with a curious gait, taking three steps forward and two backward each time. After the image has been returned to the church at midnight, there is dancing and feasting till dawn.

Feria en Jalisco

From October 22 to 25 Ciudad Guzmán in the state of Jalisco, Mexico, presents a fair at which a great number of regional dances are performed. Two of the most interesting are those of the *Sonajeros* and the *Paixtles*.

The *Sonajeros* (literally, "rattlers") take their name from the *sonaja* (rattle) which each dancer carries. It consists of a long wooden stick with handles at both ends and four groups of metal pieces between. The dancers wear white trousers with wide red cuffs, red sashes, white shirts trimmed with rows of many-colored ribbons, and black painted aprons in both front and back. About fifteen dance at one time in single file. To the music of drum and flute, the dancers shake their rattles and perform a great variety of interesting and vigorous steps.

In the dance of the *Paixtles* (moss-covered ones) the men are covered, except for their arms, by a huge cape of moss and wooden or paper masks. They are supposed to represent sorcerers with animal power, in spite of the human features of the masks. They carry a shepherd's staff carved with an animal's head and hung with bells that jingle as they strike the ground rhythmically during the dance. From time to time they emit weird beast-like cries. The costumes are so cumbersome that only the simplest of steps can be performed.

Nossa Senhora da Penha

On a 300-foot-high granite boulder on the outskirts of Rio de Janeiro stands the prim but enormously wealthy little church of Nossa Senhora da Penha (Our Lady of the Rock). There are several different stories explaining the selection of this particular spot for the church. According to one version, a hunter about to be swallowed by an enormous snake implored the Virgin to save him. She caused a little lizard, who was sunning himself on the rock, to drop on the snake's head, frightening it away. Another version has the man being attacked by both a venomous snake and a scorpion. The Virgin heard his appeal and came to his aid, placing a foot on each of his enemies. According to still another legend, a traveler who fell asleep at the base of the rock was saved from a vicious crocodile by the miraculous intercession of the Virgin.

Whatever the reason for this shrine, it is the scene of impressive pilgrimages every Sunday in October, and the festivities are considered next in importance to Carnival. At the base of the rock is a large square which, during the month of October, is crowded with stalls and food-and-drink bars. From here ascends a flight of 365 steps carved out of the rock itself. It is an impressive sight to watch the pilgrims climbing with huge wax candles and wax representations of parts of the body cured by the Virgin. Though prohibited by the authorities, some still go all the way on their knees in fulfillment of a pledge. It is said that one time a man tripped on the top step and rolled all the way down to the bottom. Thinking that he was fulfilling a vow, everyone stepped aside considerately to let him pass. On the slopes of the hill are numerous little huts where there is constant music, singing, and dancing. There are Ferris wheels, carrousels, entertainment booths of all kinds, and the inevitable fireworks. On the first Sunday in November a final festival is held for the proprietors of the stalls and vendors of food and drinks.

NOVEMBER

ALL SAINTS AND ALL SOULS

THOUGH NOVEMBER 1 bears the title of All Saints' Day (Día de Todos los Santos) and November 2 All Souls' Day (Día de las Animas) or Day of the Dead (Día de Difuntos), the two days are considered as one holiday throughout Latin America. The first day is generally a religious holiday celebrated by special masses and the second a memorial day during which people visit the cemeteries carrying flowers and candles to the graves of their departed ones. In the Andean countries it is customary to bring food also, and people feast, dance, and make merry in the cemeteries until dawn of the third. In some places food and drinks are sold at special stands set up on the grounds.

Andean Indians often pray to their dead for good crops and set up altars of their favorite foods, of which the dead may partake in spirit. In the village of Huarocondo, Peru, the Indians take offerings of roasted pig, tamales, potatoes, corn, cheese, and eggs to the church to be blessed by the priest and then left for the dead.

In Arequipa and Cuzco, Peru, many of the young men take a cake made in the form of a baby and decorated with colored candies to the homes of their girl friends and stage a mock baptismal ceremony. This entering into the ritual relationship of *compadrazgo*, or godfathership, often facilitates the much more desired union of matrimony. In the village of Tomaiquiche, near Huánuco, young men go out at dawn on the second to serenade their girl friends and are rewarded when the girls throw open the doors or windows and sprinkle them with urine which is kept in a closed vessel in every house for its curative properties.

The Indian village of Todos Santos in Guatemala adds the last day of October in order to have a three-day celebration in honor of the dead. Men in elaborate costumes and masks perform the colorful Deer Dance; villagers standing on the sidelines are almost as colorful themselves in their traditional red turban and red-and-white striped pants topped by a black woolen garment. On All Souls' Day, families bring their offerings to church—flowers of various kinds, ears of corn, squash, and cut pieces of orange—and arrange them carefully on the floor. Then they pour a little coffee into some of the blossoms and sprinkle the whole arrangement with brandy. After mass, everyone in town gathers in or near the plaza to watch the rooster race. Ropes are stretched across the street and from them live roosters are hung up by their feet. As men on horseback gallop by, they are supposed to reach up with one hand and jerk off the head of a rooster. The team that acquires the most heads wins the race, and individual riders are awarded the bodies of the birds that they have killed.

In Mexico, where people know how to make light of even the most serious matters, the two-day celebration in honor of the dead is utterly charming and gay. It is believed that the deceased deserve a vacation as much as the living, so once a year they return to earth and in spirit join in the family fun and partake of delicious dishes prepared especially in their honor.

Altars are set up within the homes on October 31. They are decorated with candles and bright orange marigolds (the *zempoalxochitl* or "flower of the dead") and laden with all kinds of goodies. As November 1 is the Day of the Little Dead, unseen visitors on the night of the thirty-first are the souls of dead children, and they always find an abundance of cookies, candies, milk, and honey. Often there is a special *tamal* spiced with seeds known as the "seeds of happiness." Placed near the food are toys for them to play with when they have finished eating.

On the following night, which is for adult souls, the fare is a little more substantial—*mole* (heavy chocolate and chili sauce with turkey), various puddings, *pan de muertos* (plain coffeecake made more or less in the form of a skull and cross-bones), and the native drink, pulque. Families and their friends celebrate both nights, often talking to the departed ones in a most realistic manner. The family rarely touches the food left by the spirits but gives it to friends or neighbors and in return receives the loot from their altars. Friends often call in the daytime as well as at night and are offered a taste of the "food for the dead."

For several days before the first of November, Death leers invitingly from every bakery window and from stalls in markets and along the streets. Besides the traditional *pan de muertos* there are thousands of sugar skulls with bright tinsel eyes and names across their forehead. It is considered quite proper and not the least bit superstitious to present one's friends with these macabre namesakes. There are fancy funeral processions made of chocolate with tiny wreaths of candied fruit on the hearses, and coffins made of every kind of candy. Children beg their parents for death's-head masks, small gilt skeletons that dance up and down on strings or pop out of a box when the lid is touched, tiny funeral processions that go round and round as a handle is turned, miniature altars with offerings of food on them, and the many other ingenious toys sold at this time.

Death is the theme also for advertisements in newspapers and magazines, and in some cities mock obituaries or satirical verses known as *calaveras* (literally, "skulls") are sold on the streets and in the market places for a few centavos apiece. These poke fun at well-known persons and at times no one is spared, not even the priests. Often the *calaveras* are illustrated with engravings made by Mexico's best artists.

The theater also joins in the fiestas for the dead with presentations of the lugubrious play *Don Juan Tenorio*, which is filled with violent death, voices echoing from tombs, and ghosts materializing. It is not the great work of Tirso de Molina, however, but a version of José Zorrilla which ends with a repentent Don Juan, redeemed by his love for the beautiful nun Inés, who takes him to heaven with her. This Spanish classic also appears in radio or television versions, but it is interspersed with acid comments subtly worked in among José Zorrilla's beautiful verses.

In some parts of the country graves are adorned on November first, and in others, on the second. Throughout the cemeteries, yellow is the outstanding color—yellow marigolds and yellow candles everywhere. Purple seems to be a second choice, and there are many flowers of this color too. Roads leading to the cemeteries seem to be crawling with monstrous floral pieces which almost completely hide the man staggering along beneath them. In some villages in the states of Veracruz and Puebla, paths of marigold petals connect the cemetery with all the houses that have been visited by death during the year.

In the town of Milpa Alta, near Mexico City, huge bonfires are built in the streets on the night of November 2nd. Small boys run through town holding up lighted jack-o-lanterns and asking for pennies much like our own Halloween celebrants. Attractive lanterns made in the shape of houses or other objects are hung in trees to guide dead souls home with their light. A little farther on, toward Toluca, in the town of Mixquic, gigantic cardboard skeletons which stand guard all day at the gates of the cemetery are burned with great festivity. The fires soon die down, and the cemetery becomes a fairyland of twinkling candlelights with here and there a shadowy figure watching over the grave of a loved one.

Villages in Oaxaca are noted for their very unusual altars to the dead which sometimes fill almost an entire room. Long lengths of sugar cane are used in the decorations, and on various levels or steps of the altar designs are made in real or artificial flowers, maize, or cactus leaves. The tempting dishes on the altars are taken to the cemetery on the night of the second and left there for the dead.

Many of the Indian communities have a more sober approach to the festival of the dead. The Zapotecs in Yalalag celebrate for nine nights before the second. Each night between midnight and 3:00 a.m. a ghostly procession leaves the church and heads for the cemetery. Unearthly musical discords fill the air as high-pitched wailing voices emanate from the white-shrouded marchers. The path leading to the cemetery is like a terrestrial Milky Way, ablaze with the lights of candles and pine torches. Headed by the image of the Virgen del Carmen and accompanied by the weird music of flute and drum, the spectral figures ascend the hill, stopping now and then while the shaman offers special prayers to the dead in both Spanish and Zapotec.

Probably the best known celebration for the dead in Mexico is that of Janitzio Island in Lake Pátzcuaro. Though tourists have done their best to spoil it with their rude ways and popping flashbulbs, it has somehow managed to retain most of its picturesqueness. Shortly after midnight on the first, women begin to appear carrying baskets of food covered with attractively embroidered napkins, small wooden frameworks hung with fruit of all kinds, bundles of orange flowers, and candles. The women are Tarascan Indians and wear the beautiful costume of the region—heavy woolen skirts intricately pleated across the back, bright satin blouses, and several necklaces. Followed by their children, the women make their way to the cemetery. Though there are neither grave markers nor headstones, each woman seems to know where her dead lie. Carefully cleaning the graves, the women arrange the flowers and offerings of food in attractive patterns and set up lighted candles. At first there are just a few lights here and there, but gradually they grow into pools of golden glow which burn huge holes in the blue darkness. The women and children spend the rest of the night sitting quietly on the graves while the men sing Tarascan songs nearby.

At the crack of dawn a priest appears and blesses all the graves. The women gather up their offerings, deposit them at one of the churches, and go back to their homes. Each of the churches has a large wooden framework hung with fruit and arrangements of flowers and candles for the dead who have no relatives or who are no longer in their graves.

One of the favorite foods of the "dead" around Lake Pátzcuaro is wild duck, and on the morning of the first of November there is a duck hunt in which several villages take part. Shortly before dawn, native dugout canoes of all sizes set out from the shores of the lake. Paddling silently, the Tarascan men surround the ducks, gradually closing the circles. At a given signal each man hurls a harpoon-like weapon called Atlatl. A favorite Mexican weapon since 2000 B.C., this four-pointed bamboo spear stands upright in the water when it hits its mark. The men are so skilled at throwing it that the lake is often left almost duckless in a few hours. The ducks are cooked with a special orange and spice flavoring that gives a distinctive and delicious taste to the meat. The white fish in Lake Pátzcuaro are also known for their delicious flavor but are not fished for during these days because of the superstition that people who have drowned in the lake will come up in the nets.

Carnival in Cartagena

The most important celebration in the old, walled city of Cartagena, Colombia, is the annual carnival which takes place on November 11, the anniversary of the declaration of independence. For four days a remarkable zaniness takes over. Thousands of costumed men, women, and children fill the streets, dancing to the sound of drums and maracas. There are parades of floats, flower battles, and much general excitement caused by the *buscapies* (feet searchers). These popular Colombian firecrackers are made of a plant stalk hollowed out and filled with powder. They are lighted at one end and hop about chasing everyone off the street. These festivities coincide with the National Beauty Contest, which is always held in Cartagena, and the lovely queens are the center of attraction at dances and on floats. Though the holiday lasts officially for only four days, the public often manages to continue the general merrymaking for several consecutive Saturdays and Sundays.

Virgen del Amparo

Inhabitants of Sacaba, Bolivia, eagerly await the seventeenth of November, which is the day of their patron, the Virgin of Amparo. Though a crudely carved image whose features leave much to the imagination, the Virgin possesses an elegant wardrobe. Only for this fiesta, however, is she allowed to wear her dress of gold filigree featuring intricate patterns of leaves and flowers.

On the morning of the fiesta (occasionally the third Sunday of November instead of the 17th), groups of dancers begin to appear, each with its own musicians. There are usually several groups of *cambas*—Quechua men in suits hung with multicolored scarves and mirrors, red sashes decorated with mirrors and glass beads, and straw hats which hang from their necks and bob up and down on their backs. Holding a long arrow or spear in one hand, they gyrate rapidly and form different figures. There are also *cullacas*, or mixed groups in which the women wear the bright full skirts of the cholla or mestizo women of the Altiplano and join the men in a monotonous dance. Devils in hideous blue, white, green, and black masks run about clearing spaces for the dancers, and *jucumaris* (bears) in thick llama skins amble through the crowd nearly suffocating, no doubt, in the oppressing heat.

At about two in the afternoon the procession leaves the church, and the dancers line up on both sides, the *cambas* with their long arrows interwoven to form a kind of barricade. Several stops are made while the priest offers prayers and the musicians sing and play liturgical pieces composed especially for this occasion.

On the eighteenth (or third Monday) the dancers come out again, and the procession takes place as before except that it is in the morning this time. In the afternoon everyone goes to El Calvario, a spot located on the river about three-quarters of a mile west of Sacaba. Here mature men and women as well as children set about gathering pebbles from the bank. With these they construct miniature houses of different kinds using twigs or leafy branches for the roof. With tiny toy implements they dig holes in which they "plant" branches of peach, plum, and orange trees, creating sizable orchards. On some of the properties, which have been designated as farms, toy cows, sheep, and other animals are set out. As each piece of property grows, the owners suddenly become boundary conscious, and many a real or pretended skirmish takes place over the location of the markers. When the whole community is laid out, complete with well-marked roads, a few business transactions usually take place. These involve little or no money but are taken quite seriously. Many of the young folk decide to combine their wealth, and there is a sudden rash of weddings with improvised notaries and priests. It's all in fun, of course, but as the fiesta reaches its last stage and dancing begins on the hard ground near the river, many a happily-whirling couple is thinking that it could all come true with the help of the Virgin of Amparo.

Santa Catarina

Many Latin American towns celebrate the day of St. Catherine on November 25. In Apopa, El Salvador, things get started on the twenty-second with one of the *velaciones* which are so common throughout the country. These half-religious, half-profane affairs are organized gatherings at one of the larger country homes to honor the saint and to collect money for the day of its fiesta.

An elaborate setting is arranged for the altar of the saint who is an honored guest during these festivities. A green bower is formed of palm branches and aromatic plants. Bouquets of wild flowers, small Chinese lanterns, and little flags of colored paper are added. From the ceiling hang garlands of white and red flowers intermixed with little chains of paper. With everyone grouped around the altar, a simple religious ceremony takes place, ending with the praying of three rosaries. After this everyone scatters throughout the house and patios. Women go from group to group carrying big pots of black coffee, trays of steaming tamales, and fritters of various kinds. There is always a good supply of *chachacaste*, a clandestine whisky considered much tastier than the famous name brands. When everyone has had his fill, the dancing begins in the patio, usually accompanied by an accordion and a few guitars. Before the evening is over the country troubadour puts in an appearance, and everyone sits around him, wide-eyed, as he sings of the black eyes of a charming señorita, of the white towers of a little country church, of the shining feathers of a beautiful bird, or of a hammock stretched out beside the sea.

Farther north, the Otomí Indians of Pahuatlán, Mexico, celebrate St. Catherine's Day with an interesting dance called *Acatlaxquis* (reed throwers). The dancers (ten or more young men) wear their ordinary white shirts and pants with short red over-trousers. Two red bandannas are tied crosswise across the chest while a third serves as a loin-cloth. Heavy sandals and conical paper hats trimmed with colored streamers complete the costume. Each dancer carries an *acatlaxque*, which consists of one large reed (about a yard long) with a dozen or more slender reeds fastened to it and all ornamented with brilliant feathers. They are put together in such a way that when the dancer throws them out, the reeds slide out one by one and form a huge arch.

The central figure of the dance is a small girl, called la Maringuilla—in reality, a boy in a long white dress carrying a gourd containing a wooden snake. Commencing inside the church, the dancers form two rows and perform several intricate steps to the music of a flute and drum. As they move into the atrium, they first dance back and forth in one long row and finally form a circle around the Maringuilla while one of the men holds the snake over her head. After a while she is lifted onto a small wooden platform which the dancers encircle. At the climax of the dance, the reeds are thrown out to form an arched dome over her head. This action is repeated several times to the accompaniment of ringing church bells and bursting rockets.

Manger-yam

Of all the things grown in Haiti, the yam is probably the most significant. In addition to being the most vital of all staples, it is a link with the past and a symbol of fertility. The yam was brought to the New World from Africa, where it has always been a staff of life among those who live by agriculture. When the yam crop is good in Haiti there is plenty of food for the winter months and a general sense of well-being; when it is poor, there is a feeling of insecurity and sometimes even hunger. Everything depends upon the family ancestors, for they have the power to enhance the crops or to blight them. To make sure that the ancestors remain in the proper frame of mind, they are always the honored guests at the Manger-yam, or annual harvest feast.

This takes place at the time of the annual harvest in November. No yams may be eaten before the feast or the crops will spoil and those who eat them become ill.

In some regions the Manger-yam takes place in the peristyle of the voodoo priest or houngan and is given for the community at large. In other places it is held in the homes of the peasants with a houngan in attendance. Wherever it takes place, all those who have strayed away from home are obligated to return for this occasion. In a sense, the fate of the entire family depends upon a succcessful appeal to the ancestral dead, and the solidarity of the living in this effort is considered vital. Though strictly a voodoo rite, Catholics and Protestants alike participate.

During the service the yams are washed, cut into small pieces and placed in dishes or calabash bowls. The yams are first offered to the recent and well-remembered dead, next to those who can be recalled only by name, and then to those whose names have been forgotten. After the dead of Haiti are taken care of, the dead of Africa are invoked, and a special table is set aside for the very ancient dead who must move slowly and may take a long time to arrive. Next it is the turn of the family *loa*, the African deities who protect their household, and finally the members of the family receive their symbolic portions. In the evening the yams are cooked with fish and everyone enjoys a feast.

Though the celebration of Manger-yam varies in different places and at different times, it usually lasts for about two days and comprises the usual elements of any important voodoo service—African prayers, libations, sacrifices, consecrations, singing, dancing, and possessions.

DECEMBER

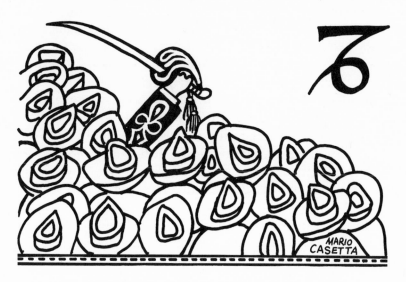

MARIO CASETTA

LA INMACULADA CONCEPCION

DECEMBER 8 IS AN especially important day in Latin America because it is the day of the Immaculate Conception of the Virgin Mary. In some places, such as San Juan de los Lagos, Mexico, it is the most important festival of the year, and the celebrating begins long before the appointed day.

During the last week of November, the town of San Juan de los Lagos begins getting ready for its annual fair. Each of the streets where the fair takes place is given a special name. On the "Calle de Alegría" (Joy Street) there are Punch and Judy shows, side shows, games of chance, refreshment stands, and musical groups. The "Calle del Azúcar" (Sugar Street) has sweets to delight the most exigent palate: grape conserves from Aguascalientes, jellies of Celaya, sweetmeats of nuts from Pachuca, sweets of quince and guava from Tabasco, little sugar loaves from Linares and Monterrey, the highly-prized *alfajor* (a candy made of

173

nuts and honey) from Colima, and the specialties of many other places in Mexico.

On the "Calle de la Loza" (Dishware Street) are found objects of every kind: richly imaginative pottery from Guadalajara, Toluca, and even places as far away as Oaxaca; lovely lacquer wear from Olinalá and Uruapan; interesting chocolate beaters from Teocaltiche. The "Calle de las Pieles" (Street of Hides) exhibits skins of almost every animal from the alligator to the dog. In addition there are beautifully made saddles, halters, bridles, chaps, lassos, spurs, and even knives and daggers. The "Calle de Mazatlán" is reserved for the luxury items: rich brocades, silks, crepes, Irish linen, embroidered shawls from Spain, toys and objects of fine crystal.

During the fiesta the church is ablaze with the lights of hundreds of candles. On the morning of the eighth, the image of the Virgin goes out in procession on her litter of silver. She is carried on the shoulders of the priests under a canopy of silver cloth with gold fringes. In the afternoon two silver cups are placed on the altar. Into one are put a dozen or more scraps of paper bearing names of devout members of the community. Into the other are put the same number of papers, but they are blank except for one which says "Fiesta de Nuestra Señora de San Juan." The papers are drawn simultaneously from both cups, and the person bearing the name of the fiesta will be in charge of the following year's celebration. It is a much solicited honor, and the announcement is greeted with ringing of bells and gunfire. After the drawing the Virgin is lowered so that the public can kiss her. Usually not everyone can be accommodated on the one afternoon, so the ceremony is continued for another day or two.

Although Our Lady of San Juan is more diminutive than most (only eleven inches high) and a humble mixture of cornstalks and a special gum used by the Tarascan Indians, she is greatly venerated in her section of Mexico. It is told that the image was once repaired by angels after it had brought an acrobat's daughter back to life.

According to the tradition, in the year 1634 a traveling circus troupe was putting on a performance in San Juan de los Lagos. The acrobat's little daughter, Cristina, stole everyone's heart from the beginning by her grace and beauty. At one point in the show she whirled in the air over a board studded with knife points and let herself fall in such a way that her small body went between the blades without being touched. The audience went wild and begged her to do it again. Not realizing that such a dangerous act should not be repeated the same day, she tried it again but slipped and landed chest down on the knife blades. Though everyone rushed to her aid, she died soon afterward from loss of blood.

While the girl's body was in the chapel awaiting burial, an old Indian woman rushed in saying: "Wait! The Cihuapilli will bring her back to life." She left but returned a moment later carrying a dilapidated image which she placed on the girl's chest. Soon afterward the girl opened her eyes and sat up. Overjoyed at having his daughter back, the acrobat asked permission to take the image to Guadalajara and have some sculptor restore it. He had barely arrived at an inn there when two boys came up and asked if he would like to have them arrange for the restoration. Astonished that they should know his mission, the acrobat handed the image over to them. When he awoke the next morning, the image was in his room, completely restored, and the people in the inn said that the angels had done this during the night.

When the Virgin returned to San Juan she continued to perform miracles, and as her good deeds multiplied so did the number of pilgrims that came to her shrine. They carried away everything that they thought Her Holy Presence might have touched, including the bricks of the walls of the sanctuary. It was at that time that the custom started of making little earthenware bars stamped with the image of the Virgin. These are touched to the miraculous statue and carried away and cherished by the thousands of pilgrims who go there each year.

Another Mexican town that goes all out for December 8 is Pátzcuaro in Michoacán. The honored image in this case is called Nuestra Señora de la Salud (Our Lady of Health) and was made in the same manner as the Virgin of San Juan de los Lagos. This method of making religious images from cornstalks held together with gum from an orchid plant was developed by the Tarascan Indians in order to have their images light enough to carry with them whenever they went to war or on pilgrimages.

Each year Pátzcuaro celebrates the eighth of December with a fair, bullfights, rodeos, cockfights, regattas on the lake, native dances, and usually parades of floats based on religious or historical themes. One year, for instance, there were titles such as "Columbus proposes to Ferdinand and Isabella the discovery of the New World," and "The famous women of the Bible pay tribute to the Mother of God."

The whole town dresses up with flags, flowers, and streamers of different colors. Doors of houses that are usually kept closed are thrown wide open displaying colorful hangings made of such things as leaves, flowers, handkerchiefs, or corrugated paper. At little tables along the streets women serve hot cinnamon water and other refreshments. On the eve of the eighth the *monigotes* appear. These are boys masked and dressed in white garments who clown about on stilts to the amusement of both young and old. Groups of girls dressed as angels sing hymns and dance at the foot of the altar of the Virgin. Outside the church other groups perform such dances as the *Viejitos, Moros y Cristianos, Listones, Arrieros, Mojigangas, Sembradores,* and *Negritos.*

In Central America, a noteworthy celebration is that of Juticalpa in Honduras. Here, too, the festivities begin several days before the eighth. Food and drink stalls are set up in the plaza, and the bursting of rockets and popping of firecrackers accentuate each day's activities. At night, care-

fully prepared fireworks fill the air with cascades of sparkling colored lights. Each day is sponsored by one of the
guilds which also offers the prizes for the day's contest. On
one day the main feature is the "Triangle"—a balancing
contest on ropes strung in the shape of a triangle. On other
days there are games such as climbing a greased pole, catching a greased pig, ribbon races, egg-in-spoon races, and sack
races. There are also straight horse racing, bicycle racing,
bullfights, and parades of floats and people in costumes and
masks. On the seventh there is an interesting equestrian
parade, and things reach a climax on the eighth with the
religious celebrations and procession of the image.

In Paraguay the eighth of December is known as the day
of the Virgin of Caacupé, and festivals take place in the town
of the same name. People from all over Paraguay make an
annual pilgrimage to this shrine, many of them walking for
weeks to get there. In addition to the religious services and
processions there are the usual secular amusements found
at fairs all over Latin America.

Several towns in Argentina have special fiestas on the
eighth of December, but the most popular one is that of the
Virgen del Valle in the town of Catamarca. This miraculous
image was found by the Spaniards in 1620 in a cave not far
from town. The face of the Virgin is dark and broad, with
narrowed eyes. She is obviously no importation from Europe but the work of an Indian craftsman modeled after one
of his own race. Each village in the province of Catamarca
and in neighboring ones (Salta, Jujuy, Tucumán, and Santiago del Estero) has a replica of the statue, and these are
taken to Catamarca in procession for the December festivities. As the pilgrims go on foot, those from farthest away
have to set out some time in November. Most of them go in
fiesta costume, some decked out in colored feathers, and
nearly all carry pennants and flags of brilliant hues. They
play native instruments such as the *quena* (a sort of flute)
and *charango* (a guitar-like stringed instrument) along the

way and sing the popular *huaynitos, carnavalitos,* and *vidalas*. At the town of Catamarca they continue to sing, dance, and enter into many of the competitive games. The highlight of the fiesta, of course, is the procession on the eighth in which the original image is escorted through town and greeted by thousands of white handkerchiefs tossed in the air.

In Brazil, one of the most outstanding December 8 celebrations is that which takes place in Salvador. In addition to the colorful processions typical of this region, one can usually see the famous *capoeiristas* perform. The dance known as *capoeira* is really more like jujitsu wrestling in which the men attack and defend themselves with extraordinary agility. The dancers stand in a semicircle around the first two contestants, who compete with vigorous movements until one succeeds in tripping his adversary with his feet or legs. The movements are made in time to a rhythmic song of several stanzas and accompanied by an *urucungo* drum or a *berimbau*. The latter is a flexible wooden bow with wire "string" from which hangs a tiny copper gourd or coin. The player holds this in his left hand and strikes the wire with a thin stick.

Día de las Playas

In Uruguay the eighth of December is known as Día de las Playas (Day of the Beaches). It marks the official opening of the bathing season, and there are ceremonies in which the priest blesses the waters. There are regattas in the different ports, horsemanship competitions in some places, and an international shooting contest at Carrasco.

Virgen de Guadalupe

The Virgin of Guadalupe, patroness of Mexico and of all the Americas, is by far the best known of Latin America's treasured virgins and for years her shrine, just outside of Mexico City, has been the most important pilgrim shrine in the Western Hemisphere. It is not surprising, therefore, that the day commemorating her appearance, December 12, is the most important day on Mexico's fiesta calendar.

According to tradition, on the morning of December 9, 1531, a humble Indian convert named Juan Diego was crossing Tepeyac Hill when he heard lovely music and a voice calling his name. It gave him an eerie feeling for he was standing on the very spot where several years before there had been a shrine to the Aztec goddess, Tonantzin. She had been the favorite deity of all the Indians in that region, and when she and her shrine were destroyed at the same time as all the other pagan idols, the natives felt a deep sense of loss.

It was not Tonantzin who called to Juan Diego, however, but the Blessed Virgin who suddenly appeared on the rocks, radiant as the sun. She asked him to tell the bishop that she wanted a church built on this very spot so that she could be near his people to protect them. Juan had difficulty getting the bishop to listen to his story and was unable to convince him of the vision. When he returned to the hill the Virgin was waiting for him and told him not to be discouraged but to try again. Juan went again to the bishop, but he was sent away and told not to return unless he could bring a token from the Virgin.

Juan was not able to return to the hill right away because of illness in his family, but the Virgin came to him and told him to go to the place where he had first seen her and to pick some roses as a token for the bishop. He did as he was told and was astonished to find roses growing among the rocks where only cactus had grown before. Wrapping the roses in his tilma, or cape, he hurried with them to the bishop. There, just as he unfolded the cape, the image of the Virgin of Guadalupe appeared upon it. The bishop fell upon his knees and begged forgiveness for not having believed Juan the first time.

A chapel was built on Tepeyac Hill and Indians were converted by the thousands. At first, the personalities of the Virgin and Tonantzin were so confused in the minds of the natives that some of the priests thought the shrine should be abolished. The Virgin was so miraculous, however, that she quickly established herself.

Today an eighteenth-century chapel stands on the spot where the Virgin is said to have appeared, but the tilma bearing her image is enshrined in the great green and gold basilica at the foot of the hill. It is said that the colors of this luminous painting, which measures about six feet by two feet, are unobtainable from any known pigments, and it has been impossible to duplicate them. It is not understood how any paint could have produced such fine work on such coarse cloth. Certainly skeptics are puzzled at the excellent condition of the picture which was hung, without any kind of preservative, for over four centuries in a climate where other paintings, even carefully protected, begin to deteriorate within a few years.

There is probably not a town in Mexico without its Guadalupe church, and the twelfth of December is celebrated everywhere. Naturally the most impressive ceremonies are those at the shrine itself, to which thousands of pilgrims come at this time of the year. Festivities usually begin a week ahead of time and end on the big day. On the night of the eleventh, the main boulevard leading to the shrine from the capital is jammed with pedestrians. Many of the groups are in a festive mood, laughing and singing along the way. In contrast there are always the penitents who "kneel" their way to the shrine, some with horribly lacerated and bloody knees. Every once in a while an Indian bystander will throw down a serape or other garment in the path of one of the penitents. This is not so much from compassion as from the belief that the self-inflicted torture makes the knees and the blood of the penitent holy. Whatever object they touch will absorb this holiness and bring blessings to its owner.

As the fiesta-goers near the end of their journey, a deafening din greets their ears. Various sources of music compete in discordant tones; singing and laughter of happy celebrants ring out in the night air. It is a regular fair with entertainment booths of all kinds and various rides designed to upset the equilibrium of all who venture upon them. Among the booths offering things for sale, one can find every kind of sacred and profane object from rosaries to chamber pots. Most interesting of all are the *"gorditas de la Virgen"* (literally "little fat ones of the Virgin"). These are tasty little corn cakes made in the shape of the Holy Virgin and wrapped in colored papers.

The religious significance of the occasion is not forgotten in the merry-making, however, and there is a constant stream of worshipers passing in and out of the church. Because of the crowds, no one is allowed to stay for more than a minute, and at times only the strongest and most intrepid can even elbow their way in.

Around midnight, groups of Indian dancers begin to perform in the plaza. Most numerous of these are the *concheros* who dance in shifts and perform continually until the end of the fiesta.

Competing with the Basilica as a religious center of attraction is the Capilla del Pocito (Chapel of the Little Well). This well, which is about a block away from the big church, is said to have opened underneath the feet of the Virgin during one of her appearances. Here the healthy as well as the sick drink of its brackish waters. Many of the sick pour it over their sores and take it home in bottles. It is said that any stranger who drinks this water will be sure to return to Mexico.

Since the Virgin of Guadalupe is the special patroness of the Indians, her day is specially celebrated by the Indian population of most of Central America. In El Salvador the day is referred to as Día de los Indios (Day of the Indians). In this country and in the neighboring one of Honduras, children often masquerade as savages with their bodies and faces smeared with paint, feathers in their hair, and bows and arrows in their hands. Others wear colorful native costumes and carry large baskets of fruit and flowers or cages

with birds in them. There are always special services in the
Guadalupe churches.

Virgen de la Soledad

December is the big month of the year in the town of
Oaxaca, Mexico, and it is hard to tell when one fiesta ends
and another begins, for there is one continuous round of
festivities from Guadalupe Day on the twelfth clear up to
the sixth of January. The eighteenth, however, rightfully
belongs to the Virgin of Solitude, and it is to see her that
thousands of Indians arrive from all the far corners of the
state. This Virgin, who is the patroness of the whole state of
Oaxaca and the most beautiful of Mexico's famous Virgins,
first appeared in the city in 1543.

A man leading twelve burros arrived in town one night
and the next morning, to his amazement, found a thirteenth
burro with his animals. The strange beast died almost immediately, and the man hastened to see what was in the
huge chest it had been carrying. It was a lovely image of the
Virgin. The priests had a church for her erected on the spot
which the miraculous burro had evidently chosen. Later,
near the end of the seventeeth century, this early church was
replaced by the present tawny golden baroque structure.
The spot where the Virgin was found happened to be directly over a rich silver mine, and at the right of the main aisle
of the church can be seen a sealed entrance. It is said that
the early priests worked the mine at night and brought the
silver out through an underground passage opening into the
church.

The entire interior of the church is a glowing frame for
this waxen, almost life-size image which stands in a glass-
and-gold enclosure. She possesses a wardrobe fit for a queen
—gowns of velvet and satin embroidered in gold and studded with precious stones, priceless pearls and diamond jewelry. With her holiday costume she wears a diamond and
emerald studded golden crown. In colonial times she was
treated like a queen and her ladies-in-waiting, chosen from

the Spanish aristocracy, carefully disrobed her at night and dressed her again in the morning. Oaxaqueños know, however, that in spite of her regal appearance, this lovely lady is not without her human foibles. She is the special patron saint of sailors and has been known to disappear from her niche at night and return just before dawn with salt water on her dress.

The fiesta of Our Lady of Solitude gets under way several days before the eighteenth. Near the church are the usual Ferris wheel, merry-go-round, shooting galleries, and the various gambling games which Mexicans dearly love. There are food booths and vendors of candles and other religious objects. The *buñuelos* appear at this time and can be bought all during the holiday season. They are crisp cakes which have been fried in lard and are sold on individual plates. It is the custom to eat the *buñuelo*, make a wish, and then smash the plate for luck. At times the streets near the center of town are almost covered with bits of shattered pottery.

For several evenings there are processions known as *calendas*. These come from the various barrios, or sections of town, and join together near the main square. There are men and women carrying brightly colored paper lanterns lighted with candles, others with poles topped with beautiful figures of birds, boats, and other objects skillfully wrought of flowers, leaves, or colored paper. There are usually floats with various themes and often huge papier-mâché caricatures.

The evening ends with a *castillo* that is really a castle. Spanish soldiers spin round and round on the battlements and fire toy cannons while tiers of pinwheels ignite and shower cataracts of red and green. In a final deafening salvo, rockets at the top of the castle take off and fill the darkness with bursting stars.

Santo Tomás

Chichicastenango, Guatemala, is one Indian town that is picturesque and colorful even when nothing much is happening, but it is especially interesting during the fiesta of St. Thomas from December 18 to 21. The ceremonial costumes of the men of this town are woven of pure black wool and elaborately embroidered with the symbols of the Quiché Indians. With their scarlet sashes and headdresses, the men present a striking picture as they stand on the dazzling white church steps swinging pots of incense or shooting off rockets. The women wear a long loose-fitting *huipil* with an attractive yoke woven of bright red wool. Though most of the Indians that flock to Chichi for this fiesta are Quichés, there are representatives of other ethnic groups from the various sections of the country.

Each day several of the images are taken out in procession on gaudy crimson-canopied litters hung with peacock or ostrich feathers, mirrors, tinsel, and paper flowers. At the end of the line of popular saints is an image representing God Himself—a white-bearded figure strongly resembling a department store Santa Claus. Marimbas and *chirimías* accompany the marchers and continue to play the rest of the day and night.

For this fiesta a rope is strung from the church tower to a stake at the foot of the steps, and all day long a funny little toy horse and horseman go jogging up and down it, never quite reaching the top or touching the ground at the bottom. This little man, who is carved out of wood and gaily painted, is called Tsijolaj. Actually there are many different spellings of his name, because the word is a phonetic rendering of the Quiché name. He wears the elegant costume of a Spanish gentlman with strings of coins looped about his neck and a large leather bag slung from his shoulder. Most of the natives have no idea what he represents and if asked the reason for this wild ride will answer as always, *"porque es costumbre"* (because it is the custom). Those who do have explanations have not been able to get together on their stories. Some say that Tsijolaj represents a priest who came one time to make gifts of money, and that explains the necklaces of old silver coins. According to others he represents a Spaniard named Santos Pérez who came to this area after the Conquest and first taught the Indians how to make fireworks. He lived the rest of his days on a farm outside Chichi and on feast days would come riding in on his horse with a leather bag full of rockets. The old Spaniard grew rich on his fireworks and his farming, and the coins symbolize his wealth.

A third story has Tsijolaj a messenger sent with offerings to propitiate the Sun God so that the sun will shine again after the long rainy season. In all probability Tsijolaj is a combination of a pagan messenger and the old Spaniard. The Quiché word for fire forms a part of his name and could refer to either the fireworks or the sun. Certainly his ride embodies the whole idea of rising toward the sky and the sun, and after the Spaniards introduced horses, which are so much swifter than men, it was natural that the messenger be given one of these animals to hasten him on his way.

At any rate, Tsijolaj's keepers are the fireworks-makers, and several times during the fiesta one of them will remove the figure from the rope and do a peculiar jigging dance with him. Usually he is danced with during the processions also.

Another interesting feature of this fiesta is the *Palo Volador* (Flying Pole Dance), similar to that done in Mexico during Corpus Christi but with only two fliers. The selection and bringing in of the tree, as in the Mexican dance and in the *Baile del Venado* in Santa Cruz del Quiché in August, is an extremely important ritual and must be accompanied by sacrifices. There is an additional stipulation, and that is that no woman must ever approach the pole. The flight itself has become like any ride at a fair, for anyone who wishes may fly from the pole for a nominal fee of two cents.

Virgen del Rosario

One of the most picturesque fiestas in Chile and certainly the most famous one is that given on December 26 in Andacollo in honor of the Rosario Virgin. The population of this mining town swells to an estimated 150,000 at this time of the year as visitors come not only from other parts of Chile but from the Bolivian highlands and Argentina as well.

The festivities are really a continuation of the Christmas activities that fill the week before the twenty-sixth, and the Rosario fiesta usually goes on for at least three days and nights. Open-air eating stands mushroom; merry-go-rounds, Ferris wheels, Japanese pool tables, gambling tents, and other amusements are set up. Special horse races and cock fights are staged for the occasion. As dancers in vivid red, blue, and green costumes whirl through the streets, the Virgin is carried in an elaborately carved frame of massed roses. She is beautifully gowned and wears a gold crown set with emeralds and other precious stones. The numerous dancers at this fiesta belong to organizations known as *chinos* which are further divided into groups known as *danzantes turbantes*.

San Esteban

In the province of Santiago del Estero, Argentina, there is an unusual ceremony on December 26, the day of St. Sebastian. It is called Sumamao after its location on a branch of the Rio Dulce. Originally it took place in a deserted chapel near the river, but it is now sponsored by a ranch owner and a special altar is erected on his ranch.

On the day of the fiesta, the image of San Esteban is placed on the altar which has been decorated with flowers, fresh branches, and fruits. Leading up to the altar is a long row of arches formed by tying together the tops of small trees that have been stripped of their branches. From each arch hang several *ichas* (cakes made in the shape of dolls).

Soon after dawn the blare of trumpets announces the first of the activities. Two groups of horsemen known as *alfereces* and *promesantes* ride in slow procession through the arches while other riders, called *celebrantes*, dash about shouting. All this is done to the accompaniment of native trumpets, violins, and accordions. Following this is the consecration during which the ranch owner with great ceremony presents each of the *alfereces* and *promesantes* with an *icha*. When that is completed, the populace storms the arches, seizes the remaining *ichas*, and feasts upon them.

At this point several men called *indios* disappear into the woods. Later they come out running and beating their calves with stout branches. Followed by the shouts and trumpets of the horsemen, they run to the altar where they kneel before the saint, kiss his robe, and deposit their branches. The ranch owner makes several cuts in their calves with a knife while women offer holy water and fragrant branches.

Fiesta del Yancunú

Along the north coast of Honduras there is an interesting dance called *Baile del Yancunú* which is performed from December 25 until January 6 although it has nothing to do with the Christian celebration of Christmas. The inhabitants of this part of the country are mainly Caribs, descendants of Negroes brought over from the Island of St. Vincent during colonial times. The dance, which is similar to that done by some of the African tribes, is a ritual designed to assure prosperity for the coming year. These people believe that if they do not give these performances they will be faced with poverty and other misfortunes. Ordinarily only men take part in the dance. They wear long-sleeved shirts of shrieking colors, kilt-like skirts with stockings up to their knees, and use masks of metallic cloth painted with different colors. From various parts of their bodies hang strings of seashells, especially from their knees, and these make a rustling sound as they dance. Each group consists of from six to twelve dancers and four drummers who hit their instruments with the palms of their hands. All dance at the same time while shouting and singing in their own dialect. At times they make a circle, and pairs take turns dancing the principal role in the center.

Jeu Jeu

The town of Izalco in El Salvador also has a pagan Christmas-time ceremony which is known as El Tabal or Jeu Jeu. Between Christmas and Epiphany the natives have a nightly procession in which they carry *garruchas*. The *garrucha* is the trunk of a special kind of tree which grows tall and slender and at regular intervals has five straight branches coming out from the same place. The trees are selected and cut two or three weeks in advance, stripped of their bark and exposed to the sun until they turn white. Then, with vegetable dyes, stripes are traced along their entire length. When everything is ready, choice ears of corn (preferably colored) which are to be used in sowing the second crop are hung from the branches of the *garruchas*. With their offerings, the members of the different *cofradías* march, singing and accompanied by drums and *dulzainas* (a type of flageolet), to the Church of la Asunción to greet the Holy Child. They feel that the seeds carried on the *garruchas* will produce much better corn for having received His blessing.

As a part of these ceremonies there is a dance done by thirteen men dressed in skirts of grass or palm leaves to represent savages. They wear numerous bracelets and leg ornaments made of shells and have gilt crowns trimmed with feathers. Twelve men dance in a circle around their leader, leaping wildly and flourishing their bows and arrows. At regular intervals the air is pierced by the shrill cries of "¡Jeu! ¡Jeu!" which is said to mean, "Let the rains come! Let the rains come!"

Santos Inocentes

In many parts of the world Holy Innocents' Day, December 28, is considered the unluckiest day of the year. It was the day which was set aside in memory of the children who were slaughtered by King Herod, and it has been felt that any undertaking begun on this day would be doomed to failure. At one time the holiday had such ominous connota-

tions that even the day of the week on which it fell was
tainted for the next twelve months.

In Latin America the Día de los Santos Inocentes is one of
great merriment—a sort of April Fool's Day. People play
practical jokes on their friends, or they may order things sent
to a fictitious address. Girls who receive packages from their
boy friends on this day should not be surprised if the gift
turns out to be a mouse or a frog. There are hoax editions of
the newspapers and all sorts of crazy announcements on the
radio, and there are always enough unsuspecting people to
make the effort worthwhile.

Chimbángueles de San Benito

Several towns of the state of Zulia, Venezuela, and especially Bobures, celebrate on December 29 the Fiesta of the
Black St. Benito. The merrymaking begins two days ahead
of time when gaudy decorations of all kinds are put up in
the streets and white flags placed in the windows of the
houses. The festivities are under the supervision of the
chimbángueles, or vassals of the saint, who are divided hier-
archically into a *jefe* (chief), *capitanes* (captains), *capi-
tanas* (female captains), *mayordomos* (major-domos), and
esclavos (slaves).

On the twenty-ninth, after early morning mass, the *chimbángueles* place the image of San Benito on a litter and adorn
it with real flowers. Then, doing a peculiar jogging dance,
they carry the saint through the streets of town. As they suddenly jump, advance and retreat, so does the image they are
carrying. Others dance along behind the litter, and groups
of women shake green branches in the face of the saint.
Everything is done to the beat of the drums—seven in number and each of a different tone. No one stops dancing for an
instant. Off and on during the long procession they sing
short verses in praise of the saint and sprinkle him with
aromatic substances. Some even offer him drinks of the local
whisky. Most of these groups of *chimbángueles* derive di-

rectly from the brotherhoods which the Venezuelan Negroes formed upon their arrival from Africa for the preservation of their ancient religious practices.

New Year's Eve

New Year's Eve celebrations are as diverse as the communities which observe them, but all have one thing in common—the feeling that one cycle of living is finished and a new one is beginning.

Nowhere perhaps are the hopes for the year to come more vividly portrayed than in Mitla, Mexico. On New Year's Eve the darkness just outside of town is pierced by a thousand lights—warm lights of bonfires, each one surrounded by a family of Zapotec Indians; moving lights of pinewood torches carried by those still arriving; and, almost overshadowed by all the greater brightness, small flickering lights of candles. From every direction people have been arriving for hours. Some have come by bus or on bicycles but most on burros, by oxcart, or on foot.

In the center of all the glowing lights is a stone cross called Cruz de Pedimientos or Petition Cross. Each family stops here first. After gently laying an offering of flowers on the rapidly mounting pile, they blow incense in the four directions. This accomplished, they find a place on the crowded slope. After hurriedly eating a few tortillas and beans, they settle down to the task of making their material request for the coming year. To explain clearly their desires to God, each family makes clever and often realistic miniatures. Houses are constructed out of sticks with grass for the roof; pigs, sheep, goats, burros, oxen, and even farming implements are cleverly fashioned with twigs, seeds, and bits of sugar cane; fields of corn or maguey are carefully laid out with straws to represent the plants. The Zapotecs of mountain villages who are not able to come here to visit the cross at Matatlán make their offerings in the enchanted caves near their villages.

New Year's Eve is also the time when many of the Indian tribes install their new local officials. In the Bolivian Andes, those who have completed their traditional command go out in groups carrying pearl-studded rosaries and large figures of such things as eagles, condors, or fish. The actual changing of authority is accompanied by strange ritual dances performed to the music of their primitive instruments. Colorful celebrations take place also in the vicinity of San Cristóbal las Casas in southern Mexico and at Todos Santos in Guatemala.

In Sonsonate, El Salvador, members of the Cofradía de la Vera Cruz begin at noon on the thirty-first to construct the arbor in which their ceremony will take place. Decorated oxcarts arrive from nearby fincas carrying forked poles, sticks, palm leaves, creeping vines, and other materials. Here at midnight the outgoing *alcalde mayor* turns over his staff of authority to the incoming one. The *cofrades*, dressed in native costumes trimmed with colored paper and wearing live iguanas around the crowns of their straw hats, spend a good part of the night obtaining contributions for their organization. Anyone out on the streets that night is in danger of being abducted. The victim is brought before the *alcalde mayor*, accused of some imaginary crime and forced to pay a fine in accordance with his economic status. Afterward he is invited to join in the singing, dancing, eating, and drinking.

Among the non-Indian population of Latin America, and especially in the large cities, New Year's Eve is celebrated as in this country, with public and private clubs filled to overflowing. However, as these countries are over ninety per cent Catholic, most of the population also attend midnight mass.

CHRISTMAS

I N OUR COUNTRY Christmas is usually associated with snow, or at least with winter, but in South America this holiday (called *Navidad*) comes in the middle of summer and at the hottest time of the year. Even in Mexico and Central America, December is the beginning of the dry season and a time of bright flowers and ripe fruits. The main difference between our Christmas and that of the other Americas, however, is that here the commercial aspects of the holiday completely overshadow its real significance. In these other countries it is primarily a religious holiday.

In almost all the countries, festivities begin about mid-December when families set up manger scenes in their homes. These are called *nacimientos*, *pesebres*, or *portales* in Spanish-speaking countries, *presepios* or *lapinhas* in Brazil. Haiti, of course, uses the French word, *crèches*. This custom of erecting nativity scenes, which is familiar throughout the Christian world, dates back to 1223 when St. Francis of Assisi made the first scene to help make the story of Bethlehem more realistic for the townspeople of Greccio, Italy.

A *nacimiento* may be very simple, consisting only of images of Joseph, Mary, the Christ Child, and perhaps a cow or two to indicate the stable, or it may include the whole countryside around Bethlehem with figures of the Three Wise Men, angels, shepherds, sheep, and other animals. In the state of Mérida, Venezuela, it is not unusual to find King Herod also, going about his grizzly task of beheading babies.

Just as we accumulate more and lovelier ornaments for our Christmas trees, the Latin American family collects more little figures until at times an entire room has to be given over to the scene. Green carpet or paper is laid over boxes or tabletops with little mounds here and there to give the appearance of hills and dales. Over this is spread moss, real or artificial grass, and little trickles of white sand to define the roads. Lakes and rivers are usually represented by mirrors, only the most elaborate scenes having real water. Cotton may be stuck on the blue backdrop to represent clouds, and there is always a bright star to guide the Magi. Most interesting are the glaring anachronisms in many of the *nacimientos*—electric trains speeding furiously across the pastoral countryside, sailboats and modern steamers on the lakes, even jets flying perilously close to the picturesque stable. There are never any two scenes exactly alike; each one expresses in some way the personality of its creator.

The figures used in the *nacimientos* are of various materials such as clay, wood, plaster, porcelain, rubber, cardboard, and plastic. In most places, even the humblest of scenes with crude clay or cardboard figures has an exquisite porcelain Christ Child. In wealthy families, all of the pieces are apt to be works of art, brought over from Spain and passed down from generation to generation. Probably the tiniest figures seen anywhere are those made by the natives of Ilobasco, El Salvador, and used in nativity scenes throughout the country. Though often so tiny that two or three dozen can be placed in the palm of a hand, the figures seem almost to move, each one going seriously about his business whether it be work or play. Against a background of typical Salvadorian countryside one sees a whole village of diminutive tile-roofed houses. On the veranda of one sits a placid gentleman, reading a newspaper and smoking a cigar; several women are carrying water from the well while others are doing the family washing in the crystal stream that runs through the village; a group of musicians plays in the town square where a few Indian women have spread out luscious-looking pineapples, mangoes, and oranges for sale; one woman is busy making tortillas. Out on the road a boy drives his pigs before him while a burro loaded with wood picks his way slowly through the dust; a yoke of oxen drags its heavy cart up the hill. The road comes to an end at the little white church at the top of the hill, and there within its portals are the Christmas manger and the images of the Holy Family. These figures, like all the others, were patiently and lovingly molded from lumps of clay, painted with native dyes, and clothed with cloth woven on native looms.

In Paraguay and Peru the making of nativity scenes is usually delayed until the twenty-fourth. No matter what day they are set up, however, the manger is generally empty until midnight of Christmas Eve when the Infant Jesus "is born." In many parts of Mexico He is laid in the manger by specially chosen godparents. The *nacimientos* are left up until January 6 when the Wise Men, who have inched ahead a little each day, finally reach the Holy Family. On that day the Mexican godparents must give a party for everyone in the household.

Besides the nativity scenes in the homes, larger versions are often erected in the churches and sometimes in public squares also. Viña del Mar and other cities in Chile have unusually lovely outdoor scenes in which the various parts are played and sung by young people of the town.

During the last fifteen or twenty years Christmas trees have been gaining in popularity, especially in Argentina, Brazil, Colombia, Peru, Guatemala, Nicaragua, Haiti, and Mexico. These are used in addition to the *nacimientos* rather than in place of them. Even Santa is beginning to share the spotlight with the traditional gift givers, the Three Kings, in many parts of Argentina, Brazil, Paraguay, Mexico, and Haiti. He is usually known as Papá Noel and has his own ingenious means of entry, for houses in those countries rarely have chimneys. All this, of course, leads to a wonderful (for the children) duplicity of gift-giving, for most parents are loath to do away with the custom of having the Kings bring the presents later on the sixth of January.

In addition to the setting up of the *nacimientos*, there are other activities that go on for several days or nights before the twenty-fifth. In Mexico, El Salvador, Honduras, and Nicaragua, the night of the sixteenth marks the beginning of the *posadas* which take place on nine consecutive nights. Posada means "inn" or "lodging," and the celebration commemorates the attempt of Mary and Joseph to find shelter in Bethlehem. Though *posadas* are held within the homes, they are never a one-family affair. Relatives and intimate friends get together and each night go to a different house, repeating the same ritual.

As soon as they arrive the guests are divided into two groups—the innkeepers and the pilgrims. When it is dark the pilgrims line up outside behind two children who carry a small litter with the figures of Mary, Joseph, and the angel. Carrying lighted candles and singing litanies, the pilgrims march through the halls or patios until they come to the closed door behind which the innkeepers are stationed. They knock on the door and sing a song which goes something life this:

> In the name of Heaven
> We beg lodging
> My beloved wife is weary.

The people inside, also singing, anwer:

> This is no inn. Go away!
> We dare not open.
> We are afraid of thieves.

The pilgrims sing:

> We are so tired.
> We have come from Nazareth.
> Please open. My beloved wife is weary.

Inside they answer:

> Please go away, and stop bothering us.
> Or the master may come and
> Drive you away with sticks.

This time the pilgrims sing:

> My beloved wife is Mary,
> Queen of heaven
> She will be mother of the Holy Child.

At this, the door is thrown open and the chorus inside sings:

> Come in, holy pilgrims.
> Come into our humble dwelling.
> Come into our hearts.
> The night is one of joy, of joy
> For here beneath our roof
> We shelter the Mother of God.

The pilgrims enter, a few prayers are said, and thus ends the religious part of the *posada*. Refreshments are served and usually followed by social dancing. In Mexico there is always a *piñata* as a climax to each night's activities.

In small villages, *posadas* are often held in the church as the native huts cannot accommodate such gatherings. In a few of the larger towns they are given both in homes and in the church. In the latter, the procession stops at side altars which have been covered with curtains to represent the inns from which the holy pilgrims were turned away.

Posadas in San Miguel de Allende, Mexico, are a real community project. Each night there are processions through town symbolizing the journey of Mary and Joseph in search of lodging. There are tableaux of the Nativity on floats complete with living sheep and goats, hundreds of children in gay shepherd costumes singing the *posada* carols, men and boys carrying lighted lanterns or huge surrealistic heads made of papier-mâché. The town band provides the music, and rockets are set off from rooftops as the procession passes. The route is always announced ahead of time, and the rooftops and windows of the houses on those streets are decorated with paper lanterns and streamers. Most important of the decorations are the *piñatas* suspended overhead, waiting to be broken open and shower their sweets upon the paraders below.

Colombia is another country in which the Christmas season officially opens on December 16. In the evenings friends gather at each other's homes to sing the traditional Spanish carols known as *villancicos* and then pray together at the *pesebre*. Afterward they adjourn to the street or patio to wave sparklers, shoot off Roman candles and firecrackers. In Popayán and other towns in the Department of Cauca, there are groups of wandering minstrels called *chirimías* who appear at this time. The name comes from the musical instrument, chirimía (an ancient sort of oboe or flageolet). This has been replaced by the *flauta de carrizo* (cane flute), however, as the solo instrument of the group. The *chirimías* are made up of young boys who play in the streets for pennies. Often one of the group dresses as a devil with a fearsome mask and long tail. He carries a small bag to collect the coins and uses his tail to lash those who do not pay.

In this part of Colombia also there are special games associated with the *novena* of Christmas. They are called *aguinaldos*, which literally means "Christmas gifts"; and in every case the loser must reward the winner. There are usually just two participants—friends who decide upon a game ahead of time and set a certain time limit. One game which is very popular is called *Palito en boca* (little stick in the mouth). When two friends happen to meet, one will challenge the other by saying *"Palito en boca,"* and if the friend cannot produce the evidence he will have to pay the forfeit.

These games usually last for several days so that there will be a chance for several encounters. *Hablar y no contestar* (to speak and not answer) consists of asking the opponent some very urgent question in the hope that he will be caught off guard and break his silence. In *Dar y recibir* (to give and receive), neither can give anything to nor receive anything from the other. *Estatua* (statue) often becomes quite hilarious, for at the cry of *"Estatua"* the other person must remain in the position in which he was caught.

The most exciting of the games is *Aguinaldos gritados* (shouted Christmas gifts) which takes place most often on Christmas Eve. Two people decide upon an hour and a meeting place for the game. Then each finds several friends of the same height and build as himself and they all dress alike —as ghosts, pirates, Indians, or whatever they can dream up. This group is called a *comparsa*. The two *comparsas* meet at the scheduled time and place, and the leader of each tries to discover and unmask his opponent. Naturally there is no talking as the voices would give them away. The first to identify his friend shouts *"Mis aguinaldos"* and that ends the game. The loser usually has to treat the winning team to a party.

The town of Oaxaca, Mexico, adds a humorous note to its pre-Christmas activities with a special celebration called *Noche de Rábanos* (Radish Night) on the twenty-third. All around the *zócalo*, or plaza, are gaily decorated stalls festooned with enormous radishes. These have been carved into extraordinary forms, all bearing some resemblance to people or animals. Some of the "radish people" are clothed in typical costumes, but others go quite nude, and what the sculptors lack in artistry they make up in detail. Some are real masterpieces and represent such things as men riding elephants or burros. There are also stalls with other objects seen only on this one night: lovely birds made of tiny everlasting flowers, miniature animals of seeds or straw or feathers, various fanciful creations of fluted cellophane. It is a big night for eating *buñuelos* and shattering the plates, a ceremony begun a week before during the fiesta for the Virgin of Solitude.

On Christmas Eve, which is called *la Nochebuena* (the good night) all activities reach a climax. The exciting *aguinaldos gritados* mark the end of the holiday games in Colombia. In Mexico and Central America the last of the *posadas* take place. In addition, the Mexican towns of Querétaro and Celaya have spectacular parades featuring elaborate floats with living tableaux of biblical scenes such as the Garden of Eden, the Annunciation, Belshazzar's Banquet, Solomon's Judgment, or the Ten Commandments. Oaxaca sees the last of its *calendas* with torchlight processions organized by each of the town's thirty-five churches. Each section has its bearers of paper lanterns, a band of some sort, and a float bearing the nativity scene. It may be set in a blazing star or on a tropical beach, or it may be a copy of an old church painting. The tableaux use mostly children who play their parts with the greatest dignity.

In Táchira, Venezuela, people dress as shepherds and shepherdesses on Christmas Eve and go from house to house singing Christmas carols. In many of the Andean villages and in small towns of Mexico, Panama and other Central American countries, groups of children dress as shepherds and shepherdesses and perform a simple dance in the main aisle of the church.

In San José, Costa Rica, the pre-midnight celebration of Christmas Eve is purely secular. People of the lower and middle classes promenade along the main street of the capital throwing confetti at each other. Some wear masks, many have paper hats and horns. On the edge of town at La Sabana, the annual Christmas fair, with the usual amusements, attracts large crowds of celebrants.

The Christmas Eve procession in Antigua, Guatemala, is also a popular affair with marchers dressed in costumes and floats with humorous themes. For years the poorer classes amused themselves by burlesquing the town's aristocrats, and members of the wealthy families even donated their typical hats or canes to make the caricatures more authentic.

All activities, whether sacred or secular, come to a halt at midnight on Christmas Eve when all good Catholics hurry to the churches for the *Misa de gallo* (Mass of the Cock). In many places this is immediately followed by fireworks, the blowing of whistles or ringing of bells. After this, families return home for their special Christmas supper.

Though chicken, turkey, and roast pig are traditional throughout most of the Americas, each country has its own time-honored dishes to make up the rest of the Christmas Eve feast. Brazilian families have fried shrimp or *cuscuz* (a steamed fish pie made of corn meal, cassava flour, sardines, shrimp, and seasonings) and a bewildering assortment of mouth-watering desserts. Venezuelan tables are laden with *hallacas* (a sort of corn meal pie stuffed with pork, chicken, and any number of delicious ingredients), *jamón planchado* (ironed ham), and a dessert made from green papaya and brown sugar called *dulce de lechoza*. *Tamales* with chocolate is the favorite Christmas dish in Mexico, and they vary in each section of the country. There are the rich *tamales* of the north, containing pork and chicken and spiced with chili; the fluffy, light *tamales* of Mexico City, made with chicken or often with fruit centers; the rich, dark *tamales* of Vera Cruz or Oaxaca, which are baked in folded banana leaves. Mexican families also have *bacalao* (codfish cooked with tomato, olives, capers, and seasonings), *revoltijo* (a dish of prickly-pear, shrimp, rosemary, chili, and potatoes), a special Christmas Eve salad consisting of mixed fruit with peanuts and beets. Panamanians too have tamales for Christmas, and also sweet sausages cooked in Malaga wine, hot chocolate, and a sweet Christmas bread made in the shape of rings and decorated with sugar and fruits. Nicaraguans associate the meal with *nacatamales* (a kind of *tamale* made of ground corn with a filling of turkey, chicken or pork, and raisins, almonds, olives, and chili) and *sopa borracha* (literally, "drunken soup") which consists of slices of a plain cake made with corn meal or rice flour and covered with a rum-flavored syrup. In Argentina there is a traditional torta made of flour, eggs, raisins, and nuts, and various confections made of dried fruits and nuts. In Chile a favorite main dish is lobster brought from the Juan Fernández Islands. Country people usually have roast duck with apple stuffing or in some places an exciting Araucanian dish known as *curanto*. To prepare this, deep pits are dug in sand, lined with scented herbs and leaves and then filled with layers of eggs, fowl, fish, clams, oysters, mutton, beef, pork, and every available vegetable. Hot stones are tossed on top of the ingredients, and the whole thing is covered tightly. Whole wheelbarrows of the finished product are wheeled to guests seated at long plank tables set up outdoors. Paraguay is the big exception to the rule of the post-midnight meal, and city people there prefer to have their Christmas supper before going to the *Misa de gallo*.

Since most people have been up all night eating, singing, and dancing, either in their homes or in clubs, Christmas Day is comparatively quiet. In many places religious or civic organizations put on parties in the afternoon for underprivileged children and distribute gifts. In Popayán, Colombia, there is a special children's parade on Christmas Day. Loaded with noise-makers and balloons, they march up the zigzag path to the Church of Belén, high on a hilltop above the town. In Lima, Peru, the year's greatest bullfight takes place and is followed by a religious procession bearing a statue of the Virgin.

Holiday activities continue at full swing clear up to the sixth of January. City folk enjoy parties in private clubs and in homes; country folk have various kinds of folkloric diversions. In Mexico and El Salvador, Christmas marks the beginning of the *pastorelas* and *pastores*. These are modern versions of a medieval miracle play brought from Europe in the early days of the Conquest. The *pastorela* (pastoral) is usually given in a public square, in the atrium of a church, or in someone's patio. The participants are young people of the more prominent families, and there are elaborate costumes for the shepherds, angels, archangels, and devils that go to make up the cast. The folk version is called *pastores* (shepherds) or *coloquio* (colloquy) and is performed in very small towns or on ranches by itinerant actors who move to a different village each night. Though the plot is basically the same as that of the *pastorela*, the speech is that of the simple peasants who play the parts.

The entire plot of the *pastores* revolves around the shepherds who visited the Christ Child, and a great part of it is in song. At the beginning the story of the Christ Child's birth is sung, and the shepherds begin to prepare for the journey. The devil, who sits off to one side, hears them discussing their plans and lashes his long tail furiously. At this point there is usually a comic interlude during which an old hermit does take-offs of people in the audience. It grows late and as the shepherds are beginning to doze, the Archangel Michael comes to warn them that the devil is lurking about. Soon afterward the devil himself appears, in disguise, and begs for food. He forbids the shepherds to go to visit the manger and gets in a violent argument with the hermit, who comes to their defense. Finally the Archangel returns and engages the devil in a clattery sword duel. The latter is then driven away with a firecracker tied to his tail, and the shepherds journey to the manger and present their gifts to the Christ Child.

The length of the performance varies from half an hour to several hours. An unusually repetitious but interesting performance seen in the mountain regions of Guanajuato goes on for two or three days and covers all Biblical history from Adam and Eve up to the birth of Christ. These folk plays are given all during the last week of December and often go on into January.

In some of the more isolated towns of northern Brazil there are still vestiges of the old miracle plays. The shepherds have been changed into shepherdesses, however, and the plot expanded to include a gypsy's attempt to kidnap the Child. In Panamanian provincial towns the play has gradually been shrinking until there is little left but a dance or procession of children dressed as long-ago shepherds in the main aisle of the church. In hidden corners of the Venezuelan Andes there is an interesting play which revolves around the Child's first steps, which they naively assume to have been taken a few days after birth.

Christmas, thus, like all the other important holidays, is celebrated a little bit differently in each locality, for every fiesta reflects the customs of the region in which it takes place. The future will undoubtedly bring about many changes in present-day fiestas, especially those in or near the big cities. The age-old traditions of the Indian population, however, will probably be safe for at least several more decades. Fortunately, in many places (especially in the Andes) the non-Indian population is scornful of the native celebrations, considering their ceremonies barbaric and their dances nothing but a scandalous form of amusement. Thanks to this interpretation and to their non-intervention the ceremonies can live on with their true meaning or with what still remains of their original significance.

FIESTAS OF ARGENTINA
See text for additional information

DATE:	PLACE:	NAME:	EVENTS:

Jan. 1-2 / *La Rioja* / San Nicolás y El Niño / *religious processions*

Feb. 2 / *Humahuaca & Los Molinos* / La Candelaria / *processions on horseback*

movable / *various places* / *Carnival / street celebrations, folk dances*

March / *Mendoza* / *La Vendimia / wine festival, parades, regional dances*

March 10 / *Leones* / *Fiesta del Trigo / wheat festival, parades, crowning of queen*

movable / *all over* / Holy Week / *processions*

15 days after Easter / *Catamarca* / Virgen del Valle / *pilgrimage, processions*

April / *Valle de Calingasta (near San Juan)* / Fiesta de la Manzana / *apple festival, parade, floats, queen*

May 3 / *Provinces of La Rioja & Santiago del Estero* / Invención de la *Santa Cruz / processions*

May 19-25 / *La Rioja* / Semana de La Rioja / *regional dances, crowning of queen*

May 21 / *Luján* / Nuestra Señora de Luján / *pilgrimage, processions*

June / *all over* / Corpus Christi / *processions*

June 24 / *Quebrada de Humahuaca* / San Juan Bautista / *bonfires, processions of "Indians"*

July 16 / *Itatí* / *Nuestra Señora de Itatí / pilgrimage, fair, parades*

July 25 / *Provinces of Salta & Jujuy* / Santiago Apóstol / *processions, games*

July 26 / *Tilcara (Humahuaca)* / Santa Ana / *religious ceremonies, fair of miniatures*

Sept. / *Resistencia* / Fiesta del Algodón / *cotton festival*

Sept. 6-15 / *Salta* / Señor del Milagro y Nuestra Señora del Milagro / *fair, processions*

Sept. 8 / *Mendoza* / Virgen del Carmen de Cuyo / *procession*

Sept. 21 / *principal cities* / Día del Estudiante / *street dancing, picnics, open air art exhibits*

Sept. 24 / *Córdoba* / Nuestra Señora de la Merced / *procession*

Sept. 29 / *Tucumán* / San Miguel

Sept. 30 / *Córdoba & Paraná* / San Gerónimo

October / *Rosario* / Semana de Rosario

Oct. 31 / *Delta del Tigre (near B.A.)* / Día del Isleño

Oct. or Nov. / *Tucumán* / Fiesta de la Zafra / *parades, crowning of queen, choreographic spectacle*

Nov. 10 / *Mar del Plata, Azul & Bahía Blanca* / Día de la Tradición

Nov. 10-15 / *San Antonio de Areco* / Semana de la Tradición

Nov. 10-15 / *La Plata* / Semana de La Plata

Nov. 23 / *Sumampa* / Nuestra Señora de Sumampa / *procession*

Nov. 29-Dec. 8 / *Catamarca* / *La Virgen del Valle / *pilgrimages, processions, dances, contests*

Dec. 8 / *Tuama* / Inmaculada Concepción / *processions, horsemen*

Dec. 26 / *Sumamao* / *San Estéban / *costumed processions, folk play*

Dec. 26 / *provinces of Catamarca, La Rioja & San Juan* / Virgen de Andacollo / *processions*

FIESTAS OF BOLIVIA

See text for additional information
**Described in text under a different fiesta*

Jan. 1 / *Laja* / Fiesta de los Trucasiris / *Indian dances, parades*

Jan. 2 / *Ilabaya* / Dulce Nombre de Jesús / *Indian dances*

Jan. 17 / *Caquiaviri* / San Antonio Abad / *Indian dances: "Pallapallas," "Wacathokoris"*

Jan. 20-25 / *La Paz* / *Alacitas / *fair of miniatures, Indian dances*

Feb. 2 / *Copacabana* / *Virgen de la Candelaria / *fair, Indian dances*

Feb. 10-15 / *Oruro & Potosí* / miner's holiday / *barbecues, regional dances*

movable / *various towns* / *Carnival / *parades, Indian dances,* *"Diablada"*

movable / *all over* / *Holy Week / *religious ceremonies & Indian rituals*

April 30 / *Escoma* / Santa Catalina

May 3 / *Italaque* / *Santa Cruz / *Sicuri tests*

May 3 / *Copacabana* / Santa Cruz / *Indian dances: "Cullahuas," "Morenos," *"Sicuris," "Pusipías," "Llipis"*

June / *various towns* / *Corpus Christi / *processions, Indian dances*

June 13 / *Sorata and Jesús de Machaca* / San Antonio

June 24 / *various towns* / *San Juan / *bonfires, water games*

June 29 /*Achacachi and Tiquina* / San Pedro y San Pablo / *Indian dances*

July 16 / *La Paz* / Virgen del Carmen / *procession*

July 16 / *Charazani* / Virgen del Carmen / *Indian dances: "Morenada," "Kantus," "Chatris," "Kena-Kenas"*

July 16 / *Umala* / Virgen del Carmen / *dances such as "Morenada"*
July 25 / *Achocalla* / Santiago / *"Danzantes," "Morenada," "Llameros"*
July 25 / *Quime* / Santiago / ***"Diablada," "Morenada,"* ***"Sicuris"*
July 25 / *Upinguayo* / Santiago / *Indian dances*
July 26 / *Umala* / Santa Ana
Aug. 1-7 / *Copacabana* / *Virgen de Copacabana / *processions, Indian dances*
Aug. 5-7 / *mining regions* /*Independencia / *masquerades, carnival celebrations, Indian dances*
Aug. 15 / *Sapahaqui* / Asunción / *dances such as "Los Huitucus"*
Aug. 15 / *Italaque* / Asunción / *dances*
Aug. 25 / *Cohoni and Chulumani* / San Bartolomé
Aug. 30 / *Kaata* / Santa Rosa / *dances: "Chunchos," "Chatris"*
Sept. (1st Sund., Mon. & Tues.) / *Tarija* / *San Roque / *procession, Indian dances such as "Chunchos"*
Sept. (2nd Sund.) / *Tarija* / *San Roque / *procession, Indian dances*
Sept. 8 / *Mocomoco* / La Natividad de Nuestra Señora / *dances: "Chunchos," "Cullahuas," "Ilameros"*
Sept. 8 / *Kasani* / La Natividad de Nuestra Señora / *dances: "Llameros," "Morenos," "Llipis,"* ***"Sicuris"*
Sept. 14 / *Yaco & Laja* / Exaltación de la Santa Cruz / *Indian dances*
Sept. 24 / *Carhuiza* / Nuestra Señora de la Merced
Sept. 29 / *Chulina* / San Miguel / *dances: "Huacathokoris," "Choquelas," "Kantus"*
Oct. (1st Sund.) / *Aukapata* / El Rosario / *Indian dances*
Oct. 4 / *Tajma* / San Francisco de Asis
Nov. 1 / *various places* / *Todos los Santos
Nov. 2 / *various places* / *Día de los Difuntos / *celebrations in the cemeteries*
Nov. 16 / *Huancané* / San Cristóbal / *religious procession, Indian dances*
Nov. 17-18 or 3rd Sund. / *Sacaba* / *Virgen del Amparo / *procession, Indian dances, mock weddings*
Nov. 21 / *Sorata* / Nuestra Señora de los Remedios / *dances such as "Cullahuas"*
Nov. 22 / *Guaqui* / Santa Cecilia / *religious procession*
Nov. 30 / *Pucarani* / San Andrés / *religious procession*
Dec. 4 / *Sapahaqui & Umala* / Santa Bárbara
Dec. 8 / *Laja & Sapahaqui* / La Purísima / *Indian dances*
Dec. 9 / *Laja* / Nuestra Señora de Chijipata / *Indian dances*
Dec. 13 / *Ancoraimes* / Santa Lucía

FIESTAS OF BRAZIL

See text for additional information
**Described in text under a different fiesta*

DATE: PLACE: NAME: EVENTS:

Jan. 1 / *Salvador* / Senhor Bom Jesus dos Navegantes / *water pageant, religious processions*

Jan. 6 / *Alagoas, Recife and Maranhao* / *Reis / *"Bumba meu boi" *(folk play)*, dances

Jan. 11-20 / *Salvador* / Nosso Senhor do Bom Fin / *processions, popular amusements*, **"rodas de capoeira"

Jan. 20 / *Rio* / São Sebastião / *processions, fireworks*

movable / *Rio, Recife, Belém, Salvador & São Paulo* / *Carnival / *parades, floats, indigenous dances*

March 19 / *Fortaleza* / São José / *fireworks & popular celebration* if it has rained

movable / *all over* / Holy Week / *processions (famous passion play at Fazenda Nova)*

Mon. after Easter / *Aparecida do Norte* / *São Benedito / *parades*, *"congadas" & *"moçambiques"

April 16 / *Mogi das Cruzes* / Persimmon Festival

50 days after Easter / *Tietê* / *Festa do Divino / *procession of fishermen, regatta*

May (all month) / *all over* / *Month of Mary / *processions*, *votive masts

May (various days) / *Belém* / special saints / *processions*, *votive masts, fireworks

May (all month) / *Poços de Caldas* / São Benedito / *pilgrimages, fair, processions on Sundays*

May 24 / *Salvador* / Nossa Senhora Auxiliadora / *processions*

June 1-13 / *Salvador* / Santo Antonio / *processions and religious ceremonies*

June 24 / *all over* / *São João / **votive masts, processions, fireworks, bonfires, dances*

June 24/ *São Luiz, Recife, Alagoas, & Maranhao* / São João / **"Bumba meu boi"

June 28 / *same as above* / São Pedro / **"Bumba meu boi"

June 29 / *Rio & most fishing towns* / São Pedro / *processions of decorated boats*

July 16 / *Recife* / Our Lady of Mt. Carmel

Aug. 3-5 / *near São Paulo* / Festa de Pirapora / *popular amusements, dances*

Aug. 4 / *Iguape* / unknown / *water pageant*

Aug. 8 / *São José do Pardo* / São Roque

Aug. 15 / *southern part of state of São Paulo* / *Nossa *Senhora dos* Navegantes / *water pageant*

Aug. 15 / *Outeiro da Gloria* / Assumption

Aug. 16 / *Olinda* / São Roque

Aug. 15-30 / *Rio* / Nossa Senhora da Gloria / *processions, expositions, fair*

Aug. (last Fri.) / *Salvador* / **Aguas de Oxalá / *candomblé purification rite*

Sept. 1-15 / *São Luis* / São José do Ribamar / *pilgrimage, processions,* **"*moçambiques*"

Sept. 8 / *Curitiba* / Nossa Senhora da Luz

Sept. 9 / *Saquarema* / Our Lady of Nazare

Sept. (last Fri.) / *Salvador* / *Aguas de Oxalá / *candomblé purification rite*

Oct. 4 / *Canindé* / São Francisco / *pilgrimage, procession*

Oct. (last Sund.) / *Fortaleza* / Bom Jesus dos Aflitos / *procession*

Oct. (every Sund.) / *Rio* / *Nossa Senhora da Penha / *pilgrimages, fair, fireworks*

Oct. (2nd Sund. + 2 weeks) / *Belém* / *Festa da Luz / *fair, pilgrimage, processions*

Nov. (1st Sund.) / *Rio* / *Nossa Senhora da Penha / *fair & festa for vendors*

Nov. 16 / *São Luis* / Espíto Santo / **"*moçambique*" & *other dances*

Dec. 3 / *Fortaleza* / Bom Jesus dos Aflitos

Dec. 8 / *Salvador* / *Nossa Senhora da Conceicão da Praia / "*rodas de samba*" & *"*rodas de capoeira*"

Dec. 18-26 / *Quatipurú* / São Benedito / *procession, "marujada" dancers, various folk dances*

FIESTAS OF CHILE
See text for additional information

Jan. 1 / *Valparaíso* / New Year's / *procession of decorated boats, "Chinos" dancers in streets*

Jan. 20 / *Santiago* / Día del Roto Chileno / *fireworks, parade, dancing of "cueca"*

Feb. 2 / *San Fernando* / Candelaria / "*Danza de los Chinos*"

Feb. 2 / *Chiloé* / Candelaria / *religious procession, regattas*

Jan. or Feb. / *Southern Chile* / Wheat harvest festivals

Week of Feb. 12 / *Valdivia* / Semana Valdiviana / *regattas, rodeos, races & other sports, torchlight processions*

March or April / *Curicó, Talca, Linares & other places* / Vendimia / *wine festival*

movable / *all over* / Holy Week / *processions (passion in the streets of Valparaíso)*

May 3 / *various places* / Santa Cruz / *"Danza de los Chinos"*

June 29 / *almost all ports* / *San Pedro / *processions on land or water*

June 29 / *Concón* / San Pedro / *procession, "Danza de los Chinos"*

July 16 / *various places* / Virgen del Carmen / *processions*

July 16 / *La Tirana* / *Virgen de la Tirana / *native dances such as "Chinos," processions*

Sept. 8 / *Aiquina* / Candelaria / *"Danza de los Chinos," procession*

Sept. 18-20 / *all over* / *Independencia / *rodeos, barbecues, parades, fireworks, street dancing*

Dec. 26 / *Andacollo* / *Virgen del Rosario / *processions, "Chinos" and other native dances, concessions, races, cockfights*

FIESTAS OF COLOMBIA
See text for additional information

Jan. 5 / *Popayán* / *Día de Negritos / *parades of masked people, "Chirimías," "Devils"*

Jan. 6 / *Popayán* / *Fiesta de los Blanquitos / *merrymaking in streets, flour battles*

Jan. 6 / *Quibdó* / *Día de los Reyes / *masquerades, floats, folk dances*

End of Jan. & beg. of Feb. / *Manizales* / Feria del Café / *bullfights, Olympic games, floats, rodeos, cockfights, folklore competitions*

Jan. 25-Feb. 2 / *Cartagena* / *Candelaria / *pilgrimage, "Cumbia"*

movable / *Barranquilla & Guajira* / *Carnival / *Negro dances, masquerades, street dancing*

movable / *All over (best in Popayán)* / *Holy Week / *processions & other religious observances*

April 4 / *Río Frío* / *San Isidro / *procession*

June / *All over* / *Corpus Christi / *parades, blessing of animals, erection of street altars*

June 29 / *Espinal & Ibagué* / San Pedro y San Pablo / *native dances, games and contests*

July 16 / *Cartagena & elsewhere* / Nuestra Señora del Carmen / *processions*

July 19-24 / *Cúcuta* / Feria / *typical fair*

Aug. 15-27 / *San Bernardo* / Feria / *typical fair*

Aug. 31-Sept. 18 / *Santa Rosa* / Feria / *typical fair*

DATE:	PLACE:	NAME:	EVENTS:

Sept. 9 / *Cartagena* / San Pedro Claver / *procession*

Sept. 19-24 / *Camarones* / Feria / *typical fair*

Sept. 26-Oct. 4 / *Quibdó* / San Francisco de Asis / *procession, floats, masquerades, dances, contests, sports*

Nov. 10-11 / *Cartagena* / *Independencia / *parades, floats, flower battles, beauty contest*

Dec. 8 / *Neiva & Chiquinquira* / Inmaculada Concepción / *pilgrimage, fair*

Dec. 8 / *Condoto* / Inmaculada Concepción / *dances such as "Aguabajo" & "Jota"*

Dec. 16-24 / *all over* / *Christmas / *"Chirimías," special games*

Dec. 25 / *Popayán* / *Christmas / *children's parade*

Dec. 28 / *Condoto & Quibdó* / *Santos Inocentes / *masquerades, floats, folk dances*

End of Dec.-beg. of Jan. / *Cali* / Feria del Azúcar / *election of world queen of sugar*

FIESTAS OF COSTA RICA
See text for additional information

Feb. 15 / *San Isidro de Coronado* / Unknown / *procession & blessing of decorated oxcarts*

March 19 / *San José* / San José / *religious procession*

movable / *San José & elsewhere* / *Holy Week / *processions, popular celebrations*

April 11 / *Alajuela* / Día de Juan Santamaría / *fiesta and dancing*

June / *San José* / Corpus Christi / *religious procession*

June 29 / *Puntarenas* / San Pedro y San Pablo / *water carnival*

July 16 / *Puntarenas* / Virgen del Carmen / *procession of boats*

July 25 / *Guanacaste* / Unknown / *popular celebration, "Punto Guanacasteco"*

Aug. 2 / *Cartago* / *Nuestra Señora de los Angeles / *outdoor ceremony & procession, flower carpets*

Aug. 15 / *San José* / Assumption / *procession*

Sept. (1st Sat.) / *Cartago* / *Nuestra Señora de los Angeles / *procession*

Dec. 24-31 / *San José* / *Christmas / *fair, merriment in streets Christmas Eve*

FIESTAS OF THE DOMINICAN REPUBLIC
*See text for additional information

DATE: PLACE: NAME: EVENTS:

Jan. 5 / *Santo Domingo* / *Día de los Reyes / costumed parade, fireworks*

Jan. 21 / *Higüey* / Virgen de la Altagracia / *pilgrimage*

movable / *all over* / *Carnival / *general merrymaking*

Feb. 27 / *all over* / Independencia / *carnival-like activities*

movable / *all over* / *Holy Week / *processions, burning of Judas*

June / *all over* / Corpus Christi / *processions*

June 24 / *Bani* / San Juan / *dance "Sarandunga"*

June 25 / *Santiago* / Santiago / *popular celebration, "sortija"*

Sept. 24 / *Santo Cerro* / Las Mercedes / *pilgrimage, processions*

Oct. 12 / *Santo Domingo* / *Día de la Raza / *ceremonies in honor of Columbus*

FIESTAS OF ECUADOR
*See text for additional information

Jan. 6 / *all over* / Santos Inocentes / *masked entertainment in streets*

Feb. 5 / *Baños* / Our Lady of the Holy Water / *pilgrimage, processions*

movable / *all over* / *Carnival / *parades of floats*

Fri. before Holy Week / *Riobamba* / Señor del Buen Suceso / *religious procession*

movable / *all over* / *Holy Week / *processions*

April 21 / *Riobamba* / Batalla de Tapi / *fair, parades*

June / *all over* / Corpus Christi / *processions*

June 24 / *Chambo & Otavalo* / *San Juan / *Indian dances and "Diablitos"*

June 29 / *Cayambe* / San Pedro & San Pablo / *fireworks, Indian dances, regattas*

Aug. 8 / *Guápulo* / Our Lady of Guápulo / *pilgrimage, processions*

Aug. 15 / *Yaguachi* / San Jacinto de Yaguachi / *pilgrimage, processions*

Sept. 8 / *Loja* / Virgen del Cisne / *fair, processions*

Sept. 24 / *various towns* / Las Mercedes / *processions*

Oct. 10 / *Guayaquil* / Día del Montuvio / *popular fiesta, equestrian events*

Nov. 21 / *El Quinche* / Virgen del Quinche / *pilgrimages, processions*

Dec. 28 / *Quito & Guayaquil* / *Día de los Inocentes / *parade, masked entertainment in streets*

FIESTAS OF GUATEMALA

*See text for additional information
**Described in text under a different fiesta

DATE: PLACE: NAME: EVENTS:

Jan. 2 / *Santa María de Jesús* / Dulce Nombre de Jesús

Jan. 6 / *Salcajá & Chimaltenango* / Día de los Reyes

Jan. 12-15 / *Esquipulas* / *Cristo de Esquipulas / *pilgrimages, Indian rites*

Jan. 15 / *Totonicapán* / Cristo de Esquipulas

Jan. 15-18 / *Chicalajá* / Cristo de Esquipulas / **"La Culebra" and* other dances*

Jan. 17-20 / *San Antonio Sacatepéquez* / San Sebastián / *fair, Indian dances*

Jan. 21-23 / *San Raimundo* / Feria / *fair, Indian dances*

Jan. 22-25 / *Tamahú* / Feria / *fair, Indian dances*

Jan. 23-25 / *San Pedro Jocopilás* / Feria / *fair, Indian dances*

Jan. 25-29 / *Rabinal* / Feria / *fair, Indian dances*

movable / *various places (especially Mazatenango)* / *Carnival / *street celebrations, cascarones, Indian dances*

1st Fri. of Lent / *outside Antigua* / Jesús Sepultado / *pilgrimage*

2nd Fri. of Lent / *Chajul* / Cristo del Golgota / *pilgrimage*

Every Fri. of Lent / *San Felipe* / Viernes de Cuaresma / *religious celebrations*

Feb. 1-2 / *Mixco* / Feria de Morenos / *Indian dances*

Feb. 1-2 / *Chiantla* / *Candelaria / *fair, pilgrimages*

Feb. 1-2 / *Jacaltenango, San Juan, Ostuncalco, Santiago, Sacatepéquez* / Candelaria / *Indian dances*

March 6-13 / *Puerto Barrios* / Izabal Fair / *Indian dances, games*

March 19 / *Chichicastenango* / San José / *celebration of cofradías*

March 19 / *San José Pinula, San Juan Sacatepéquez, San José Chacaya* / San José / *Indian dances*

March / *Chichicastenango & elsewhere* / *corn-planting ceremonies / *Indian rituals*

Week before Holy Week / *San Pedro Sacatepéquez & Sololá* / Feria de Dolores / *fair, Indian dances*

movable / *all over* / *Holy Week / *religious processions, ceremonial burlesque*

Beg. of April / *Santa Eulalia* / *frost-sealing ceremonies / *Indian rituals*

April 23 / *Quezaltepeque* / unknown / *Indian processions*

April 24 / *San Jorge Panajachel* / unknown / *Indian dances*

April 25-30 / *San Marcos* / Feria de San Marcos / *fair, Indian dances*

May 1-5 / *Amatitlán* / *Feria de la Cruz / *pilgrimage, fair, dances, sports*

May 3 / *Chichicastenango & Chinautla* / Día de la Cruz / *Indian rites*

May 8 / *Gualán* / Apparition of the Archangel

May 15-17 / *Zacualpa* / Feria / *fair, Indian dances*

May 20 / *Patzún* / San Bernardino

May 24 / *San Martín Jilotepeque* / María Auxiliadora

June / *Guatemala City* / Corpus Christi / *procession*

June / *Palín* / Corpus Christi / **"Bull Dance"*

June / *Salamá & Ciudad Vieja* / Corpus Christi

June 10-13 / *San Antonio Aguas Calientes* / San Antonio / *fair, Indian dances*

June 12-13 / *San Antonio Sacatepéquez* / San Antonio

June 22-24 / *San Juan Chamelco & San Juan Sacatepéquez* / *San Juan / *fair, Indian dances such as "Los Gigantes"*

June 24 / *Cotzal, Comalapa, Camotán, Alotenango, Olintepeque* / San Juan Bautista / *Indian dances*

June 24 / *San Juan Ostuncalco* / San Juan Bautista / *music on rare native instruments*

June 27-29 / *San Pedro Carchá, San Pedro Sacatepéquez* / San Pedro / *fair, Indian dances*

June 29 / *San Pedro Jocopilas, Tamahú, Rabinal, Almolonga, Zacapa* / San Pedro / *Indian dances*

July 1 / *San Raimundo* / Sagrado Corazón

July 12-18 / *Huehuetenango* / Fiestas Julias / *fair, Indian dances*

July 23-25 / *Santiago Atitlán* / *Santiago / *"La Conquista" dance drama, procession*

July 23-25 / *Santiago Sacatepéquez, San Cristóbal Totonicapán, San Cristóbal Verapaz* / Santiago / *fair, Indian dances*

July 25-26 / *Chimaltenango* / Santa Ana

July 28-30 / *Momostenango* / *Santiago / *"Mejicanos," *"Bull Dance," procession*

July 29-30 / *Palín* / San Cristóbal

Aug. 1-4 / *Sacapulas & Cobán* / Santo Domingo / *fair, Indian dances*

Aug. 10 / *San Lorenzo El Cubo & San Lorenzo El Tejar* / San Lorenzo

Aug. 12-15 / *Tactic & Joyabaj* / Asunción / *Indian dances, vivid costumes*

Aug. 13-15 / *Guatemala City, Nebaj, Sololá* / Asunción / *fair, dances in villages*

Aug. 15-18 / *Almolonga* / Asunción / *fair, Indian dances*

DATE:	PLACE:	NAME:	EVENTS:

Aug. 15-20 / *Santa Cruz del Quiché* / *Fiestas Elenas / *fair*, *"*La Culebra"*, *"*El Venado"*, *"*El Convite" & other dances*

Aug. 24 / *San Juan Sacatepéquez* / Sangre de Cristo / *Indian rituals*

Aug. 25 / *Salcajá & Santa María de Jesús* / San Luis Rey

Aug. 28 / *Sumpango* / San Augustín / *Indian dances*

Aug. 29-30 / *Malacatancito* / Santa Rosa de Lima / *fair, Indian dances*

Sept. 10 / *San Antonio Palopó* / San Nicolás

Sept. 12-16 / *Quezaltenango* / Independencia / *fair, Indian dances*

Sept. 16-21 / *Salamá* / unknown / *fair, Indian dances*

Sept. 25-30 / *Totonicapán* / San Miguel / *fair, Indian dances*

Sept. 27-29 / *San Miguel Chicaj* / San Miguel / *fair, Indian dances*

Sept. 29-30 / *San Miguel Tucurú* / San Miguel / *fair, Indian dances*

Oct. 1-4 / *San Francisco El Alto & Tecpán* / San Francisco / *fair, Indian dances*

Oct. 7 / *Mixco, Quezaltenango, Chinautla* / Rosario / *procession, dances*

Oct. 10-11 / *Momostenango* / San Francisco (octava) / *Indian dances*

Oct. 15 / *Palín* / Santa Teresa

Oct. 15-18 / *Aguacatán & San Lucas Tolimán* / San Lucas / *fair, Indian dances*

mid-Oct. / *Chichicastenango* / unknown / *harvest festival, Indian rites*

Nov. 1 / *Palín* / Todos los Santos / *"Dance of the Devils"*

Nov. 1 / *Chichicastenango* / Todos los Santos / *Indian rites, appearance of **Tsijoloj*

Nov. 1 / *Todos los Santos & Panajachel*

Nov. 11 / *San Martín Chile Verde, San Martín Sacatepéquez, San Martín Jilotepeque* / San Martín

Nov. 21-22 / *Santa Cruz Quiché* / Santa Cecilia / *Indian dances*

Nov. 23-25 / *Nahualá* / Santa Catalina / *fair, Indian dances*

Nov. 24-25 / *Santa Catarina Palopó* / Santa Catalina

Nov. 25-30 / *Itzapa* / San Andrés / *fair, Indian dances*

Nov. 30 / *San Andrés Xecul* / San Andrés

Dec. 1-10 / *Zacapa* / Concepción

Dec. 6-8 / *Ciudad Vieja* / Concepción / *fair, "Baile del Gigante"*

Dec. 8 / *Chichicastenango, Tucurú, Comalapa, Sololá, Tecpán* / Concepción

Dec. 6-10 / *Retalhuleu* / Concepción / *fair, dances*

Dec. 12 / *Chichicastenango, Santa Cruz Quiché, Comalapa* / Guadalupe

Dec. 16-20 / *Comalapa* / Santo Tomás / *fair, Indian dances*
Dec. 18-21 / *Chichicastenango* / *Santo Tomás / *processions, Indian rites, "Palo Volador", *Tsijoloj*
Dec. 19 / *Quezaltepeque* / San Francisco
Dec. 27-29 / *San Pedro Sacatepéquez* / unknown
Dec. 31 / *Todos Santos* / election of municipal officers / **"*El Venado*"

FIESTAS OF HAITI
See text for additional information

movable / *all over* / *Carnival / *celebrations in streets*
Sat. & Sund. nites of Lent / *all over rural areas* / continuation of Carnival / *"Rara"*
March 19 / *Port-au-Prince* / St. Joseph / *religious ceremonies, *cockfights*
movable / *all over* / *Holy Week / *"*Rara*," *Judas hunts*
June 26 / *Bel Air* / Notre Dame du Perpétuel Secours
June 29 / *Petionville* / St. Pierre
June / *Port-au-Prince* / Corpus Christi / *procession*
Around July 16 / *Ville Bonheur* / *Saut d'eau / *pilgrimage, Catholic & voodoo rites*
July 26 / *Port-au-Prince* / Ste. Anne
November / *various places* / *Manger-yam / *voodoo rites*

FIESTAS OF HONDURAS
See text for additional information

Jan. 6 / *San Francisco de la Paz* / San Francisco de Asis / *procession*
Feb. 2 / *Suyapa* / Virgen de Suyapa / *procession*
movable / *Trujillo* / Ash Wednesday / *"Las Tiras" dance drama*
movable / *all over* / *Holy Week / *processions*
April 25 / *Taulabé* / San Gaspar / *procession*
May 15 / *La Ceiba* / San Isidro
June 13 / *San Pedro Sula* / San Antonio de Padua
June 13 / *Tela* / San Antonio de Padua
June 24 / *Trujillo* / San Juan / *"Las Tiras" dance drama*
June 29 / *San Pedro Sula* / San Pedro / *procession*
July 25 / *Yoro* / Santiago

Sept. 7-14 / *El Progreso* / Feria de las Mercedes / *fair, processions*

Oct. 3 / *Catacamos* / San Francisco

Oct. 21-30 / *La Paz* / Feria de la Paz / *fair, processions*

Nov. 1 / *all over* / Todos los Santos / *decoration of images*

Nov. 2 / *all over* / *Día de Difuntos / *decoration of cemeteries*

Dec. 7-24 / *Comayagüela* / Concepción / *fair, processions*

Week of Dec. 8 / *Juticalpa* / *Inmaculada Concepción / *fair, fireworks, contests, parades, floats*

Dec. 12 / *various places* / Virgen de Guadalupe / *procession of children in Indian costumes*

Dec. 16-24 / *all over* / *Christmas / *posadas*

Dec. 25-Jan. 6 / *north coast towns* / *Christmas / *"*Yancunú*" (*native dance*)

FIESTAS OF MEXICO

*See text for additional information
**Described in text under a different fiesta

Jan. 1 / *Tlaxcoapan, Hgo.* / Año Nuevo / *dances such as "Segadores," "Vaqueros," & "Contradanzas"*

Jan. 1 / *Dolores Hidalgo, Gto.* / Feria / *usually dances such as "Comanches," "Torito," "Compadres"*

Jan. 1-5 / *Chalma, Mex.* / Pilgrimage to Señor de *Chalma / *pilgrimage, many native dances*

Jan. 1-7 / *Joyutla, Mor.* / Feria / *fair, **rodeo, cockfights, Indian dances*

Jan. 5-12 / *Irapuato, Gto.* / Fundación de la Ciudad / *fair, bullfights, floats, athletic contests*

Jan. 6 / *many places & of special interest in Chiconcoac (Mex.), Los Reyes (Mex.), Matehuala (S.L.P.) and Xochitepec (Mor.)* / *Día de los Reyes or Santos Reyes / *processions, *piñatas, native dances*

Jan. 6 / *Coatlan del Río, Mor.* / Santos Reyes / *fair, dances such as "Mojigangas"*

Jan. 6-7 / *Almoloya del Río, Mex.* / Santos Reyes / *fair, native dances*

Jan. 6-15 / *Temascaltepec, Mex.* / Señor del Perdón / *fair, dances: "Tecomates," "Arcos," **"Moros y Cristianos"*

Jan. 10-20 / *Moroleón, Gto.* / Fundación de la Ciudad / *parade of floats, bullfights, horse races, regional dances*

Jan. 12-Feb. 12 / *Celaya, Gto.* / unknown / *short plays & dances every night in the Tierras Negras section of the city*

Jan. 15 / *Tenango, Mex.* / Padre Jesús de Tenango / *fair, native dances, plays, bullfights, cockfights*

Jan. 15 / *Ocoyoacac, Mex.* / unknown / *native dances: "Chalmeritos," "Arrieros," "Negritos," & **"Moros y Cristianos"*

Jan. 17 / *various places* / *San Antonio Abad / *blessing of animals*

Jan. 17-25 / *León, Gto.* / Fundación de la Ciudad / *fair, dancing, bullfights, cockfights*

Jan. 18-20 / *Taxco, Gro.* / Santa Prisca and San Sebastián / *native dances*

Jan. 18-20 / *Asientos, Ags.* / unknown / ***"Matachines"*

Jan. 20-25 / *Tehuantepec, Oax.* / San Sebastián / *dances*

Jan. 20 / *Tepetlixpa, Mex.* / San Sebastián / *fair, dances: "Aztecas," "Pastores," "Negros," "Vaqueros"*

Jan. 20 / *Tenosique, Tab.* / *San Sebastián / *dances, games*

Jan. 20 / *Guanajuato, Gto.* / San Sebastián / *celebration re-enacting a famous robbery, fireworks, dances*

Jan. 20 / *Chamula, Chiapas* / San Sebastián / *native dances*

Jan. 20 / *San Luis Potosi, S.L.P.* / San Sebastián / *native dances*

week around Jan. 21 / *Dzitas, Yuc.* / *Santa Inés / *"Jarana," *"Torito," *"Turkey Dance," Indian rituals*

Jan. 24 / *Indaparapeo, Mich.* / Nuestro Señor de la Paz / *parade of floats, dances*

Jan. 3rd Wed. / *San Felipe del Progreso, Mex.* / Fiesta titular / *fair, "Apaches," "Santiagueros," "Las Cintas," "Los Arcos," "Pastoras"*

Jan. 3rd Sund. / *Amacueca, Jal.* / unknown / *fair, bullfights, **rodeo, regional dances*

Jan. 3rd Sund. / *Asientos, Ags.* / unknown / ***"Matachines"*

Jan. 25 / *Palmatlán, Pue.* / unknown / ***"Voladores"*

Jan. 25 / *Axochiapan, Mor.* / unknown / *fair, "Cicuanes," "Doce Pares de Francia"*

Jan. 25-28 / *Cuilapan, Oax.* / unknown / ***"Plume Dance"*

Jan. 25-Feb. 2 / *Talpa de Allende, Jal.* / Candelaria / *pilgrimage, fair, native dances*

Jan. 25-Feb. 2 / *Arenal, Jal.* / Candelaria / *fair, cockfights, bullfights, "La Conquista," **Jarabe Tapatío"*

Jan. 29 / *Pahuatlán, Pue.* / unknown / *"Santiagueros," "Tocotines," **"Quetzales"*

Jan. last Sund. / *Tonatico, Mex.* / unknown / *bullfights, cockfights, **"Moros y Cristianos," "Pastores"*

movable / *Mazatlán, Sin.* / *Carnival / *flower & confetti battles, popular celebrations* movable / *Tepeyanco, Tlax.* / *Carnival / *"*Paragüeros*"

movable / *Santa Ana Chiautempan, Tlax.* / *Carnival / *"*Catrines*"

movable / *Acapulco, Veracruz, & Mérida* / *Carnival / *street celebrations, masquerades*

movable / *Huejotzingo, Pue.* / *Carnival / *folk play by entire town*

Feb. 1 / *Comitan, Chis.* / Fiesta patronal / *procession, usually native dances*

Feb. 1-2 / *Tlacotalpan, Ver.* / *Candelaria / *procession of grotesque figures, **rodeo, native dances, especially *"Huapangos"*

Feb. 1-8 / *Tzintzuntzan, Mich.* / *Candelaria / *Indian regatta on Lake Pátzcuaro, *"Viejitos", "Negritos", *"Sembradores"*

Feb. 1-12 / *San Juan de los Lagos, Jal.* / *Candelaria / *pilgrimage, fair, dances such as *"Moros y Cristianos"*

Feb. 2 / *Arandas, Jal.* / Candelaria / *bullfight, horse races, "La Conquista", "Los Palitos"*

Feb. 2 / *Taxco, Gro.* / Candelaria / *blessing of animals, popular fiesta*

Feb. 2 / *Sombrerete, Zac.* / Candelaria / *fair, "Los Monarcas"*

Feb. 2 / *Colomé, Sin.* / Candelaria / *fair, bullfights, horse races, cockfights, "Venado"*

Feb. 1st Fri. / **Chalma, Mex.* / unknown / *pilgrimage, fair, native dances*

Feb. 27 / *Ocoyoacac, Mex.* / unknown / *"Vaqueros", "Apaches", and other dances*

Feb. 29-March 3 / *Yautepec, Mor.* / Feria / *fair, "Chinelos"*

March 1-5 / *Durango, Dgo.* / Feria / *fair, native dances*

March 3 / *Amecameca, Mex.* / unknown / *regional dances*

March, 2nd week / *Etla, Oax.* / Our Lord of the Cliffs / *native dances, especially **"Plume Dance"*

March 10-20 / *Huauchinango, Pue.* / Santo Entierro / *flower fair, usually **"Voladores"*

March 11-19 / *Talpa, Jal.* / Virgen de Talpa / *pilgrimage, **rodeos, cockfights, native dances*

March 12 / *San Gregorio Atlapulco (near capital)* / Santo Patrón / *dances such as "Vaqueros"*

March 15 / *Cuyutlán, Col.* / Feria / *fair, dances, regattas*

March 18 / *Tepaltzingo, Mor.* / Feria / *fair, native dances*

March 18 / *Taxco, Gro.* / Chavarrieta / *procession, dances*

March 19 / *Cuautla, Mor.* / San José / *folk play on horseback*

March 19 / *Coahuayana, Mich.* / San José / *bullfights, cockfights, "Pastores"*

March 19 / *Honey, Pue.* / San José / **"*Voladores*"

March 29 / *Taxco, Gro.* / Santa Veracruz / "*Pastores*," "*Tres Potencias*"

movable / *Taxco, Gro.* / *Holy Week / *processions, pageants, dances, *castillos*

movable / *Malinalco, Mex.* / *Holy Week / *passion play*

movable / *Ixtapalapa, D.F.* / *Holy Week / *passion play*

movable / *Tzintzuntzan, Mich.* / *Holy Week / *passion play*

movable / *Cherán, Mich.* / *Holy Week / *primitive rites*

movable (during Holy Week) / *Tepoztlán, Mor.* / *Fiesta del Brinco / *native dances*

movable / *Towns in Sonora* / *Holy Week / *"*Pascolas*"

April 4 / *San Isidro, Mor.* / San Isidro / *decoration and blessing of bulls*

April 5 / *Ticul, Yuc.* / Feria del Tabaco / *fair, bullfights, native dances*

April 9 / *Santiago de las Peñas, Oax.* / Señor de las Peñas / *pilgrimage, dances such as* **"*Plume Dance*"

April 16 / *Coyocac, Mor.* / unknown / "*Chinelos*"

April 20-26 / *Tuxtla, Chis.* / Feria / *fair, native dances*

April 25-May 5 / *Aguascalientes, Ags.* / Feria de San Marcos / *fair, bullfights, cockfights, native dances*

April 30 / *Tepatitlán, Jal.* / Señor de la Misericordia / *native dances*

May 1-5 / *Cuyutlán, Col.* / unknown / *regattas, floats, dances*

May 1-10 / *Morelia, Mich.* / State Fair / *historical pageants, floats, dances*

May 2-3 / *Tlacotepéc, Pue.* / Santa Cruz / *torchlight parades*

May 2-3 / *Amatlán de los Reyes, Ver.* / Santa Cruz / **"*Moros y Cristianos*," "*Zapateados*," **"*Jaranas*"

May 3 / *Valle del Bravo, Mex.* / Santa Cruz / *fair, parade of decorated oxen, flower battles, regional dances*

May 3 / *all over* / *Santa Cruz / *decoration of buildings and small celebrations*

May 3 / *Maxcanú, Yuc.* / Santa Cruz / *fair, bullfights,* **"*Vaquerías*"

May 3 / *Parras, Coa.* / Santa Cruz / *mock battle,* "*Pastorelas*," "*Matlachines*"

May 3 / *Santa Cruz Atizapán, Mex.* / Santa Cruz / *fair,* "*Pastores*," "*Tecomates*," "*Arrieros*"

May 3 / *Calkini, Camp.* / *El Cux de Lerma / *pig's head ceremony, dances*

May 3 / *Atolinga, Zac.* / Santa Cruz / *fair,* "*La Palma*," "*Los Mecos*"

May 3 / *Parral, Chih.* / Santa Cruz / *fair,* **"*Matachines*"

May 3-15 / *Gomez Palacio, Dgo.* / Fiestas de Mayo / *"Plumas," "El Arco"*

May 3-4 / *Santiago Tianguistenco, (near capital)* / Santa Cruz / **"Moros y Cristianos," "Apaches"*

May 3-5 / *Nogales, Son.* / Fiesta de las Flores / *fair, floats, flower battle*

May 5 / *Puebla, Pue.* / *Cinco de Mayo / *sham battle and other celebrations*

May 5 / *Peñon, Mexico City* / *Cinco de Mayo / *folk play*

May 5 / *Fortin, Ver.* / Cinco de Mayo / *flower battles*

May 6 / *Tepoztlán, Mor.* / unknown / *native dances*

May, 2nd week / *Abala, Yuc.* / Mes de María / *bullfights,* **"Vaquerías"*

May 10-20 / *Etchojoa, Son.* / Espíritu Santo / *fair, "Venado,"* **"Pascolas"*

May 15 / *Acapantzingo, Mor.* / San Isidro Labrador / *sowing festival, folk play, native dances*

May 15 / *Metepec, Mex.* / *San Isidro Labrador / *decoration and blessing of oxen*

May 17-22 / *Tixkokob, Yuc.* / Feria / *regional dances*

May 18-25 / *Juchitan, Oax.* / San Vicente Ferrer / *spring festival, pageants, velas*

May 20 / *Abasolo, Gto.* / Nuestra Señora de la Luz / *fair, "Panaderos"*

May 25 / *Santa Maria del Oro, Nay.* / Fiesta titular / *fair, "La Conquista"*

May 31 / *Guanajuato, Gto.* / Virgen de Guanajuato / *processions*

June 1-30 / *Motul, Yuc.* / Sacred Heart of Jesus / *popular celebrations, processions*

June 2 / *Ojinaga, Chih.* / Aniversario de la Fundación / *popular fair*

June, 2nd week / *Río Verde, S.L.P.* / San Antonio / *cockfights, horse racing, native dances*

June 13 / *San Antonio Tultitlán, Mor.* / San Antonio / *native dances*

June 13 / *San Antonio Calpulalpan, Tlax.* / San Antonio / **"Moros y Cristianos"*

June 13 / *Teoloyucan, Mex.* / San Antonio / *fair, horse races, "Pastores," "Santiagueros"*

June 13-29 / *Uruapan, Mich.* / San Antonio / *procession with decorated oxen, "Negritos"*

June 13 / *Casas Grandes, Chih.* / San Antonio / *"Pastores" and other native dances*

June 13   *Charapan, Mich.* / San Antonio / *native dances*

221

June 23-29 / *Guanajuato, Gto.* / Verbena de San Juan / *fair, dances, athletic events, picnics at dam*

June 24 / *Cuncunul, Yuc.* / San Juan / *fair, regional dances*

June 24 / *Libres, Pue.* / San Juan / *fair, floats, cockfights, bullfights,* **rodeo, serenatas, ***"Matachines"*

June 24 / *Tehuantepec, Oax.* / San Juan / *flower battles, decorated oxcarts, torchlight parades*

June 24 / *Navojoa, Son.* / San Juan / *"Venado," "Coyote,"* **"Pascolas"*

June 29 / *Tlaxcoapan, Hgo.* / San Pedro / *fair, "Segadores," "Vaqueros," "Conquistadores," "Contradanzas"*

June 29 / *Guadalajara, Jal. & San Pedro Tlaquepaque* / San Pedro / *fair, mariachis, cockfights, bullfights, serenatas, flower battles*

June 29 / *Cacalchén, Yuc.* / San Pedro y San Pablo / *fair, regional dances*

June 29 / *San Pablo Oxtotepec, D.F.* / San Pedro y San Pablo / *"Aztecas," "Pastoras,"* **"Concheros," and others*

June 29 / *La Barca, Jal.* / San Pedro y San Pablo / *regional dances*

June 29 / *San Pedro Cántaros, Oax.* / San Pedro y San Pablo / *regional dances*

June 29 / *Tehuacán, Pue.* / San Pedro y San Pablo / *bullfights, cockfights, greased-pole climb,* **rodeos, fireworks, boxing*

June / *Mexico City* / *Corpus Christi / *children's processions*

June / *Tzintzuntzan, Mich.* / *Corpus Christi / *unusual parade*

June / *Paracho, Mich.* / *Corpus Christi / *unusual parade*

June / *Papantla, Ver.* / *Corpus Christi / *"Voladores,"* *"Quetzales"*

June / *Pahuatlán, Pue.* / *Corpus Christi / *"Voladores"*

June / *Texcoco, Mex.* / Corpus Christi / *fair, horse races, bullfights,* **"Moros y Cristianos," "Vaqueros," "Serranitos,"* **"Sembradores"*

July 1-13 / *Huamantla, Tlax.* / unknown / *fair, native dances, bullfights*

July 3 / *Oaxaca, Oax.* / San Marcial / ***"Plume Dance," cockfights*

July 4 / *Lagos de Moreno, Jal.* / Señor del Refugio / *unknown*

July 7-15 / *Comitán, Chris.* / San Fermín / *native dances*

July 8 / *Teotitlán del Valle, Oax.* / unknown / ***"Plume Dance"*

July 8-16 / *Motul, Yuc.* / Our Lady of Mt. Carmel / *regional dances such as "Jarana Yucateca"*

July 11 / *Angangueo, Mich.* / Día del Minero / *fair, horse races, bullfights, serenatas, dances*

July 15 / *San Juan Teotihuacán, Mex.* / Divino Redentor / *fair, "Apaches,"* **"Moros y Cristianos," fireworks*

July 16 / *Tehuacán, Pue.* / Virgen de Carmen / *castillos, toritos*

July 16 / *Guitiérrez Zamora, Ver.* / Virgen de Carmen / *regional dances*

July 16 / *Mexico City* / Our Lady of Mt. Carmen / *religious festival & fair in the Plaza del Estudiante*

July 19 / *Juchitan, Oax.* / St. Vincent de Paul / *almost pagan harvest festival, Tirada de frutas*

July 19 / *Playa Vicente, Ver.* / St. Vincent de Paul / *dances such as "Bamba," **"Huapangos"*

July-Mon. after 16th for 1 week / *Oaxaca, Oax.* / Lunes del Cerro / **"Plume Dance" and others, athletic events*

July 24-25 / *Candela, Coa.* / Santiago / ***"Matachines"*

July 24 / *Torréon, Coa.* / Santiago / ***"Moros y Cristianos" and other dances*

July 25 / *Ocoyoacac, Mex.* / Santiago / *"Chalmeritos," "Arrieros," "Negritos," **"Moros y Cristianos"*

July 25 / *Cuilapan, Oax.* / Santiago / *fair, **"Plume Dance" and others*

July 25 / *Chilacalapa, Gro.* / Santiago / *"Tecuanes," "Vaqueros," **"Moros y Cristianos," "Negritos," and other dances*

July 25 / *Chalco, Mex.* / Santiago / *fair, horse races, **rodeos, **"Moros y Cristianos," "Franceses," "Vitores"*

July 25 / *Ciudad Valles, S.L.P.* / Santiago / *native dances*

July 25 / *Santiago, Baja Calif.* / Santiago / *fair, games*

July 25 / *Coatzintla, Ver.* / Santiago / ***"Voladores" and other dances*

July 25 / *Silao, Gto.* / Fundación de la Ciudad / *floats, flower battles, serenatas, regional dances*

July 26 / *Santa Ana Tlacotenco, D.F.* / Santa Ana / *fair, regional dances, serenatas*

July 31 / *Guanajuato, Gto.* / San Ignacio / *popular celebrations*

Aug. 1-7 / *Saltillo, Coa.* / **Señor de la Capilla* / *fair, native dances, religious plays, cockfights, *"Matachines"*

Aug. 2 / *Tulancingo, Hgo.* / Nuestra Señora de los Angeles / *fair, native dances, cockfights, bullfights*

Aug. 4 / *Uayma, Yuc.* / Santo Domingo / *fair, dances*

Aug. 6 / *Lagos de Moreno, Jal.* / unknown / *fair, **rodeos, bullfights*

Aug. 6 / *Malinalco, Mex.* / unknown / *fair, regional dances*

Aug. 8 / *Paracho, Mich.* / unknown / *parade of decorated bulls*

Aug. 8-16 / *Mérida, Yuc.* / Asunción / ***"Jarana," processions*

Aug. 10-15 / *Amozoc, Pue.* / Asunción / ***"Moros y Cristianos" and other dances, **rodeos, cockfights, bullfights*

Aug. 10-20 / *Zacatlán, Pue.* / Feria de la Manzana / *fair, queen, native dances, cockfights*

Aug. 15 / *Sanahct, Yuc.* / Asunción / *fair, regional dances*

Aug. 15 / *Sudzal, Yuc.* / Asunción / *fair, regional dances*

Aug. 15 / *Tlapacoyan, Pue.* / Asunción / *fair,* "Santiagueros", **"Moros y Cristianos", "Tejoneros", **"Quetzales", "Toreadores", **"Voladores"

Aug. 15 / *Huamantla, Tlax.* / Asunción / *flower tapestries in church*

Aug. 13-16 / *Juchitan, Oax.* / Velas Agostos / *folk dances, processions*

Aug. 15-16 / *Izamal, Yuc.* / Nuestra Señora de Izamal / *fair, bullfights,* **"Vaquerías"

Aug. 21 / *Mexico City* / *Homage to Cuauhtémoc / *"Concheros"

Aug. 24 / *Juanacatlán, Jal.* / San Bartolomé / "Danza de los Cuares"

Aug. 24 / *Villa Cuauhtémoc, Mex.* / San Bartolomé / *fair,* **rodeo, "Apaches", "Caporales", "Pastores"

Aug. 28 / **Chalma, Mex. / unknown / *pilgrimage, dances*

Aug. 31 / *Oaxaca, Oax.* / San Ramón / *pets dressed up and paraded to church*

Sept. 1-8 / *Tepoztlán, Mor.* / *Natividad / *Aztec dance drama*

Sept. 1-8 / *Cuzama, Yuc.* / Natividad / *fair, regional dances*

Sept. 1-8 / *San Bartolo Naucalpan, Mex.* / *Virgen de los Remedios / *fair,* **"Concheros" *and other dances*

Sept. 3 / *Juchitan, Oax.* / Vela Pineda / "Zandunga", "Llorona", "Tortuga"

Sept. 6-15 / *Zacatecas, Zac.* / Santa Patrona / *fair, processions*

Sept. 6 / *Putla, Oax.* / unknown / *lantern processions, floats*

Sept. 8 / *Totolán, Jal.* / Natividad / **"Matachines", **"Viejitos", "Pastoras", "Amazonas", "Guajitos", "Reyes"

Sept. 8 / *Los Remedios, Mex.* / Virgen de los Remedios / *pilgrimage, dance drama*

Sept. 8-11 / *Tixtla, Gro.* / Natividad / *dances such as* "Gachupines", "Gallitos", "Cabezones", "Vaqueros", "Pescados"

Sept. 8-9 / *Cholula, Pue.* / Virgen de los Remedios / *fair, regional dances*

Sept. 10-Oct. 7 / *Ramos Arizpe, Coa.* / unknown / *fair, cockfights, bullfights,* **"Matachines"

Sept. 10-16 / *Chihuahua, Chih.* / Fiestas Patrias / *fair, parades, dances, serenatas, bullfights*

Sept. 12-14 / *San Juan Nuevo, Mich.* / unknown / **"Concheros", "Romans", "Aztecs"

Sept. 14 / *various places* / *Día de los Charros / *rodeos, parades, *"Jarabe Tapatío"

Sept. 14 / *Querétaro, Qro.* / unknown / *regional dances*

224

Sept. 15-16 / *Acatlán de Juarez, Jal.* / Fiestas Patrias / *fair, serenatas,* **rodeos,* *"La Conquista," "Los Palitos," mariachis*

Sept. 16 / *all over* / *Independencia / *"Grito de Dolores," fireworks*

Sept. 16 / *Querétaro, San Miguel Allende & Dolores Hidalgo* / *Independencia / *historical pageant covering all three towns*

Sept. 16-29 / *San Miguel Allende, Gto.* / *Independencia / *parades, floats,* **rodeos, bullfights,* **"Concheros"*

Sept. 22-30 / *Ciudad Doctor Hernández Alvarez, Gto.* / San Miguel / *fair, "Comanches," "Malinches,"* **"Moros y Cristianos,"* **"Sonajeros," "Cuadrillas"*

Sept. 29-Oct. 2 / *San Miguel Allende, Gto.* / *San Miguel / *parades, street dancing, cockfights,* **"Concheros," "Rayados"*

Sept. 29 / *Ocoyoacac, Mex.* / San Miguel / *"Chalmeritos," "Arrieros," "Negritos,"* **"Moros y Cristianos"*

Sept. 29 / *Hoctún, Yuc.* / San Miguel / *fair, bullfights, regional dances*

Sept. 29 / *Atlixco, Pue.* / San Miguel / *bullfights, cockfights, rodeos, regional dances*

Sept. 29 / *Tlalpam, Mex.* / San Miguel / *"Doce Pares de Francia" and other dances*

Sept. 29 / *Uruapan, Mich.* / San Miguel / **"Viejitos,"* **"Canacuas,"* **"Moros y Cristianos"*

Sept. 29 / *Atlautla, Mex.* / San Miguel / *fair, serenatas, charro events, "Doce Pares de Francia," "Apaches," "Vaqueros," "Negritos," "Pastorcitas," "Pecado Original"*

Sept. 29 / *Cocula, Jal.* / San Miguel / *mariachi contest, bullfights, "La Conquista"*

Sept. 29 / **Chalma, Mex.* / San Miguel / *pilgrimage and native dances*

Sept. 29 / *Jesus María, Nay.* / *San Miguel / *"Maromeros" and **"Las Palmas"*

Sept. 29 / *Tuxtla, Chis.* / *San Miguel / *devil dancers*

Sept. 30 / *Coatepec, Ver.* / San Jerónimo / *"Tocotines" and other dances*

Oct. all month / *Atzcapotzalco, D.F.* / Virgen del Rosario / *fair, horse races, dances*

Oct. 1-7 / *Ciudad Delicias, Chih.* / Feria del Algodón / *parades of floats, bullfights, horse races, serenatas, regional dances*

Oct. 1-30 / *Pachuca, Hgo.* / San Francisco / *fair, races, kermesses, cockfights*

Oct. 2-6 / *Cuetzalán, Pue.* / San Francisco / *native dances*

Oct. 3 / *Ocotlán, Jal.* / Señor de la Misericordia / *fair, bullfights,* **rodeos, serenatas, regional dances*

Oct. 3-4 / *Olinalá, Gro.* / San Francisco / *"Mojigangas" and other dances*

Oct. 4 for one week / *Amixtlán, Pue.* / Harvest festival / *little known dances such as "Hunters," "Olmecas," "Reapers"*

Oct. 4 / *Valle de Bravo, Mex.* / San Francisco / *parade of decorated oxen, flower battles, native dances*

Oct. 4 / *Uruapan, Mich.* / *San Francisco / *parade of decorated oxen, **"Viejitos," ***"Moros y Cristianos," *"Canacuas"*

Oct. 4 / *Tala, Jal.* / Fiesta titular / *fair, **rodeos, "La Conquista," ***"Sonajeros," "Pastores," "Huehuenches," "Chayacates"*

Oct. 4 / *Atil, Son.* / San Francisco / *horse races, "Venado," ***"Pascolas"*

Oct. 4 / *Telchac, Yuc.* / San Francisco / *regional dances*

Oct. 4-5 / *Guadalajara and Zapopan, Jal.* / *Virgen de Zapopan / *processions, **rodeos, bullfights, "La Conquista," "Los Piteros"*

Oct. 7-15 / *Alvarado, Ver.* / Our Lady of the Rosary / *regattas, parades, masquerades, cockfights, dances*

Oct. 10 / *Ocoyoacac, Mex.* / unknown / *"Chalmeritos," "Arrieros," "Negritos," ***"Moros y Cristianos"*

Oct. 10-12 / *Santa María del Tule and Tlacolula, Oax.* / unknown / *regional dances*

Oct. 22 / *Apatzingán, Mich.* / Fiesta patriótica / *bullfights, greased-pole climbing, parades, dances*

Oct. 22-25 / *Ciudad Guzmán, Jal.* / *Feria de octubre / *parade with floats, "La Conquista," *"Paixtles," "Pastores," *"Sonajeros," "La América"*

Oct. 24 / *Church of San Rafael, Mexico City* / San Rafael / *gay street fair, sometimes native dances*

Nov. 1-2 / *All over—best in Mixquic (D.F.), Amecameca, Oaxaca, Toluca, Chiapas, Janitzio (Lake Pátzcuaro)* / *Todos Santos / *see Chapter 13*

Nov. 1 / *Cortazar, Gto.* / Todos Santos / *fair, regional dances*

Nov. 4 / *Altamirano, Chis.* / unknown / *regional dances*

Nov. 3-12 / *Texelucan, Pue.* / San Martín / *fair, regional dances, serenatas, **rodeos, bullfights*

Nov. 8-13 / *Tecax, Yuc.* / San Diego / *regional dances, bullfights*

Nov. 11 / *San Martín de las Pirámides, Mex.* / Fiesta titular / *fair, regional dances, **rodeos, cockfights, horse races*

Nov. 13 / *San Diego de la Unión, Gto.* / Fiesta patronal / *floats, athletic events, serenatas*

Nov. 16 / *Villa Juárez, S.L.P.* / Santa Gertrudis / *fair, bullfights*

Nov. 2nd Sund.-3rd Sund. / *Guanajuato, Gto.* / Virgen de Guanajuato / *processions*

Nov. 20 / *Francisco I. Madero, Dgo.* / Fundación de la ciudad / *parade of floats*

Nov. 20 / *Coalcomán, Mich.* / Fiestas patrias / *fair, regional dances*

Nov. 25 / *Asunción Ixtaltepec, Oax.* / Fiesta patronal / *fair, parade*

Nov. 25 / *Pahuatlán, Hgo.* / *Santa Catarina / *"Acatlaxquis"*

Nov. 25-30 / *San Marcos, Gro.* / San Marcos / *"Tlacololeros," "Tlamiques," "Diablos," "Doce Pares de Francia,"* **"Moros y Cristianos," "Cockerels"*

Nov. 28-Dec. 13 / *San Juan de los Lagos, Jal.* / *San Juan de los Lagos / *cockfights, pilgrimages, fair, processions,* **rodeos, bullfights, regional dances*

Nov. 30 / *Mixquic, D.F.* / Fiesta Titular / *fair, regional dances*

Nov. 30 / *San Andrés Cabecera Nueva, Oax.* / Fiesta titular / *fair, regional dances*

Nov. 30-Dec. 8 / *Champotón, Camp.* / Concepción / *fair, processions*

Dec. 1 / *Dolores Hidalgo, Gto.* / Señor del Llanito / *procession, "Apaches"*

Dec. 1-8 / *Compostela, Nay.* / Señor de la Misericordia / *fair, dances such as "La Conquista"*

Dec. 1st week / *Taxco, Gro.* / Feria de la Plata / *silver fair and exposition, crowning of queen, regional dances*

Dec. 3-12 / *Tecalitlán, Jal.* / Guadalupe / *bullfights, horse races, "La Conquista,"* **"Sonajeros,"* **"Moros y Cristianos," "Tecomates," "La América"*

Dec. 5-9 / *San Francisco del Rincón, Gto.* / Fundación de la ciudad / *parade of floats, cockfights, bullfights, horse races, serenatas, regional dances*

Dec. 5-15 / *Iguala, Gro.* / unknown / *fair, plays, cockfights, bullfights, native dances*

Dec. 6 / *San Miguel Zinacantepec, Mex.* / Nuestra Señora del Rayo / *fair, "Apaches," "Pastores," "Pastoras"*

Dec. 7-13 / *Chiautla, Pue.* / La Purísima / **"Moros y Cristianos," "Vaqueros," "Doce Pares de Francis," "Tecuanes," "Las Moras"*

Dec. 8 / *Tenancingo, Mex.* / La Purísima / *fair, bullfights, cockfights,* **"Moros y Cristianos"*

Dec. 8 / *Pátzcuaro, Mich.* / *Nuestra Señora de la Salud / *fair, parade of floats, bullfights,* **rodeos, cockfights, regattas,* **"Viejitos,"* **"Moros y Cristianos," "Los Listones," "Las Mojigangas," "Arrieros," "Negritos," "La Conquista,"* **"Sembradores"*

Dec. 8 / *Zapotlán de Juárez, Hgo.* / La Purísima / *fair, ribbon races,* "Los Lanceros"

Dec. 8 / *San Juan de los Lagos, Jal.* / La Purísima / *regional dances*

Dec. 8 / *Atotonilco El Alto, Jal.* / La Purísima / *fair, charro events,* **rodeos, regional dances*

Dec. 8-14 / *Tuxtla, Chis.* / Guadalupe / *fair, sports events, serenatas, regional dances*

Dec. 8-12 / *Otumba, Mex.* / La Purísima and Guadalupe / *serenatas,* **rodeos,* "Apaches", "Santiagueros"

Dec. 8-12 / *Jaumave, Tamps.* / La Purísima / *fair,* "Caballitos", "Infantes"

Dec. 10-12 / *Parral, Chih.* / *Guadalupe / *fair, processions*

Dec. 12 / *Villa García, Zac.* / *Guadalupe / *fair, bullfights, cockfights,* "Chichimecas", "Mayas", "La Conquista", "Toltecas"

Dec. 12 / *Villa de Guadalupe* / *Guadalupe / *fair, pilgrimages,* **"Concheros" and many other dances*

Dec. 12 / *Jilotepec, Mex.* / *Guadalupe / *fair, horse races, ribbon races,* "Pastoras", "Xhitas", "Santiagueros", "Luas", "Eles", "Apaches"

Dec. 12 / *Villamar, Mich.* / *Guadalupe / "Guajes", "Tejedoras", "Guares"

Dec. 12-13 / *Jonacatepec, Mor.* / *Guadalupe / *fair,* "Los Vaqueritos"

Dec. 15-31 / *Querétaro, Qro.* / *Christmas / *unusual *posadas, parade of floats, floral games, fair, bullfights, regional dances*

Dec. 15-31 / *Quiroga, Mich.* / *Christmas / *floats with Biblical scenes,* **"Viejitos",* **"Moros y Cristianos",* "Los Listones" and other *dances*

Dec. 16-24 / *all over* / *Christmas / *posadas*

Dec. 16-24 / *Puruándiro, Mich.* / *Christmas / *floats,* "Las Macanas", "Los Reyes Magos", "Negros", "Mojigangas"

Dec. 16-25 / *Oaxaca, Oax.* / *Christmas / *processions, *calendas, parades, Radish Festival on night of 23rd*

Dec. 18 / *Oaxaca, Oax.* / *Virgen de la Soledad / *procession,* "Apaches" and other dances

Dec. 23-Jan. 2 / *Venustiano Carranza, Jal.* / Fiesta de Fin de Año / *fair, bullfights,* **"Sonajeros"*

Dec. 24-Jan. 1 / *Yuriria, Gto.* / *Christmas / *floats, *pastorelas, serenatas*

Dec. 30-Jan. 9./ *Tizimín, Yuc.* / Los Reyes / *fair, bullfights, serenatas,* **"Vaquerías"*

Dec. 31 / *Mitla, Oax.* / *New Year's Eve / *pagan rites on hill*

FIESTAS OF NICARAGUA
See text for additional information

DATE: PLACE: NAME: EVENTS:

Jan. 20 / *Chinandega & Rivas* / San Sebastián / *native dances such as "Toro Huaco", "Diablitos" and "Macho Ratón"*

movable / *Everywhere (most impressive in León and Granada)* / Holy Week / *processions*

May 3 / *Jinotega & Corinto* / Día de la Cruz

June / *all over* / Corpus Christi / *processions*

June 24 / *León* / San Juan

June 29 / *León* / San Pedro

July 1 / *Granada* / La Santísima / *procession*

July 24-26 / *Jinotepe* / annual fair / *typical fair*

July 26 / *Chinandega* / Santa Ana / *procession*

Aug. 1-10 / *Managua* / Santo Domingo / *carnival, bullfights, folk festival*

Aug. 14-30 / *Granada* / Santo Domingo / *carnival, parades, native dances*

Aug. 15 / *all over* / Assumption / *processions*

Aug. 15 / *Ocotal, Juigalpa & Masaya* / Santo Domingo

Sept. 24 / *Matagalpa* / Virgen de la Merced

Sept. 30 / *Masaya* / San Gerónimo / *procession, "Toro Venado", "Toro Huaco", Mantudos" and "Zopilote" dances*

Oct. 1st Sund. / *Granada* / unknown

Nov. 29-Dec. 7 / *all over* / La Purísima / *processions, dances, merry-making in the streets on the 7th of December*

Dec. 16-24 / *all over* / *Christmas / *posadas*

FIESTAS OF PANAMA
See text for additional information

Jan. 6 / *Santiago* / Tres Reyes

Jan. 15 / *Antón* / *Esquipulas / *religious procession*

Jan. 20 / *Ocú* / San Sebastián / *gathering of montunos, religious celebrations*

Jan. 20 / *San Carlos* / San Sebastián / *fair*

movable / *Panama City* / *Carnival / *street celebrations, floats, *"Tamborito"*

1st Sund. in Lent / *Atalaya* / Jesús Nazareno / *procession*

Feb. 2 / *La Pintada, Montijo, Las Lajas, Pacora, Chepillo, Tonosí* / Candelaria / *religious processions*

229

Feb. 12 / *Chiriquí* / *Balserías / *tribal contests*

March 8 / *Natá* / San Juan de Dios / *religious celebrations*

March 19 / *El Valle, Soná, Montijo* / San José / *processions*

March 19 / *David* / San José / *carnival, election of queen*

movable / *all over* / *Holy Week / *processions, horseplay in rural areas*

April 2 / *Chorrera & Río de Jesús* / San Francisco de Paula

April 16 / *Nombre de Dios* / Santo Toribio / *religious celebrations*

April 20 / *Antón* / Nuestra Señora de Perpetuo Socorro / *procession*

May 1 / *Portobelo* / San Felipe de Portobelo / *procession*

May 2 / *Otoque Oriente* / Nuestra Señora de Fátima / *procession*

May 3 / *Pacora, Chepillo, Cabuya* / Santa Cruz / *religious celebrations*

May 15 / *Ocú, Capira, Taboga* / San Isidro Labrador

June 13 / *Puerto Armuelles & Peñablanca* / San Antonio

June / *Villa de los Santos* / Corpus Christi / *"Dance of the Devils," "Moctezumas"*

June 24 / *Chitré & Penonomé* / San Juan Bautista / *religious and popular celebrations*

June 29 / *Los Pozos & La Colorada* / San Pedro y San Pablo / *procession*

July 16 / *Taboga, San Carlos, Pocri, Bocas del Toro* / Virgen del Carmen / *processions*

July 20 / *Las Tablas* / Santa Librada

July 25 / *Chepo* / San Cristóbal / *procession*

Aug. 10 / *El Caño* / San Lorenzo

Aug. 16 / *Las Minas, Tonosí* / San Roque / *religious celebrations*

Aug. 25 / *Ponuga* / San Luis

Aug. 30 / *Higo, San Carlos, Ocú, Penonomé* / Santa Rosa de Lima / *processions*

Sept. 3 / *San Carlos* / Fiesta del Higo / *popular celebration*

Sept. 11 / *Otoque Oriente* / San Nicolás / *procession*

Sept. 18 / *Pocri* / Santo Tomás

Sept. 24 / *Guararé* / Nuestra Señora de las Mercedes / *folklore contest*

Sept. 29 / *San·Miguel, Boquerón, Monagrillo* / San Miguel

Oct. 4 / *San Miguel* / Nuestra Señora del Rosario / *procession*

Oct. 21 / *Portobelo* / *Cristo Negro / *procession*

Dec. 4 / *Las Minas* / Santa Bárbara

Dec. 6 / *Arraiján* / San Nicolás

Dec. 8 / *Pacora & Penonomé* / Inmaculada Conceptión / *processions*

FIESTAS OF PARAGUAY

See text for additional information

DATE: PLACE: NAME: EVENTS:

Jan. 6 / *Tobatí* / *Reyes Magos / *religious procession, races and games,* "*Cambá ra'angá*"

Feb. 2 / *Capitá* / Candelaria / *religious procession*

Feb. 3 / *all over* / *San Blas / *processions, horse races, bullfight farce, ("Sortija" in the town of Itá)*

movable / *Asunción and other places* / Carnival / *parades, floats, water games*

movable / *all over* / *Holy Week / *religious processions and popular celebrations*

May 24 / *Tobatí* / María Auxiliadora / *horse races, dances, processions*

June / *Asunción* / Corpus Christi / *religious processions*

June 24 / *many small towns* / *San Juan / *processions,* *"*Toro Candil*"

June 29 / *many small towns* / San Pedro / *processions, "Toro Candil"*

Aug. 10 / *San Lorenzo* / San Lorenzo / *procession*

Aug. 15 / *all over* / Assumption / *processions*

Sept. 21 / *Asunción* / Spring Festival of Students / *folk dances, crowning of queen, athletic events*

Sept. 29 / *Tobatí* / San Miguel / *procession*

1st Sund. in Oct. / *Luque* / Virgen del Rosario / *procession*

Dec. 8 / *Caacupé* / Inmaculada Concepción / *pilgrimages, religious processions*

Dec. 8 / *Tobatí* / Inmaculada Concepción / *procession, games, popular celebration*

FIESTAS OF PERU

See text for additional information

Jan. 1 / *Juaja & Concepción* / Shajteo / *picnics, native dances*

Jan. 6 / *Tiabaya* / Pear festival

Jan. 6 / *Sicuani* / *Día de los Reyes / *race of kings on horseback*

Jan. 6 / *Cuzco* / *Dia de los Reyes / *procession, pageants of life of Christ & Incas*

Feb. 1-8 / *Puno* / *Candelaria / *processions, Indian dances*

DATE:	PLACE:	NAME:	EVENTS:

Feb. / *wine-producing areas* / *"Pisa" / *agricultural fiesta with pressing of grapes*

movable / *various places* / *Carnival / *parades and general merry-making*

movable / *Callejón de Huaylas* / Ash Wednesday / *"Cóndor rachi"*

March 7-8 / *Puno* / *San Juan de Dios / *llama parade, Sicuris*

movable / *all over* / *Holy Week / *processions & Indian rituals*

Mon. before Easter / *Cuzco* / *Señor de los Temblores / *procession*

Sund. after Easter / *Huancayo* / *Cuasimodo / *fair, Indian dances*

Sund. after Easter / *Ayacucho* / *Cuasimodo / *procession*

April 25 / *Puno & other places* / *San Marcos / *cattle marking & agricultural rituals*

April 27 / *La Villa de Macate* / *Santo Toribio / *procession, dances, fireworks*

May, 1st 2 weeks / *Moche* / *San Isidro / *processions, devil dancers*

May, every Sund. / *Pucará* / Santa Cruz / *decoration of crosses and processions*

May 3 / *Huaráz* / Santa Cruz / *decoration & blessing of crosses*

May 3 / *Puno* / Santa Cruz / *market of miniatures*

May 3 / *Eten* / *Santa Cruz / *procession, dances*

June 2 / *Eten* / *Apparition of Infant Jesus / *procession, Indian dances, fireworks*

June 24 / *Lima* / *Día del Indio / *torchlight picnics, Indian dances*

June 24 / *Cuzco* / *Día del Indio / *Inca Inti Raymi ceremony, dances*

June 24 / *all over* / *San Juan / *bonfires, bathing, divination*

June 29 / *Ichu, Callao* / San Pedro / *procession, dances*

June / *Cuzco* / *Corpus Christi / *procession*

July 6-8 / *Huaylas* / *Santa Isabel / *mock naval battle*

July 16 / *Pucará* / *Virgen del Carmen / *fair and fiesta*

July 16-18 / *Paucartambo* / *Virgen del Carmen / *Indian dances*

July 24-25 / *Lampa* / *Santiago / *processions, Indian dances, bonfires*

July 25 / *Huancayo* / Santiago / *cattle marking*

July 28 / *Lima* / Independencia / *street fair, bullfights, games*

July 28-Aug. 1 / *Arequipa* / Independencia / *parades, floats*

July 28-Aug. 1 / *Curahuasi* / Independencia / *condor vs. bull fight, special games*

July / *wine-producing areas* / *"poda" / *agricultural fiesta, pruning grape vines*

Aug. 4 / *Arequipa* / Santo Domingo / *processions*

Aug. 6 / *Motupe* / Holy Cross / *pilgrimage, Indian dances*
Aug. 15 / *all over* / Assumption / *processions*
Aug. 16 / *San Gerónimo* / San Roque / *procession, fireworks, dances*
Aug. 22 / *Callejón de Huaylas* / Santo Toribio / *fireworks, dances*
Aug. 30 / *Lima* / *Santa Rosa / *procession, dances*
Sept. 1-8 / *Sapallanga* / *Virgin of the Nativity
Sept. 8 / *Chavín de Pariarca* / *Virgin of the Nativity / *sham battle on horseback*
Sept. 8 / *Chumbivilcas & Baños del Inca* / *Virgin of the Nativity / *procession, dances, fireworks*
Sept. 14 / *Huaráz* / Exaltation of the Cross / *decoration & blessing of crosses*
Sept. 18 / *Eten* / *Apparition of the Infant Jesus / *Indian dances: "Pastores", "Serranitos", "Faroles"*
Sept. 24 / *Cuzco* / Our Lady of Mercy / *procession*
Oct. 4 / *Arequipa* / *San Francisco de Asís / *procession, dances, fireworks, bullfights*
Oct. 18-19 / *Lima* / *Señor de los Milagros / *procession*
Oct. 18 / *Callao* / Señor del Mar / *procession*
Oct. 28 / *Lima* / *Señor de los Milagros / *procession*
Nov. 2 / *Puno, Arequipa, Cuzco, Huánuco & other places* / Todos los Santos / *celebrations in cemetery*
Dec. 4-5 / *San Sebastián* / Santa Barbara / *wake over bones, processions*
Dec. 8 / *various towns* / Inmaculada Concepción / *processions*
Dec. 28 / *all over* / *Santos Inocentes / *practical jokes*

FIESTAS OF EL SALVADOR
*See text for additional information
**Described in text under a different fiesta

Jan. 1-6 / *Tepecoyo* / Fiesta patronal
Jan. 6 / *Guatajiagua* / Día de los Reyes
Jan. 12 / *Cojutepeque* / San Sebastián / *parade, floats, crowning of Sugar Cane Queen*
Jan. 14-15 / *San Vicente* / Señor de *Esquipulas / **"La Partesana" and other dances*
Jan. 16-18 / *San Antonio Abad* / *San Antonio Abad / *masked dances, processions, floats*
Jan. 17-20 / *Apastepeque* / San Sebastián / *"Moros y Cristianos"*
Jan. 17-20 / *Villa Delgado* / *San Sebastián / *dances, processions, "El Torito Pinto"*

Jan. 17-21 / *Tacuba* / San Sebastián / *"Las Tortugas," "El Venado," "El Tigre,"* ***"Tunco de Monte"*

Jan. 20-Feb. 5 / *Sonsonante* / Candelaria

Jan. 24-28 / *San Julián* / San Juan Obispo

Jan. 28-Feb. 2 / *Moncagua* / Candelaria / *"Jaripeo"*

Feb. 1-15 / *San Pedro Nonualco* / *Nombre de Jesús / *dances, processions*

Feb. 24 / *Metapan* / Señor de Ostua

March 1-8 / *Sesori* / Corazón de Jesús

March 17-19 /*Ataco* / San José / *"El Toro Lucero"*

movable / *all over* / *Holy Week / *processions ("La Judea" in Tejutepeque)*

April 22-May 3 / *San Juan Nonualco* / Santa Cruz / *"El Tigre"* and *"El Venado"*

May (all month) / *San Vicente* / *Flores de Mayo / *processions, flower battles, etc.*

May 3 / *all over* / *El Día de la Cruz / *processions, dances*

May 12-14 / *Pasaquina* / La Ascensión

May 21-22 / *Apastepeque* / *Santa Rita / **"Tunco de Monte"*

May, 3rd Sund. / *Ilobasco* / Los Desemparados

June 15-24 / *San Juan Nonualco* / San Juan

June 15-30 / *Cojutepeque* / San Juan

June 24 / *Chalatenango* / San Juan / *procession*

June 26-29 / *San Pedro Nonualco* / San Pedro

June 27-29 / *Moncagua* / San Pedro / *"Moros y Cristianos"* and *"El Negrito"*

July 16-22 / *Tacuba* / Santa María Magdalena / *"Moros y Cristianos"* and other dances

July 17-19 / *San Vicente* / *Muerte del Señor San José / *religious pageant*

July 17-26 / *Santa Ana* / Santa Ana

July 19-25 / *Apastepeque* / Santiago / *"La Vaquita"* and other dances

July 23-25 / *Guatajiagua* / Santiago / *"La Yegüita"*

July 24-25 / *Villa Delgado* / Santiago / *"Moros y Cristianos"*

Aug. 1-6 / *San Salvador* / *Fiesta Agostinas / *processions, parades of floats, Indian dances, piñatas in parks, fireworks*

Aug. 8-15 / *Sensuntepeque* / El Tránsito

Aug. 10-20 / *Izalco* / Ascensión

Aug. 15-16 / *Mejicanos* / Virgen del Tránsito / *"Moros y Cristianos"*

Aug. 15-30 / *Cojutepeque* / San Juan / *"Moros y Cristianos"* and ***"Tunco de Monte"*

Sept. 13-16 / *Panchimalco* / Santa Cruz de Roma / *processions, races, "Moros y Cristianos", "Los Chapetones"*

Sept. 20-21 / *Santiago Texacuangos* / San Mateo / *"Las Pulgas"*

Sept. 26-29 / *Villa Delgado* / San Miguel / *Indian dances*

Oct. 16-18 / *Ataco* / San Lucas / *"Moros y Cristianos"*

Oct. 18-19 / *El Rosario* / Virgen del Rosario

Oct. 21 / *Jicalapa* / Santa Ursula / *pilgrimages, "Historia de la Batalla"*

Oct. 21-Nov. 5 / *Chalatenango* / Todos los Santos

Nov. 1-2 / *San Vicente* / Todos los Santos / *fair, "Moros y Cristianos"*

Nov. 12-16 / *Ilopango* / San Cristóbal

Nov. 20-25 / *Santa Catarina Masahuat* / *Santa Catarina / *velaciones, processions*

Nov. 27-30 / *Apaneca* / San Andrés / *"Las Chichimecas", "Moros y Cristianos"*

Dec. 1-2 / *San Vicente* / de los Santos / *procession, Indian dances*

Dec. 1-10 / *Izalco* / Virgen de Concepción / *Indian rituals*

Dec. 7-8 / *Quezaltepeque and Ilobasco* / Virgen de Concepción

Dec. 8-16 / *Ataco* / Virgen de Concepción

Dec. 11-20 / *Izalco* / Virgen de los Remedios / *Indian rituals*

Dec. 12 / *San Salvador* / Día del Indio / *folklore costumes worn to church of Guadalupe*

Dec. 14-15 / *Candelaria* / Dulce Nombre de María

Dec. 16-Jan. 6 / *all over* / *Christmas / *posadas, miracle plays*

Dec. 19-25 / *Santa Tecla* / *Christmas

Dec. 25 / *Izalco* / *Christmas / *"El Tabal" or "Jeu Jeu"*

Dec. 27-30 / *Apaneca* / San Andrés

Dec. 31 / *Armenia* / San Silvestre

Dec. 31 / *Sonsonate* / Vela de la Vara / *Indian rituals*

FIESTAS OF URUGUAY

See text for additional information

movable / *Montevideo* / *Carnival / *parades, floats, tableaux*

movable / *all over* / Holy Week / *processions*

March or April (usually Holy Week) / *Punta del Este* / *Fiesta del Mar / *parade of boats, fireworks, crowning of queen*

March or April (Holy Week) / *Montevideo* / *Semana Criolla / *Gaucho exhibitions, dances, etc.*

235

June / *various places* / Corpus Christi / *processions*

Nov. 2 / *various places* / Todos los Santos / *decoration of cemeteries*

Dec. 8 / *Carrasco* / *Día de las Playas / *regattas, popular celebrations*

FIESTAS OF VENEZUELA

*See text for additional information

Jan. 1 / *State of Falcon* / New Year's / *street celebrations, fireworks*

Jan. 6 / *all over (best in Independencia)* / *Día de Reyes / *street pageants*

Feb. 2 / *near Mérida* / Candelaria / *native dances*

movable / *Caracas* / *Carnival / *street celebrations, games & contests*

March 19 / *all over* / San José / *religious celebrations, games & races*

movable / *all over* / *Holy Week / *processions*

May / *all over* / *Velorio de Cruz / *popular celebrations, dancing*

May 15 / *Mérida & Lagunillas* / *San Isidro / *processions, native dances such as Maypole dance*

June / *San Francisco de Yare* / *Corpus Christi / *Devil dancers*

June (8 days after Corpus Christi) / *San Francisco de Yare* / *Devil dancers*

June 13 / *El Tocuyo* / San Antonio / *"El Tamunangue" dance drama*

June 24 / *various places* / *San Juan Bautista / *baptismal ceremonies in rivers, drum dances*

June 24 / *Tocuyito* / San Juan Bautista / *"Devils"*

June 29 / *various places* / San Pablo / *resumption of St. John's Day festivities*

Aug. 14-15 / *La Asunción (Nueva Esparta)* / Assumption / *parades, religious ceremonies & popular diversions*

Aug. 15 / *various places* / Assumption / *processions*

Aug. or 1st of Sept. / *San Miguel and Bobaré* / harvest festival / *rural celebration, *"Dance of the Flutes"*

Oct. 12 / *El Pilar* / Nuestra Señora del Pilar / *processions*

Nov. 1 / *various places* / Todos los Santos / *religious ceremonies*

Dec. 28 / *San Carlos (Cojedes)* / *Santos Inocentes / *"Devils"*

Dec. 29 / *State of Zulia* / *San Benito / *Drum dance "Chimbanguele", procession*

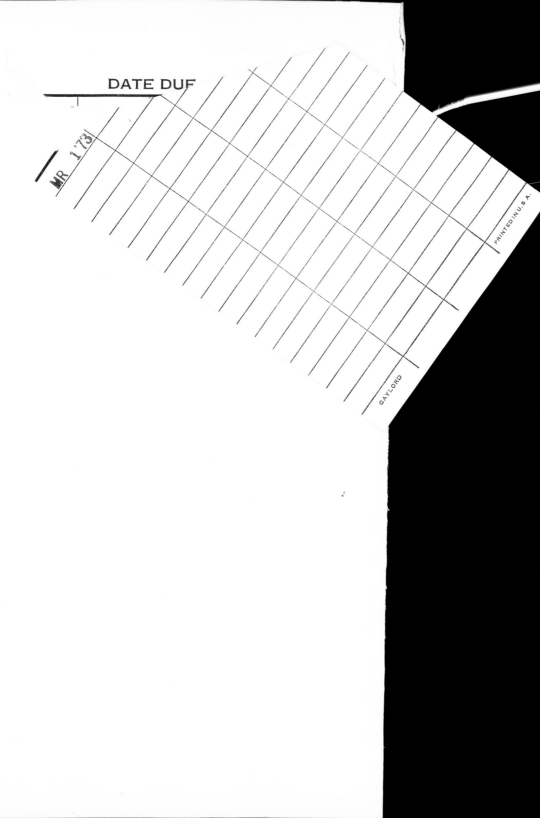

DATE DUE

MR 1731

GAYLORD

PRINTED IN U.S.A.